Get the eBooks FREE!

(PDF, ePub, Kindle, and liveBook all included)

We believe that once you buy a book from us, you should be able to read it in any format we have available. To get electronic versions of this book at no additional cost to you, purchase and then register this book at the Manning website.

Go to https://www.manning.com/freebook and follow the instructions to complete your pBook registration.

That's it!
Thanks from Manning!

Classic Computer Science Problems in Swift

Classic Computer Science Problems in Swift

ESSENTIAL TECHNIQUES FOR PRACTICING PROGRAMMERS

DAVID KOPEC

MANNING

SHELTER ISLAND

Manning Publications Co.
20 Baldwin Road
PO Box 761
Shelter Island, NY 11964

Development editor:	Jenny Stout
Review editor:	Ivan Martinović
Project editor:	Kevin Sullivan
Copyeditor:	Andy Carroll
Proofreader:	Alyson Brener
Technical proofreader:	Christopher Pickslay
Typesetter:	Gordan Salinovic
Illustrations:	Richard Shepard
Cover designer:	Marija Tudor

ISBN 9781617294891
Printed in the United States of America
1 2 3 4 5 6 7 8 9 10 – EBM – 23 22 21 20 19 18

Dedicated to the memory of IM Dr. Danny Kopec, who taught thousands in chess, computer science, and life. And with thanks to Dr. Jay Selman, who is a great uncle and was an incredible brother-in-law throughout my father's untimely passing.

brief contents

contents

acknowledgments

Thank you to the team at Manning for enabling this book to see the light of market. Thanks go especially to acquisitions editor Brian Sawyer, for believing in the book's unique concept from my first proposal and seeing "the vision." Development editor, Jennifer Stout, must also be singled out for her care and understanding throughout the book's development.

Significant improvements came to the book thanks to the careful consideration of MEAP readers and of official reviewers, including: Albert Choy, Alberto Chiesa, Arun Kumar, Becky Huett, Chad Johnston, Damian Esteban, Eric Giannini, Jeremy Gailor, Julien Pohie, Karolina Kafel, Laurence Giglio, Patrick Regan, Shawn Eion Smith, and Tahir Akhtar. Thank you to all who provided constructive and specific criticism during the book's development. Your feedback was carefully considered and incorporated.

Thank you to my family, friends, and colleagues for encouraging me during the development of this book—especially Dr. Danny Kopec, Dr. Joshua Auerbach, and Rebecca Driesen, who proofread specific chapters. Thank you to Sylvia Kopec and Rebecca Driesen for assistance with the development of diagrams in the early chapters. Thank you to my students at SUNY Suffolk and Champlain College, who have kept me inspired as a teacher.

Finally, thank you most importantly to the readers for purchasing this book. In a world of half-hearted online tutorials, I think it is important to still support the development of books that provide the same author's voice throughout a deep dive into a topic. Online tutorials are superb resources, but your purchase enables full-length, vetted, and carefully developed books to still have a place in computer science education.

about this book

Code conventions and repository

This book contains many examples of source code, both in separate examples and in-line with normal text. In both cases, source code is formatted in a `fixed-width font` `like this` to separate it from ordinary text.

In some places, original source code has been reformatted with added line breaks and reworked indentation to accommodate the available page space in the book. Wrapped code lines are often indicated with line-continuation markers (➡).

A GitHub repository with the code for the book is available: https://github.com/davecom/ClassicComputerScienceProblemsInSwift. A zip file containing the code at the time of publication is also on the publisher's website at https://www.manning.com/books/classic-computer-science-problems-in-swift.

Trademarks

Trademarked names appear in this book. Rather than use a trademark symbol with every occurrence of a trademarked name, the names are only used in an editorial fashion and to the benefit of the trademark owner, with no intention of infringement of the trademark. Apple, Xcode, Swift, Mac, iOS, iPhone, and macOS are registered trademarks of Apple Inc.

Book forum

Purchase of *Classic Computer Science Problems in Swift* includes free access to a private web forum run by Manning Publications where you can make comments about the book, ask technical questions, and receive help from the author and from other users. To access the forum, go to https://forums.manning.com/forums/classic-computer-science-problems-in-swift. You can also learn more about Manning's forums and the rules of conduct at https://forums.manning.com/forums/about.

Manning's commitment to our readers is to provide a venue where a meaningful dialogue between individual readers and between readers and the author can take place. It is not a commitment to any specific amount of participation on the part of the author, whose contribution to the forum remains voluntary (and unpaid). We suggest you try asking the author challenging questions lest his interest stray! The forum and the archives of previous discussions will be accessible from the publisher's website as long as the book is in print.

About the author

DAVID KOPEC is an assistant professor of Computer Science & Innovation at Champlain College in Burlington, Vermont. He is an experienced iOS developer and the author of *Dart for Absolute Beginners* (Apress, 2014). David holds a bachelor's degree in economics and a master's in computer science, both from Dartmouth College.

About the cover illustration

The figure on the cover of *Classic Computer Science Problems in Swift* is captioned "Habit of a Lady of Indostan." ("Indostan" was an alternate European form of "Hindustan," meaning the Indian subcontinent.) The illustration is taken from Thomas Jefferys' *A Collection of the Dresses of Different Nations, Ancient and Modern,* published in London between 1757 and 1772. The title page states that these are hand-colored copperplate engravings, heightened with gum arabic. Thomas Jefferys (1719–1771) was called "Geographer to King George III." He was an English cartographer who was the leading map supplier of his day. He engraved and printed maps for government and other official bodies and produced a wide range of commercial maps and atlases, especially of North America. His work as a mapmaker sparked an interest in local dress customs of the lands he surveyed and mapped; they are brilliantly displayed in this four-volume collection.

Fascination with faraway lands and travel for pleasure were relatively new phenomena in the eighteenth century, and collections such as this one were popular, introducing both the tourist and the armchair traveler to the inhabitants of other countries. The diversity of the drawings in Jefferys' volumes speaks vividly of the uniqueness and individuality of the world's nations centuries ago. Dress codes have changed, and the diversity by region and country, so rich at one time, has faded away. It is now often hard to tell the inhabitant of one continent from another. Perhaps, trying to view it optimistically, we have traded a cultural and visual diversity for a more varied personal life—or a more varied and interesting intellectual and technical life.

At a time when it is hard to tell one computer book from another, Manning celebrates the inventiveness and initiative of the computer business with book covers based on the rich diversity of national costumes from centuries ago, brought back to life by Jefferys' pictures.

Introduction

Thank you for purchasing *Classic Computer Science Problems in Swift: Essential techniques for practicing programmers.* Swift is at an exciting stage in its development. As the language continues to stabilize and its popularity soars, there is a need to bring traditional computer science education to the language. The problems in this intermediate book will help seasoned programmers learn the language and new programmers accelerate their CS education. This book covers such a diversity of problem-solving techniques that there is truly something for everyone.

This book is not an introduction to Swift. Apple publishes an excellent free book serving that purpose.[1] Instead, this book assumes that you have already obtained a basic working knowledge of Swift's syntax. Mastery of Swift is by no means assumed. In fact, the book's content was created with the assumption that it would serve as learning material to help one achieve such mastery. On the other hand, this book is not appropriate for complete beginners.

Why Swift?

Swift is an exciting new programming language from Apple that toes the line between the object-oriented and functional paradigms. Swift's creators have achieved a remarkable balance that, for many, is the best of both worlds. Due to its wide deployment via Apple's developer tools, its modern syntax, its amalgamation of great features from other languages, its careful paradigm balance, and its future as the main language of development for iOS and Mac applications, now is a great time to learn Swift.

---

[1] Apple Inc., *The Swift Programming Language*, http://mng.bz/6fKi.

1

Apple has called Swift the first protocol-oriented language, due to its powerful protocol feature set and the extensive use of that set in its standard library.[2] Yet, many long-time Objective-C and Java developers have little experience with functional programming, let alone protocol-oriented programming. At the same time, there are functional programmers coming into the Swift community who try to do everything the same way they would in Haskell or Scheme. They are sometimes missing more elegant, object-oriented solutions.

This book aims to serve as a bridge between these worlds by approaching classic problems that experienced programmers should be familiar with (and new programmers should become familiar with), without being dogmatic about fitting within a single paradigm in Swift. Instead, you will get a taste of all of them. A combination is the right way to approach Swift. Building bridges is the community's way forward.

What is a classic computer science problem?

Some say that computers are to computer science as telescopes are to astronomy. If that's the case, then is a programming language like a telescope lens? In any event, the term "computer science problems" is used here to mean "programming problems typically taught in an undergraduate computer science curriculum."

There are certain programming problems that are given to new programmers to solve, whether in a classroom setting during the pursuit of a bachelor's degree (in computer science, software engineering, etc.) or within the confines of an intermediate programming textbook (for example, a first book on artificial intelligence or algorithms), that have become commonplace enough to be deemed "classic." A selection of such problems is what you will find in this book.

The problems range from the trivial, which can be solved in a few lines of code, to the complex, which require the buildup of systems over multiple chapters. Some problems touch on artificial intelligence, and others simply require common sense. Some problems are practical, and other problems are fanciful.

What kinds of problems are in this book?

Chapter 1 introduces problem-solving techniques that will likely look familiar to most readers. Things like recursion, memoization, and simulation are essential building blocks of other techniques explored in later chapters.

This gentle introduction is followed by chapter 2, which focuses on search problems. Search is such a large topic that you could arguably place most problems in the book under its banner. Chapter 2 introduces the most essential search algorithms, including binary search, depth-first search, breadth-first search, and A*. These algorithms are reused throughout the rest of the book.

In chapter 3, you will build a framework for solving a broad range of problems that can be abstractly defined by variables of limited domains that have constraints

---

[2] Dave Abrahams, "Protocol-Oriented Programming in Swift" (WWDC 2015, Session 408, Apple Inc.), http://mng.bz/zWP3.

between them. This includes such classics as the eight queens problem, the Australian map-coloring problem, and the cryptarithmetic SEND+MORE=MONEY.

Chapter 4 explores the world of graph algorithms, which to the uninitiated are surprisingly broad in their applicability. In this chapter, you will build a graph data structure and then use it to solve several classic optimization problems.

Chapter 5 explores genetic algorithms, a technique that is less deterministic than most covered in the book, but that sometimes can solve a problem traditional algorithms cannot in a reasonable amount of time.

Chapter 6 covers k-means clustering and is perhaps the most algorithmically specific chapter in the book. This clustering technique is simple to implement, easy to understand, and broadly applicable.

Chapter 7 aims to explain what a neural network is, and to give the reader a taste of what a very simple neural network looks like. It does not aim to provide comprehensive coverage of this exciting and evolving field.

Finally, chapter 8 covers interesting (and fun) problems that did not quite fit anywhere else in the book.

Who is this book for?

This book is for both intermediate and experienced programmers. Experienced programmers who want to learn Swift will find comfortably familiar problems from their computer science or programming education. Fairly new programmers will be introduced to these classic problems in the language of their choice—Swift. Developers getting ready for coding interviews will likely find this book to be valuable preparation material.

In addition to professional programmers, students enrolled in undergraduate computer science programs who have an interest in Swift will likely find this book helpful. It makes no attempt to be a rigorous introduction to data structures and algorithms. *This is not a data structures and algorithms textbook*—you will not find proofs or extensive use of big-O notation within its pages. Instead, it is positioned as an approachable, hands-on tutorial to the problem-solving techniques that should be the end product of taking data structure, algorithm, and artificial intelligence classes.

Once again, a basic knowledge of Swift's syntax and semantics is assumed. A reader with zero programming experience will get little out of this book. And a programmer with zero Swift experience will almost certainly struggle. In other words, we could call *Classic Computer Science Problems in Swift* a great *second* book on Swift.

Swift versioning and tools

The source code in this book was written to adhere to version 4.1 of the Swift language. This version was released alongside Xcode 9.3 by Apple in early 2018. A GitHub repository with the code for the book is available: https://github.com/davecom/ClassicComputerScienceProblemsInSwift.

Most of the source code in this book will run on Linux (and other platforms Swift is ported to) without modification, as it only relies on Foundation (not AppKit/UIKit). The source code files are distributed as part of a Swift playground for Xcode, but the raw .swift files contained therein can be extracted for use on Linux. Cross-platform compatibility was a goal for this book, but convenience on the Mac for the majority of readers was an even greater goal.

This book does not explain how to use Xcode, build Swift projects, or use Playgrounds. There are plenty of great resources on those topics available online and in print. The ability to do these tasks is assumed throughout.

No graphics, no UI code

This book is not about learning UIKit or AppKit. The examples in the book do not require the use of either. There are no examples in this book that produce graphical output. Why? The goal is to solve the posed problems with solutions that are as concise and readable as possible. Often, doing graphics gets in the way, or makes solutions significantly more complex than they need to be to illustrate the technique or algorithm in question.

Further, to achieve cross-platform compatibility with Swift on Linux, UIKit and AppKit could not be used. At the time of writing, only Foundation was ported to Linux. The solutions here largely rely on the Swift standard library alone, with Foundation acting as a supplement in areas where the standard library is weak.

This is not a book that will teach you how to write full-scale apps. It is a book that will help you with the fundamentals of software development under Swift. It is a book that's written to stay within its scope.

Small problems

1

To get started, we will explore some simple problems that can be solved with no more than a few relatively short functions. Although these problems are small, they will still allow us to explore some interesting problem-solving techniques. Think of them as a good warmup.

1.1 The Fibonacci sequence

The Fibonacci sequence is a series of numbers such that any number, except for the first and second, is the sum of the previous two:

```
0, 1, 1, 2, 3, 5, 8, 13, 21...
```

The value of the first Fibonacci number in the series is 0. The value of the fourth Fibonacci number is 2. It follows that to get the value of any Fibonacci number, n, in the series, one can use the formula

```
fib(n) = fib(n - 1) + fib(n - 2)
```

1.1.1 A first recursive attempt

The preceding formula for computing a number in the Fibonacci sequence (illustrated in figure 1.1), a form of pseudocode, can be trivially translated into a *recursive* Swift function (a recursive function is a function that calls itself). This mechanical translation will serve as the first version of our attempt at writing a function to return a given value of the Fibonacci sequence:

```swift
func fib1(n: UInt) -> UInt {
    return fib1(n: n - 1) + fib1(n: n - 2)
}
```

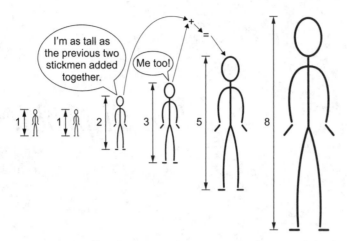

Figure 1.1   The height of each stickman is the addition of the previous two stickmen's heights added together.

> **NOTE**   fib1() uses UInt instead of Int because the Fibonacci sequence does not exist in the realm of negative integers.

If you run this function by calling it with a value, it will run forever without returning a final result. We call such a circumstance *infinite recursion*, and it is analogous to an *infinite loop*.

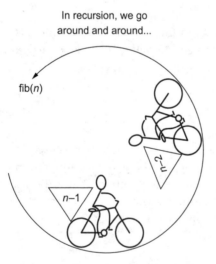

Figure 1.2   The recursive function fib(n) calls itself with the arguments n-2 and n-1.

1.1.2   *Utilizing base cases*

Notice that Xcode produces no errors regarding this Fibonacci function, fib1(). It is the duty of the programmer to avoid infinite recursion. The reason for the infinite recursion is that we never specified a base case. In a recursive function, a base case serves as a stopping point.

In the case of the Fibonacci function, we have natural base cases in the form of the special first two sequence values, 0 and 1. Neither 0 nor 1 is the sum of the previous two numbers in the sequence. Instead, they are the special first two values. Let's try specifying them as base cases:

```
func fib2(n: UInt) -> UInt {
    if (n < 2) {  // base cases
        return n
    }
    return fib2(n: n - 2) + fib2(n: n - 1)  // recursive cases
}
```

> **NOTE** The fib2() version of the Fibonacci function returns 0 as the zeroth number (fib2(n: 0)), rather than the first number, as in our original proposition. In a programming context, this kind of makes sense because we are used to sequences (such as Swift's Array type) starting with a zeroth element.

fib2() can be called successfully and will return correct results. Try calling it with some small values:

```
fib2(n: 5)
fib2(n: 10)
```

Do not try calling fib2(n: 50). It will never finish executing! Why? Every call to fib2() results in two more calls to fib2() by way of the recursive calls fib2(n: n - 1) and fib2(n: n - 2) (see figure 1.3). In other words, the call tree grows exponentially. For example, a call of fib2(n: 4) results in this entire set of calls:

```
fib2(n: 4) -> fib2(n: 3), fib2(n: 2)
fib2(n: 3) -> fib2(n: 2), fib2(n: 1)
fib2(n: 2) -> fib2(n: 1), fib2(n: 0)
fib2(n: 2) -> fib2(n: 1), fib2(n: 0)
fib2(n: 1) -> 1
fib2(n: 1) -> 1
fib2(n: 1) -> 1
fib2(n: 0) -> 0
fib2(n: 0) -> 0
```

If you count them (and as you can see if you call fib2(n: 4) in an Xcode playground), there are 9 calls to fib2() just to compute the 4th element! It gets worse. There are 15 calls required to compute element 5, 177 calls to compute element 10, and 21,891 calls to compute element 20. We can do better.

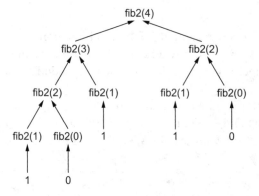

Figure 1.3   Every non-base-case call of `fib2()` results in two more calls of `fib2()`.

1.1.3   *Memoization to the rescue*

Memoization is a technique in which you store the results of computational tasks when they are completed, so that when you need them again, you can look them up instead of needing to compute them a second (or millionth) time (see figure 1.4).[1]

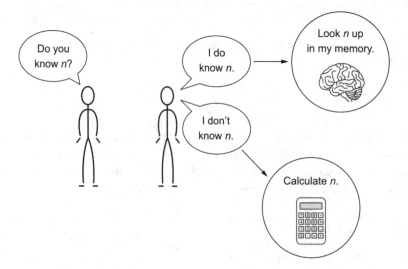

Figure 1.4   The human memoization machine

---

[1]   Donald Michie, a famous British computer scientist, coined the term *memoization*. Donald Michie, *Memo functions: a language feature with "rote-learning" properties* (Edinburgh University, Department of Machine Intelligence and Perception, 1967).

Let's create a new version of the Fibonacci function that utilizes a Swift `Dictionary` for memoization purposes.

```
var fibMemo: [UInt: UInt] = [0: 0, 1: 1]   // our old base cases
func fib3(n: UInt) -> UInt {
    if let result = fibMemo[n] {  // our new base case
        return result
    } else {
        fibMemo[n] = fib3(n: n - 1) + fib3(n: n - 2)  // memoization
    }
    return fibMemo[n]!
}
```

WARNING Using `!` to force unwrap optionals is ugly, but I do it here for convenience because it is provable that `fibMemo` will already contain a result by the time the final `return` statement is called.

You can now safely call `fib3(n: 50)`. A call to `fib3(n: 20)` will result in just 39 calls of `fib3()` as opposed to the 21,891 of `fib2()` resulting from the call `fib2(n: 20)`. `fibMemo` is prefilled with the earlier base cases of 0 and 1, saving `fib3()` from the complexity of another `if` statement.

1.1.4 *Keep it simple, Fibonacci*

There is an even more performant option. We can solve Fibonacci with an old fashioned iterative approach.

```
func fib4(n: UInt) -> UInt {
    if (n == 0) {  // special case
        return n
    }
    var last: UInt = 0, next: UInt = 1  // initially set to fib(0) & fib(1)
    for _ in 1..<n {
        (last, next) = (next, last + next)
    }
    return next
}
```

WARNING The body of the `for` loop in `fib4()` uses tuples in perhaps a bit of an overly clever way. Some may feel that it sacrifices readability for conciseness. Others may find the conciseness in and of itself more readable. The gist is, `last` is being set to the previous value of `next`, and `next` is being set to the previous value of `last` plus the previous value of `next`. This avoids the creation of a temporary variable to hold the old value of `next` after `last` is updated, but before `next` is updated.

With this approach, the body of the for loop will only run a maximum of n - 1 times. In other words, this is the most efficient version yet. Compare 19 runs of the for loop body to 21,891 recursive calls of fib2() for the 20th Fibonacci number. That could make a serious difference in a real-world application!

In the recursive solutions, we worked backward. In this iterative solution, we work forward. Sometimes recursion is the most intuitive way to solve a problem. For example, the meat of fib1() and fib2() is pretty much a mechanical translation of the original Fibonacci formula. However, naive recursive solutions can also come with significant performance costs. Remember, any problem that can be solved recursively can also be solved iteratively.

1.2   *Trivial compression*

Saving space (virtual or real) is often important. It is more efficient to use less space, and it can save money. If you are renting an apartment that is bigger than you need for your things and family, then you may "downsize" to a smaller place that is less expensive. If you are paying by the byte to store your data on a server, then you may want to compress it so that its storage costs you less. *Compression* is the act of taking data and encoding it (changing its form) in such a way that it takes up less space. *Decompression* is reversing the process, returning the data to its original form.

If it is more storage-efficient to compress data, then why is all data not compressed? There is a tradeoff between time and space. It takes time to compress a piece of data and to decompress it back into its original form. Therefore, data compression only makes sense in situations where small size is prioritized over fast execution. Think of large files being transmitted over the internet. Compressing them makes sense because it will take longer to transfer the files than it will to decompress them once received. Further, the time taken to compress the files for their storage on the original server only needs to be accounted for once.

The easiest way to compress data is to realize that its storage type uses more bits than are strictly required for its contents. For instance, if an unsigned integer that will never exceed 65,535 is being stored as a UInt (64-bit unsigned integer on most Swift platforms), it is being stored inefficiently. It could instead be stored as a UInt16 (16-bit unsigned integer). This would reduce the space consumption for the actual number by 75% (16 bits instead of 64 bits). If there are millions of such numbers being stored inefficiently, it can add up to megabytes of wasted space.

> **NOTE**   If you are a little rusty regarding binary, recall that a bit is a single value that is either a 1 or a 0. A sequence of 1s and 0s is read in base 2 to represent a number. For the purposes of this section, you do not need to do any math in base 2, but you do need to understand that the number of bits that a type stores determines how many different values it can represent. For example, 1 bit can represent 2 values (0 or 1), 2 bits can represent 4 values (00, 01, 10, 11), 3 bits can represent 8 values, and so on.

If the number of possible different values that a type is meant to represent is less than the number of values that the bits being used to store it can represent, it can likely be more efficiently stored. Consider the nucleotides that form a gene in DNA.[2] Each nucleotide can only be one of four values: A, C, G, or T (there will be more about this in chapter 2). Yet, if the gene is stored as a `String`, which can be thought of as a collection of characters, each nucleotide will be represented by a character, which generally requires 8 bits of storage. In binary, just 2 bits are needed to store a type with four possible values: 00, 01, 10, and 11 are the four different values that can be represented by 2 bits. If A is assigned 00, C is assigned 01, G is assigned 10, and T is assigned 11, then the storage required for a string of nucleotides can be reduced by 75% (8 bits to 2 bits per nucleotide).

Instead of storing our nucleotides as a `String`, they can be stored as a *bit string* (see figure 1.5). A bit string is exactly what it sounds like—an arbitrary length sequence of 1s and 0s. Unfortunately, the Swift standard library contains no off-the-shelf construct for working with bit strings of arbitrary length, but the low-level C library Core Foundation, available from Swift, contains `CFMutableBitVector`. The following code converts a `String` composed of As, Cs, Gs, and Ts into a `CFMutableBitVector` and back again.

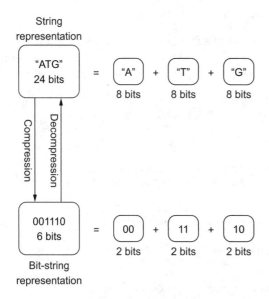

Figure 1.5 Compressing a `String` representing a gene into a 2-bit-per-nucleotide bit string.

```
struct CompressedGene {
    let length: Int
    private let bitVector: CFMutableBitVector

    init(original: String) {
        length = original.count
        // default allocator, need 2 * length number of bits
        bitVector = CFBitVectorCreateMutable(kCFAllocatorDefault, length * 2)
        CFBitVectorSetCount(bitVector, length * 2) // fills the bit vector
        ➥ with 0s
        compress(gene: original)
    }
```

A CompressedGene internally stores a sequence of nucleotides as a bit string. The init() method's main responsibility is to initialize the bit-string construct CFMutable-BitVector and call compress() to do the dirty work of actually converting the provided String of nucleotides into a bit string. CFBitVectorCreateMutable() takes an allocator and a capacity. The capacity needs to be length * 2 because we need 2 bits for every nucleotide. Confusingly, the size (how many bits *are* in it) of a CFMutableBitVector is different from its capacity (how many bits *can be* in it). CFBitVectorSetCount() sets the bit vector's size and initializes all of the bits to 0.

Next, let's look at how we can actually perform the compression.

TIP   Core Foundation constructs like CFMutableBitVector are implemented in portable C and are available in Swift on Linux. You may need to import CoreFoundation on Linux, whereas on macOS import Foundation includes it implicitly.

```
private func compress(gene: String) {
    for (index, nucleotide) in gene.uppercased().enumerated() {
        let nStart = index * 2 // start of each new nucleotide
        switch nucleotide {
        case "A": // 00
            CFBitVectorSetBitAtIndex(bitVector, nStart, 0)
            CFBitVectorSetBitAtIndex(bitVector, nStart + 1, 0)
        case "C": // 01
            CFBitVectorSetBitAtIndex(bitVector, nStart, 0)
            CFBitVectorSetBitAtIndex(bitVector, nStart + 1, 1)
        case "G": // 10
            CFBitVectorSetBitAtIndex(bitVector, nStart, 1)
            CFBitVectorSetBitAtIndex(bitVector, nStart + 1, 0)
        case "T": // 11
            CFBitVectorSetBitAtIndex(bitVector, nStart, 1)
            CFBitVectorSetBitAtIndex(bitVector, nStart + 1, 1)
        default:
            print("Unexpected character \(nucleotide) at \(index)")
        }
    }
}
```

The compress() method looks at each Character in the String of nucleotides sequentially. When it sees an A, it adds 00 to the bit string. When it sees a C, it adds 01.

And so on. Remember that 2 bits are needed for each nucleotide. As a result, the index of each `Character` in the initial `String` is multiplied by 2 to find the start of each nucleotide in the bit string.

Finally, we will implement decompression.

```
func decompress() -> String {
    var gene: String = ""
    for index in 0..<length {
        let nStart = index * 2 // start of each nucleotide
        let firstBit = CFBitVectorGetBitAtIndex(bitVector, nStart)
        let secondBit = CFBitVectorGetBitAtIndex(bitVector, nStart + 1)
        switch (firstBit, secondBit) {
        case (0, 0): // 00 A
            gene += "A"
        case (0, 1): // 01 C
            gene += "C"
        case (1, 0): // 10 G
            gene += "G"
        case (1, 1): // 11 T
            gene += "T"
        default:
            break // unreachable, but need default
        }
    }
    return gene
}
}
```

Finally, `decompress()` reads 2 bits from the bit string at a time. It assembles those bits into a tuple that is evaluated using Swift's built-in `switch` pattern-matching statement. The original `String` is reassembled and returned, completing the cycle. Let's test it out.

```
print(CompressedGene(original: "ATGAATGCC").decompress())
```

The original `String` should appear in the console after going through the compression/decompression cycle.

1.3   *Unbreakable encryption*

A one-time pad is a way of encrypting a piece of data by combining it with meaningless random dummy data in such a way that the original cannot be reconstituted without access to both the product and the dummy data. In essence, this leaves the encrypter with a key pair (one key is the product, one key is the random dummy data). One key on its own is useless—only the combination of both keys can unlock the original data. When performed correctly, a one-time pad is a form of unbreakable encryption. Figure 1.6 shows the process.

```
Original Data + Dummy Data -Encryption> Key-Pair (Dummy Data, Product)
➡ -Decryption> Original Data
```

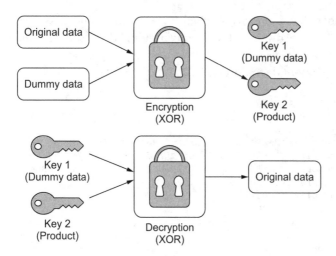

Figure 1.6   A one-time pad results in two keys that can be separated and then recombined to recreate the original data.

1.3.1   *Getting the data in order*

In this example, we will encrypt a `String` using a one-time pad. One way of thinking about a Swift `String` is as a sequence of UTF-8 bytes (with UTF-8 being a Unicode character encoding). A `String` provides a view of itself as a sequence of UTF-8 bytes through the `utf8` instance variable. This "view" is really of a sequence of `UInt8`, such that each UTF-8 byte is represented by one `UInt8`. We can therefore define a type for both our one-time pad keys and key pairs.

```
typealias OTPKey = [UInt8]
typealias OTPKeyPair = (key1: OTPKey, key2: OTPKey)
```

There are three criteria that the dummy data used in a one-time pad encryption operation must meet for the resulting product to be unbreakable. The dummy data must be the same length as the original data, truly random, and completely secret. The first and third criteria make common sense. If the dummy data repeats, because it is too short, there could be an observed pattern. If one of the keys is not truly secret (perhaps it is reused elsewhere or partially revealed), then an attacker has a clue. The second criteria poses a question all its own—can we produce truly random data? The answer for most computers is no.

In this example we will use the pseudo-random number generating function `arc4random_uniform()`, so our data will not be truly random (but close enough for our purposes). Let's work on generating a random `OTPKey` for use as dummy data.

```
func randomOTPKey(length: Int) -> OTPKey {
    var randomKey: OTPKey = OTPKey()
    for _ in 0..<length {
        let randomKeyPoint = UInt8(arc4random_uniform(UInt32(UInt8.max)))
```

the same procedure that we did from A to B. We move the top disc to A, the middle disc to C, and finally the top disc from A to C.

> **TIP** In a computer science classroom, it is not uncommon to see a little model of the towers built using dowels and plastic donuts. You can build your own model using three pencils and three pieces of paper. It may help you visualize the solution.

In our three-disc example, we had a simple base case of moving a single disc, and recursive case of moving all of the other discs (two in this case), using the third tower temporarily. We could break the recursive case into three steps:[3]

1. Move the upper n-1 discs from tower A to B (the temporary tower) using C as the in-between.
2. Move the single lowest disc from A to C.
3. Move the n-1 discs from tower B to C.

The amazing thing is that this recursive algorithm not only works for three discs, but for any number of discs. We will codify it as a function called `hanoi()` that is responsible for moving discs from one tower to another, given a third temporary tower.

```
func hanoi(from: Stack<Int>, to: Stack<Int>, temp: Stack<Int>, n: Int) {
    if n == 1 {  // base case
        to.push(from.pop()) // move 1 disk
    } else {  // recursive case
        hanoi(from: from, to: temp, temp: to, n: n-1)
        hanoi(from: from, to: to, temp: temp, n: 1)
        hanoi(from: temp, to: to, temp: from, n: n-1)
    }
}
```

After calling `hanoi()`, you should examine towers A, B, and C to verify that the discs were moved successfully.

```
hanoi(from: towerA, to: towerC, temp: towerB,  n: numDiscs)
print(towerA)
print(towerB)
print(towerC)
```

You will find that they were. In codifying the solution to the Towers of Hanoi, we did not necessarily need to understand every step required to move multiple discs from tower A to tower C. But we came to understand the general recursive algorithm for moving any number of discs, and we codified it, letting the computer do the rest. This is the power of formulating recursive solutions to problems—we often can think of solutions in an abstract manner without the drudgery of negotiating every individual action in our minds.

---

[3] "About the Towers of Hanoi," in *Surveying the Field of Computing* by Carl Burch (1999), http://mng.bz/c1i2.

Incidentally, the `hanoi()` function will execute an exponential number of times, which makes solving the problem for even 64 discs untenable. This is where the legend of the Towers of Hanoi that you can read more about in any number of sources comes from. You may also be interested in reading more about the mathematics behind its recursive solution: See Carl Burch's explanation in "About the Towers of Hanoi," http://mng.bz/c1i2.

1.6 *Real-world applications*

The various techniques presented in this chapter (recursion, memoization, compression, and manipulation at the bit level) are so common in modern software development that it is impossible to imagine the world of computing without them. Although problems can be solved without them, it is often more logical or performant to solve problems with them.

Recursion, in particular, is at the heart of not just many algorithms, but even whole programming languages. In some functional programming languages, like Scheme and Haskell, recursion takes the place of loops in procedural languages. It is worth remembering, though, that anything accomplishable with a recursive technique is also accomplishable with an iterative technique.

Memoization has been applied successfully to speed up the work of parsers (programs that interpret languages). It is useful in all fields where the result of a recent calculation will likely be asked for again. Another application of memoization is in language runtimes. Some language runtimes (versions of Prolog, for instance) will store the results of function calls automatically (*auto-memoization*), so that the function need not execute the next time the same call is made.

Compression has made an internet-connected world constrained by bandwidth more tolerable. The bit-string technique examined in section 1.2 is usable for real-world simple data types that have a limited number of possible values for which even a byte is overkill. The majority of compression algorithms, however, operate by finding patterns or structure within a data set that allow for repeated information to be eliminated. They are significantly more complicated than what is covered in section 1.2.

One-time pads are not practical for general encryption. They require both the encrypter and the decrypter to have possession of one of the same keys (the dummy data in our example) for the original data to be reconstructed, which is cumbersome and defeats the goal of most encryption schemes (keeping keys secret). But you may be interested to know that the name "one-time pad" comes from spies using real paper pads with dummy data on them to create encrypted communications during the Cold War.

These techniques are programmatic building blocks that other algorithms are built on top of. In future chapters you will see them applied liberally.

1.7 Exercises

1 Write yet another function that solves for element n of the Fibonacci sequence using a technique of your own design. Write unit tests that evaluate its correctness and performance relative to the other versions in this chapter.

2 The Core Foundation construct `CFMutableBitVector` used in section 1.2 has a C API. Write an ergonomic Swift wrapper around it. Reimplement `Compressed-Gene` using the wrapper.

3 Write a solver for The Towers of Hanoi that works for any number of towers.

4 Use a one-time pad to encrypt and decrypt images.

Search problems

2

"Search" is such a broad term that this entire book could be called "Classic Search Problems in Swift." This chapter is about core search algorithms that every programmer should know. It does not claim to be comprehensive, despite the declaratory title.

2.1   DNA search

Genes are commonly represented in computer software as a sequence of the characters A, C, G, and T. Each letter represents a *nucleotide*, and the combination of three nucleotides is called a *codon*. This is illustrated in figure 2.1. A codon codes

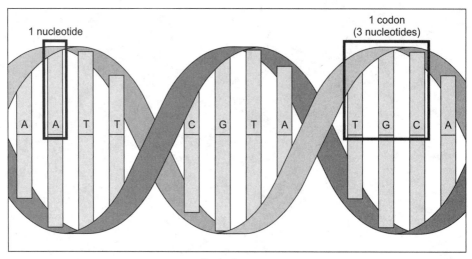

Part of a gene

Figure 2.1   A nucleotide is represented by one of the letters A, C, G, and T. A codon is composed of three nucleotides, and a gene is composed of multiple codons.

for a specific amino acid that together with other amino acids can form a *protein*. A classic task in bioinformatics software is to find a particular codon within a gene.

2.1.1 Storing DNA

We can represent a nucleotide as a simple enum with four cases.

```
enum Nucleotide: Character, Comparable {
    case A = "A", C = "C", G = "G", T = "T"
}
```

Nucleotide needs to implement the Comparable interface so that Nucleotides can be put in order. An entity that implements Comparable must override the < operator. This can be done either as a freestanding function, or as a static method inside the Comparable entity.

Here, we implement < as a freestanding function by comparing one Nucleotide's raw Character value against another's. Character has a built-in alphabetical ordering.

```
func <(lhs: Nucleotide, rhs: Nucleotide) -> Bool {
    return lhs.rawValue < rhs.rawValue
}
```

Codons can be defined as a tuple of three Nucleotides. And finally, a gene may be defined as an array of Codons.

```
typealias Codon = (Nucleotide, Nucleotide, Nucleotide)
typealias Gene = [Codon]
```

> **NOTE** Although we will later need to compare one Codon to another, we do not need to define the < operator for Codon. This is because Swift 2.2 introduced a generic implementation of < for any tuple type that contains elements of type Comparable.

Typically, genes that you find on the internet will be in a file format that contains a giant string representing all of the nucleotides in the gene's sequence. We will define such a string for an imaginary gene and call it geneSequence.

```
let geneSequence = "ACGTGGCTCTCTAACGTACGTACGTACGGGGTTTATATATACCCTAGGACTCCCTTT"
```

We will also need a utility function to convert a String into a Gene.

```
func stringToGene(_ s: String) -> Gene {
    var gene = Gene()
    for i in stride(from: 0, to: s.count, by: 3) {
        guard (i + 2) < s.count else { return gene }
        if let n1 = Nucleotide.init(rawValue: s[s.index(s.startIndex,
            offsetBy: i)]), let n2 = Nucleotide.init(rawValue:
            s[s.index(s.startIndex, offsetBy: i + 1)]), let n3 =
            Nucleotide.init(rawValue: s[s.index(s.startIndex,
            offsetBy: i + 2)]) {
```

```
            gene.append((n1, n2, n3))
        }
    }
    return gene
}
```

stringToGene() continually goes through the provided String and converts its next three characters into Codons that it adds to the end of a new Gene. If it finds that there is no Nucleotide two places into the future of the current place in s that it is examining (see the guard statement within the loop), then it knows it has reached the end of an incomplete gene, and it skips over those last one or two nucleotides.

stringToGene() can be used to convert the String geneSequence into a Gene.

```
var gene = stringToGene(geneSequence)
```

2.1.2   *Linear search*

One basic operation we may want to perform on a gene is to search it for a particular codon. The goal is to simply find out whether the codon exists within the gene or not.

A linear search goes through every element in a search space, in the order of the original data structure, until what is sought is found or the end of the data structure is reached. In effect, a linear search is the most simple, natural, and obvious way to search for something. In the worst case, a linear search will require going through every element in a data structure, so it is of O(n) complexity, where n is the number of elements in the structure. This is illustrated in figure 2.2.

It is trivial to define a function that performs a linear search. It simply must go through every element in a data structure and check for its equivalence to the item being sought. The following code defines such a function for a Gene and a Codon and then tries it out for gene and a Codon called acg.

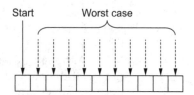

Figure 2.2   **In the worst case of a linear search, you'll sequentially look through every element of the array.**

```
func linearContains(_ array: Gene, item: Codon) -> Bool {
    for element in gene where item == element {
        return true
    }
    return false
}

let acg: Codon = (.A, .C, .G)
linearContains(gene, item: acg)
```

> **NOTE** The built-in Swift method on Sequence called contains() does a linear search and returns true if the element in question is found or false if it is not. It should be preferred to writing your own linear search function in most circumstances.

```
else {
    return true
}
```

If the element in question is not less than or greater than the middle element, that means we found it! And, of course, if the loop ran out of iterations, we return `false` (not reproduced here), indicating that it was never found.

We can try running our function with the same gene and codon, but we must remember to sort first:

```
let sortedGene = gene.sorted(by: <)
binaryContains(sortedGene, item: acg)
```

2.1.4 *A generic example*

The functions `linearContains()` and `binaryContains()` can be generalized to work with any type that implements `Comparable`. These generalized versions are nearly identical to the versions you saw before, with only their type signatures changed.

> **NOTE** As of Swift 4.0, tuples cannot be made to explicitly implement `Comparable`, so our prior types `Gene` and `Codon` cannot be used with these generic implementations.

```
func linearContains<T: Equatable>(_ array: [T], item: T) -> Bool {
    for element in array where item == element {
        return true
    }
    return false
}

func binaryContains<T: Comparable>(_ array: [T], item: T) -> Bool {
    var low = 0
    var high = array.count - 1
    while low <= high {
        let mid = (low + high) / 2
        if array[mid] < item {
            low = mid + 1
        } else if array[mid] > item {
            high = mid - 1
        } else {
            return true
        }
    }
    return false
}
```

Now you can try doing searches on other types of data.

```
linearContains([1,5,15,15,15,15,15], item: 5)
binaryContains(["a", "d", "e", "f", "g"], item: "f")
```

2.2   Maze solving

Finding a path through a maze is analogous to many common search problems in computer science. Why not literally find a path through a maze then, to illustrate the breadth-first search, depth-first search, and A* algorithms?

Our maze will be a two-dimensional array of Cell. A Cell is an enum with raw Character values where O will represent an empty space and X will represent a blocked space. There are also various other cases for illustrative purposes when printing a maze.

```
// A Cell represents the status of a grid location in the maze
enum Cell: Character {
    case Empty = "O"
    case Blocked = "X"
    case Start = "S"
    case Goal = "G"
    case Path = "P"
}

typealias Maze = [[Cell]]
```

2.2.1   Generating a random maze

The maze that is generated should be fairly sparse so that there is almost always a path from a given starting node to a given ending node (this is for testing our algorithms, after all). We'll let the caller of generateMaze() decide on the exact sparseness. When a random number beats the threshold of the sparseness parameter in question, we'll simply replace an empty space with a wall. If we do this for every possible place in the maze, statistically the sparseness of the maze as a whole will approximate the sparseness parameter supplied.

```
srand48(time(nil)) // seed random number generator

// sparseness is the approximate percentage of walls represented
// as a number between 0 and 1
func generateMaze(rows: Int, columns: Int, sparseness: Double) -> Maze {
    // initialize maze full of empty spaces
    var maze: Maze = Maze(repeating: [Cell](repeating: .Empty, count:
    ➥ columns), count: rows)
    // put walls in
    for row in 0..<rows {
        for col in 0..<columns {
            if drand48() < sparseness { //chance of wall
                maze[row][col] = .Blocked
            }
        }
    }
    return maze
}
```

Now that we have a maze, we also want a way to print it succinctly to the console. We want its characters to be close together so it looks like a real maze.

```
func printMaze(_ maze: Maze) {
    for i in 0..<maze.count {
        print(String(maze[i].map{ $0.rawValue }))
    }
}
```

Go ahead and test these maze functions.

```
var maze = generateMaze(rows: 10, columns: 10, sparseness: 0.2)
printMaze(maze)
```

2.2.2 *Miscellaneous maze minutiae*

We'll need a way to refer to an individual location in the maze. This could be a tuple of row and column, but later we will want to store a maze location in data structures that require their keys to be Hashable. Instead, therefore, we will define a custom struct for maze locations (tuples do not conform and cannot be made to conform to Hashable). All Hashable conforming types must also implement the == operator.

```
struct MazeLocation: Hashable {
    let row: Int
    let col: Int
    var hashValue: Int { return row.hashValue ^ col.hashValue }
}

func == (lhs: MazeLocation, rhs: MazeLocation) -> Bool {
    return lhs.row == rhs.row && lhs.col == rhs.col
}
```

It will be handy later to have a function that checks whether we have reached our goal during the search. In other words, we want to check whether a particular MazeLocation that the search has reached is the goal. We'll arbitrarily define the goal as always being at location 9, 9 for now.

```
let goal = MazeLocation(row: 9, col: 9)
func goalTest(ml: MazeLocation) -> Bool {
    return ml == goal
}
```

How can one move within our mazes? Let's say that one can move horizontally and vertically one space at a time from a given space in the maze. Using these criteria, a successors() function can find the possible next locations from a given MazeLocation. However, the successors() function will differ for every Maze because every Maze has a different size and set of walls. Therefore, we will define a successorsForMaze() function that returns an appropriate successors() function for the Maze in question.

```
func successorsForMaze(_ maze: Maze) -> (MazeLocation) -> [MazeLocation] {
func successors(ml: MazeLocation) -> [MazeLocation] { //no  diagonals
    var newMLs: [MazeLocation] = [MazeLocation]()
    if (ml.row + 1 < maze.count) && (maze[ml.row + 1][ml.col] != .Blocked) {
        newMLs.append(MazeLocation(row: ml.row + 1, col: ml.col))
    }
    if (ml.row - 1 >= 0) && (maze[ml.row - 1][ml.col] != .Blocked) {
        newMLs.append(MazeLocation(row: ml.row - 1, col: ml.col))
    }
    if (ml.col + 1 < maze[0].count) && (maze[ml.row][ml.col + 1] != .Blocked) {
        newMLs.append(MazeLocation(row: ml.row, col: ml.col + 1))
    }
    if (ml.col - 1 >= 0) && (maze[ml.row][ml.col - 1] != .Blocked) {
        newMLs.append(MazeLocation(row: ml.row, col: ml.col - 1))
    }

    return newMLs
}
    return successors
}
```

successors() simply checks above, below, to the right, and to the left of a MazeLocation in a Maze to see if it can find empty spaces that can be gone to from that location. It also avoids checking locations beyond the edges of the Maze. Every possible MazeLocation that it finds it puts into an array that it ultimately returns to the caller.

The pattern of successors(), a function returning a function, is unusual in Objective-C and in most pure object-oriented programming languages, but it is common in functional languages. The inner function captures data from the outer function. In this case, successors() captures maze from successorsForMaze(). Such a pattern can sometimes be confusing to implement, but ultimately it can offer more convenience for the user of an API. An alternative, equally convenient pattern would be to create a Maze class (instead of using a raw typealias) and add a successors() method to it. Neither approach is inherently wrong or right. The fact that both are possible in Swift shows its flexibility and that it straddles both the functional and object-oriented worlds.

2.2.3   *Depth-first search*

A depth-first search (DFS) is what its name suggests—a search that goes as deeply as it can before backtracking to its last decision point if it reaches a dead end. We will implement a generic depth-first search that can solve our maze problem. It will also be reusable for other problems. Figure 2.4 illustrates an in-progress depth-first search of a maze.

STACKS

The depth-first search algorithm relies on a data structure known as a *stack*. (If you read about stacks in chapter 1, feel free to skip this section). A stack is a data structure that operates under the Last-In-First-Out (LIFO) principle. Imagine a stack of papers.

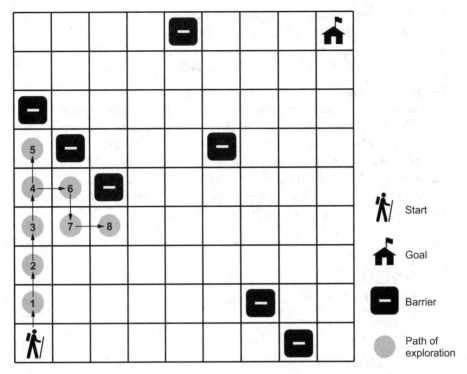

Figure 2.4 **In depth-first search, the search proceeds along a continuously deeper path until it hits a barrier and must backtrack to the last decision point.**

The last paper placed on top of the stack is the first paper pulled off the stack. It is common for a stack to be implemented on top of a more primitive data structure like a linked list. We will implement our stack on top of Swift's `Array` type.

Stacks generally have at least two operations:

- `push()`—Places an item on top of the stack
- `pop()`—Removes the item on the top of the stack and returns it

We will implement both of these, as well as an `isEmpty` property to check if the stack has any more items in it.[1]

```
public class Stack<T> {
    private var container: [T] = [T]()
    public var isEmpty: Bool { return container.isEmpty }
    public func push(thing: T) { container.append(thing) }
    public func pop() -> T { return container.removeLast() }
}
```

---

[1] These examples are based on prior code I wrote for the SwiftGraph open source project: https://github.com/davecom/SwiftGraph.

Note that implementing a stack using a Swift `Array` is as simple as always appending items onto its right end, and always removing items from its extreme right end. The `removeLast()` method on `Array` will fail if there are no longer any items in the array, so `pop()` will fail on a `Stack` if it is empty as well.

THE DFS ALGORITHM

We will need one more little tidbit before we can get to implementing DFS. We need a `Node` class that will be used to keep track of how we got from one state to another state (or from one place to another place) as we search. You can think of a `Node` as a wrapper around a state. In the case of our maze-solving problem, those states are of type `MazeLocation`. We'll call the `Node` that a state came from its parent. We will also define our `Node` class as having `cost` and `heuristic` properties and as being `Comparable` and `Hashable`, so we can reuse it later in the A* algorithm.

```
class Node<T>: Comparable, Hashable {
    let state: T
    let parent: Node?
    let cost: Float
    let heuristic: Float
    init(state: T, parent: Node?, cost: Float = 0.0, heuristic: Float = 0.0) {
        self.state = state
        self.parent = parent
        self.cost = cost
        self.heuristic = heuristic
    }

    var hashValue: Int { return Int(cost + heuristic) }
}

func < <T>(lhs: Node<T>, rhs: Node<T>) -> Bool {
    return (lhs.cost + lhs.heuristic) < (rhs.cost + rhs.heuristic)
}

func == <T>(lhs: Node<T>, rhs: Node<T>) -> Bool {
    return lhs === rhs
}
```

An in-progress depth-first search needs to keep track of two data structures: the stack of states (or "places") that we are considering searching, which we will call the frontier; and the set of states that we have already searched, which we will call visited. As long as there are more states to visit in the frontier, DFS will keep checking whether they are the goal (if a state is the goal, it will stop and return it) and adding their successors to the frontier. It will also mark each state that has already been searched as visited, so that it does not get caught in a circle, reaching states that have prior visited states as successors. If the frontier is empty, it means there is nowhere left to search.

```
func dfs<StateType:
 ➡ Hashable>(initialState: StateType, goalTestFn: (StateType)
 ➡ -> Bool, successorFn: (StateType) -> [StateType]) -> Node<StateType>? {
    // frontier is where we've yet to go
    let frontier: Stack<Node<StateType>> = Stack<Node<StateType>>()
    frontier.push(Node(state: initialState, parent: nil))
    // explored is where we've been
    var explored: Set<StateType> = Set<StateType>()
    explored.insert(initialState)

    // keep going while there is more to explore
    while !frontier.isEmpty {
        let currentNode = frontier.pop()
        let currentState = currentNode.state
        // if we found the goal, we're done
        if goalTestFn(currentState) { return currentNode }
        // check where we can go next and haven't explored
        for child in successorFn(currentState) where
        ➡ !explored.contains(child) {
            explored.insert(child)
            frontier.push(Node(state: child, parent: currentNode))
        }
    }
    return nil // never found the goal
}
```

If `dfs()` is successful, it returns the `Node` encapsulating the goal state. The path from the start to the goal can be reconstructed by working backward from this `Node` and its priors using the `parent` property.

```
func nodeToPath<StateType>(_ node: Node<StateType>) -> [StateType] {
    var path: [StateType] = [node.state]
    var node = node // local modifiable copy of reference
    // work backwards from end to front
    while let currentNode = node.parent {
        path.insert(currentNode.state, at: 0)
        node = currentNode
    }
    return path
}
```

For display purposes, it will be useful to mark up the maze with the successful path, the start state, and the goal state.

```
func markMaze(_ maze: inout Maze, path: [MazeLocation], start: MazeLocation,
➡ goal: MazeLocation) {
    for ml in path {
        maze[ml.row][ml.col] = .Path
    }
    maze[start.row][start.col] = .Start
    maze[goal.row][goal.col] = .Goal
}
```

NOTE   inout indicates that the original object passed as maze will be modified by markMaze() instead of simply being copied into a temporary variable within markMaze() and forgotten about. At optimization time, inout is analogous to "call by reference" in other programming languages. To be clear—markMaze() modifies the original maze it is passed. The changes that are made to that maze will persist after the function ends. At call time, inout arguments are passed with a preceding ampersand, &.

It has been a long journey, but we are finally ready to solve the maze.

```
let start = MazeLocation(row: 0, col: 0)

if let solution = dfs(initialState: start, goalTestFn: goalTest, successorFn:
➥ successorsForMaze(maze)) {
    let path = nodeToPath(solution)
    markMaze(&maze, path: path, start: start, goal: goal)
    printMaze(maze)
}
```

A successful solution will look something like this:

```
SPXOOOOXOO
OPPPPPPPPO
XOOOOOOOPO
OOOOXPPPPX
OXXOXPXOXO
OXPPPOOOO
PPPXXXOOOX
POOOXOOOOX
PPPPPPPPPP
OOOXOOOOOG
```

Remember, because each maze is randomly generated, not every maze has a solution.

2.2.4   *Breadth-first search*

You may notice that the solution paths to the mazes found by depth-first traversal seem unnatural. They are usually not the shortest paths. Breadth-first search (BFS) always finds the shortest path by systematically looking one layer of nodes further away from the start state each iteration of the search. There are particular problems in which a depth-first search is likely to find a solution prior to a breadth-first search, and vice versa. Therefore, choosing between the two is sometimes a trade-off between the possibility of finding a solution quickly and the certainty of finding the shortest path to the goal (if one exists). Figure 2.5 illustrates an in-progress breadth-first search of a maze.

To understand why a depth-first search sometimes returns a result faster than a breadth-first search, imagine looking for a marking on a particular layer of an onion. A searcher using a depth-first strategy may plunge a knife into the center of the onion and haphazardly examine the chunks cut out. If the marked layer happens to be near

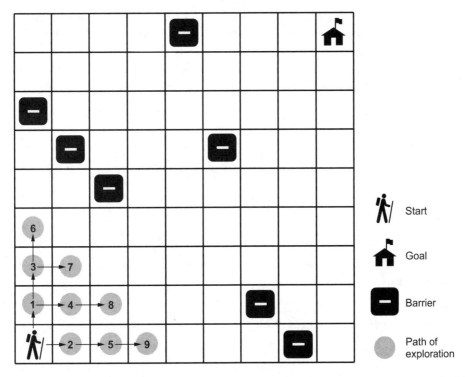

Figure 2.5 In a breadth-first search, the closest elements to the starting location are searched first.

the chunk cut out, there is a chance that the searcher will find it more quickly than another searcher using a breadth-first strategy who painstakingly peels back the onion one layer at a time.

To get a better picture of why breadth-first search always finds the shortest solution path where one exists, consider trying to find the path with the fewest number of stops between Boston and New York by train. If you keep going in the same direction and backtracking when you hit a dead end (as in depth-first search), you may first find a route all the way to Seattle before it connects back to New York. However, in a breadth-first search, you will first check all of the stations one stop away from Boston. Then you will check all of the stations two stops away from Boston. Then you will check all of the stations three stops away from Boston. This will keep going until you find New York. Therefore, when you do find New York, you will know you have found the route with the fewest stops, because you already checked all of the stations that are fewer stops away from Boston, and none of them were New York.

QUEUES

To implement BFS, a data structure known as a *queue* is required. Whereas a stack is LIFO, a queue is FIFO—First-In-First-Out. A queue is like a line to use a restroom. The first person who got in line goes to the restroom first. At a minimum, a queue has the same push() and pop() methods as a stack. In fact, our implementation for Queue (backed by a Swift Array) is almost identical to our implementation of Stack, with the only change being the removal of elements from the left end of the Array instead of the right end. The elements on the left end are the oldest elements still in the Array (in terms of arrival time), so they are the first elements popped.[2]

```
public class Queue<T> {
    private var container: [T] = [T]()
    public var isEmpty: Bool { return container.isEmpty }
    public func push(thing: T) { container.append(thing) }
    public func pop() -> T { return container.removeFirst() }
}
```

THE BFS ALGORITHM

Amazingly, the algorithm for a breadth-first search is identical to the algorithm for a depth-first search, with the frontier changed from a stack to a queue. Changing the frontier from a stack to a queue changes the order in which states are searched and ensures that the states closest to the start state are searched first.

```
func bfs<StateType:
➥ Hashable>(initialState: StateType, goalTestFn: (StateType)
➥ -> Bool, successorFn: (StateType) -> [StateType]) -> Node<StateType>? {
    // frontier is where we've yet to go
    let frontier: Queue<Node<StateType>> = Queue<Node<StateType>>()
    frontier.push(Node(state: initialState, parent: nil))
    // explored is where we've been
    var explored: Set<StateType> = Set<StateType>()
    explored.insert(initialState)
    // keep going while there is more to explore
    while !frontier.isEmpty {
        let currentNode = frontier.pop()
        let currentState = currentNode.state
        // if we found the goal, we're done
        if goalTestFn(currentState) { return currentNode }
        // check where we can go next and haven't explored
        for child in successorFn(currentState) where
        ➥ !explored.contains(child) {
            explored.insert(child)
            frontier.push(Node(state: child, parent: currentNode))
        }
    }
    return nil // never found the goal
}
```

If you try running bfs(), you will find it always finds the shortest solution to the maze in question.

---

[2] These examples are based on prior code I wrote for the SwiftGraph open source project: https://github.com/davecom/SwiftGraph.

```
var maze2 = generateMaze(rows: 10, columns: 10, sparseness: 0.2)
if let solution = bfs(initialState: start, goalTestFn: goalTest, successorFn:
    successorsForMaze(maze2)) {
    let path = nodeToPath(solution)
    markMaze(&maze2, path: path, start: start, goal: goal)
    printMaze(maze2)
}
```

2.2.5 A* search

It can be very time consuming to peel back an onion, layer-by-layer, as a breadth-first search does. Like a BFS, an A* search aims to find the shortest path from a start state to a goal state. Unlike the preceding BFS implementation, an A* search uses a combination of a cost function and a heuristic function to focus its search on pathways most likely to get to the goal quickly.

The cost function, $g(n)$, examines the cost to get to a particular state. In the case of our maze, this would be how many previous steps we had to go through to get to the state in question. The heuristic function, $h(n)$, gives an estimate of the cost to get from the state in question to the goal state. It can be proven that if $h(n)$ is an *admissible heuristic*, then the final path found will be optimal. An admissible heuristic is one that never overestimates the cost to reach the goal. (On a two-dimensional plane, one example is a straight-line distance heuristic, because a straight line is always the shortest path.)[3]

The total cost for any state being considered is $f(n)$, which is simply the combination of $g(n)$ and $h(n)$. In fact, $f(n) = g(n) + h(n)$. When choosing the next state to explore off of the frontier, A* search picks the one with the lowest $f(n)$. This is how it distinguishes itself from BFS and DFS.

PRIORITY QUEUES

To pick the state on the frontier with the lowest $f(n)$, an A* search uses a *priority queue* as the data structure for its frontier. A priority queue keeps its elements in an internal order, such that the first element popped out is always the highest priority element (in our case, the highest priority item is the one with the lowest $f(n)$). Usually this means the internal use of a binary heap, which results in $O(\lg n)$ pushes and $O(\lg n)$ pops.

Although the standard libraries of many modern programming languages contain a built-in priority queue, Swift's does not. We will not implement a priority queue from scratch. Instead we will utilize the open source project SwiftPriorityQueue, which I built.[4]

To determine the priority of a particular element versus another of its kind, Swift-PriorityQueue requires that the type of its elements implements the Swift standard library protocol Comparable. This is why the Node class was defined as Comparable and

---

[3] For more information on heuristics, see Stuart Russell and Peter Norvig, *Artificial Intelligence: A Modern Approach*, third edition (Pearson, 2010), page 94.

[4] These examples are based on prior code I wrote for the SwiftPriorityQueue open source project: https://github.com/davecom/SwiftPriorityQueue.

therefore had to implement the < operator. A Node is compared to another by looking at its respective f(n), which is simply the sum of the properties cost and heuristic.

HEURISTICS

A *heuristic* is an intuition about the way to solve a problem.[5] In the case of maze solving, a heuristic aims to choose the best maze location to search next, in the quest to get to the goal. In other words, it is an educated guess about which nodes on the frontier are closest to the goal. As was mentioned previously, if a heuristic used with an A* search produces an accurate relative result and is admissible (never overestimates the distance), then A* will deliver the shortest path. Heuristics that calculate smaller values end up leading to a search through more states, whereas heuristics closer to the exact real distance (but not over it, which would make them inadmissible) lead to a search through fewer states. Therefore, ideal heuristics come as close to the real distance as possible without ever going over it.

EUCLIDEAN DISTANCE

As we learn in geometry, the shortest path between two points is a straight line. It makes sense, then, that a straight-line heuristic will always be admissible for the maze-solving problem. The Euclidean distance, derived from the Pythagorean theorem, states that distance = $\sqrt{((\text{difference in x})^2 + (\text{difference in y})^2)}$. For our mazes, the difference in x is equivalent to the difference in columns of two maze locations, and the difference in y is equivalent to the difference in rows.

```
func euclideanDistance(ml: MazeLocation) -> Float {
    let xdist = ml.col - goal.col
    let ydist = ml.row - goal.row
    return sqrt(Float((xdist * xdist) + (ydist * ydist)))
}
```

Figure 2.6 illustrates Euclidean distance within the context of a grid, like the streets of Manhattan.

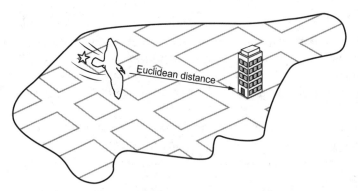

Figure 2.6 Euclidean distance is the length of a straight line from the starting point to the goal.

---

[5] For more about heuristics for A* pathfinding, check out the "Heuristics" chapter in Amit Patel's *Amit's Thoughts on Pathfinding*, http://mng.bz/z7O4.

MANHATTAN DISTANCE

Euclidean distance is great, but for our particular problem (a maze in which you can move only in one of four directions) we can do even better. The Manhattan distance is derived from navigating the streets of Manhattan, the most famous of New York City's boroughs, which is laid out in a grid pattern. To get from anywhere to anywhere in Manhattan, one needs to walk a certain number of horizontal blocks and a certain number of vertical blocks (there are almost no diagonal streets in Manhattan). The Manhattan distance is derived by simply finding the difference in rows between two maze locations and summing it with the difference in columns. Figure 2.7 illustrates Manhattan distance.

```
func manhattanDistance(ml: MazeLocation) -> Float {
    let xdist = abs(ml.col - goal.col)
    let ydist = abs(ml.row - goal.row)
    return Float(xdist + ydist)
}
```

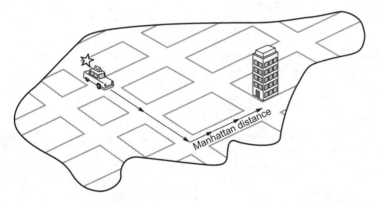

Figure 2.7   In Manhattan distance, there are no diagonals. The path must be along parallel or perpendicular lines.

Because this heuristic more accurately follows the actuality of navigating our mazes (moving vertically and horizontally instead of in diagonal straight lines), it comes closer to the actual distance from any maze location to the goal than Euclidean distance does. Therefore, when an A* search is coupled with Manhattan distance, it will result in searching through fewer states than when an A* search is coupled with Euclidean distance for our mazes. Solution paths will still be optimal, because Manhattan distance is admissible (never overestimates distance) for mazes in which only four directions of movement are allowed.

THE A* ALGORITHM

To go from BFS to A* search, we need to make several small modifications. The first is changing the frontier from a queue to a priority queue. Now the frontier will pop nodes with the lowest f(n). The second is changing the explored set to a dictionary. A dictionary will allow us to keep track of the lowest cost (g(n)) of each node we may visit. With the heuristic function now at play, it is possible some nodes may be visited twice if the heuristic is inconsistent. If the node found through the new direction has a lower cost to get to than the prior time we visited it, we will prefer the new route.

For the sake of simplicity, the function astar() does not take a cost-calculation function as a parameter. Instead, we just consider every hop in our maze to be a cost of 1. Each new Node gets assigned a cost based on this simple formula, as well as a heuristic score using a new function passed as a parameter to the search function called heuristicFn(). Other than these changes, astar() is remarkably similar to bfs().[6] Examine them side by side for comparison.

```
func astar<StateType:
    Hashable>(initialState: StateType, goalTestFn: (StateType)
    -> Bool, successorFn: (StateType) -> [StateType],
    heuristicFn: (StateType) -> Float) -> Node<StateType>? {
    // frontier is where we've yet to go
    var frontier: PriorityQueue<Node<StateType>> =
    PriorityQueue<Node<StateType>>(ascending:
    true, startingValues: [Node(state: initialState, parent:
    nil, cost: 0, heuristic: heuristicFn(initialState))])
    // explored is where we've been
    var explored = Dictionary<StateType, Float>()
    explored[initialState] = 0
    // keep going while there is more to explore
    while let currentNode = frontier.pop() {
        let currentState = currentNode.state
        // if we found the goal, we're done
        if goalTestFn(currentState) { return currentNode }
        // check where we can go next and haven't explored
        for child in successorFn(currentState) {
            let newcost = currentNode.cost + 1  //1 assumes a grid, there
    should be a cost function for more sophisticated applications
            if (explored[child] == nil) || (explored[child]! > newcost) {
                explored[child] = newcost
                frontier.push(Node(state: child, parent: currentNode,
    cost: newcost, heuristic: heuristicFn(child)))
            }
        }
    }
    return nil // never found the goal
}
```

Congratulations. If you have followed along this far, you have not only learned how to solve a maze, but also some generic search functions that you can use in many different search applications. DFS and BFS are suitable for many smaller data sets and state spaces where performance is not critical. In some situations, DFS will outperform BFS, but BFS has the advantage of always delivering an optimal path. Interestingly,

---

[6] These examples are based on prior code I wrote for the SwiftPriorityQueue open source project: https://github.com/davecom/SwiftPriorityQueue.

BFS and DFS have identical implementations, only differentiated by the use of a queue instead of a stack for the frontier. The slightly more complicated A* search, coupled with a good, consistent, admissible heuristic, not only delivers optimal paths but also far outperforms BFS.

Go ahead and try out `astar()`.

```
var maze3 = generateMaze(rows: 10, columns: 10, sparseness: 0.2)
if let solution = astar(initialState: start, goalTestFn: goalTest,
➥   successorFn: successorsForMaze(maze3), heuristicFn: manhattanDistance) {
    let path = nodeToPath(solution)
    markMaze(&maze3, path: path, start: start, goal: goal)
    printMaze(maze3)
}
```

2.3 *Missionaries and cannibals*

Three missionaries and three cannibals are on the west bank of a river. They have a canoe that can hold two people, and they all must cross to the east bank of the river. There may never be more cannibals than missionaries on either side of the river or the cannibals will eat the missionaries. Further, the canoe must have at least one person on board to cross the river. What sequence of crossings will successfully take the entire party across the river? Figure 2.8 illustrates the problem.

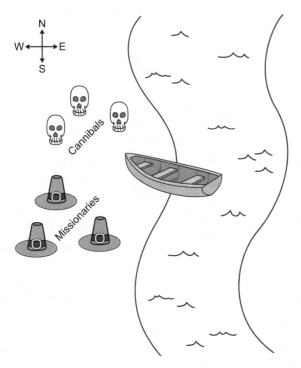

Figure 2.8 **The missionaries and cannibals must use their single canoe to take everyone across the river from west to east. If the cannibals ever outnumber the missionaries, they will eat them.**

2.3.1 *Representing the problem*

We will represent the problem by having a structure that keeps track of the west bank. How many missionaries and cannibals are on the west bank? Is the boat on the west bank? Once we have this knowledge, we can figure out what is on the east bank, because anything not on the west bank is on the east bank.

First, we will create a little convenience variable for keeping track of the maximum number of missionaries or cannibals. Then we will define the main structure.

```swift
let maxNum = 3 // max number of missionaries or cannibals

struct MCState: Hashable, CustomStringConvertible {
    let missionaries: Int
    let cannibals: Int
    let boat: Bool
    var hashValue: Int { return missionaries * 10 + cannibals + (boat ? 1000
        : 2000) }
    var description: String {
        let wm = missionaries // west bank missionaries
        let wc = cannibals // west bank cannibals
        let em = maxNum - wm // east bank missionaries
        let ec = maxNum - wc // east bank cannibals
        var description = "On the west bank there are \(wm) missionaries and
        \(wc) cannibals.\n"
        description += "On the east bank there are \(em) missionaries and
        \(ec) cannibals.\n"
        description += "The boat is on the \(boat ? "west" : "east") bank.\n"
        return description
    }
}

func ==(lhs: MCState, rhs: MCState) -> Bool {
    return lhs.hashValue == rhs.hashValue
}
```

The struct `MCState` implements `Hashable` and `CustomStringConvertible`. It implements `Hashable` because we want to be able to use it within the framework of our existing search functions and because we want to be able to distinguish one state from another. It implements `CustomStringConvertible` because we want to be able to print out a nicely formatted description of a given state in our program.

Working within the confines of our existing search functions means that we must define a function for testing whether a state is the goal state and a function for finding the successors from any state. The goal test function, as in the maze-solving problem, is quite simple. The goal is simply when there are no longer any people on the west bank of the river.

```swift
func goalTestMC(state: MCState) -> Bool {
    return state == MCState(missionaries: 0, cannibals: 0, boat: false)
}
```

To create a successors function, it is necessary to go through all of the possible moves that can be made from one bank to another, and then check if each of those moves will result in a legal state. Recall that a legal state is one in which cannibals do not out-number missionaries on either bank. To determine this, we can define a convenience function that checks if a state is legal.

```
func isLegalMC(state: MCState) -> Bool {
    let wm = state.missionaries // west bank missionaries
    let wc = state.cannibals // west bank cannibals
    let em = maxNum - wm // east bank missionaries
    let ec = maxNum - wc // east bank cannibals
    // check there's not more cannibals than missionaries
    if wm < wc && wm > 0 { return false }
    if em < ec && em > 0 { return false }
    return true
}
```

The actual successors function is a bit verbose for the sake of clarity. It tries adding every possible combination of one or two people moving across the river from the bank where the canoe currently resides. Once it has added all possible moves, it filters for the ones that are actually legal.

```
func successorsMC(state: MCState) -> [MCState] {
    let wm = state.missionaries // west bank missionaries
    let wc = state.cannibals // west bank cannibals
    let em = maxNum - wm // east bank missionaries
    let ec = maxNum - wc // east bank cannibals
    var sucs: [MCState] = [MCState]() // next states

    if state.boat { // boat on west bank
        if wm > 1 {
            sucs.append(MCState(missionaries: wm - 2, cannibals: wc, boat:
            ➥ !state.boat))
        }
        if wm > 0 {
            sucs.append(MCState(missionaries: wm - 1, cannibals: wc, boat:
            ➥ !state.boat))
        }
        if wc > 1 {
            sucs.append(MCState(missionaries: wm, cannibals: wc - 2, boat:
            ➥ !state.boat))
        }
        if wc > 0 {
            sucs.append(MCState(missionaries: wm, cannibals: wc - 1, boat:
            ➥ !state.boat))
        }
        if (wc > 0) && (wm > 0){
            sucs.append(MCState(missionaries: wm - 1, cannibals: wc - 1, boat:
            ➥ !state.boat))
        }
    } else { // boat on east bank
        if em > 1 {
```

```
                    sucs.append(MCState(missionaries: wm + 2, cannibals: wc, boat:
                    ➡ !state.boat))
            }
            if em > 0 {
                    sucs.append(MCState(missionaries: wm + 1, cannibals: wc, boat:
                    ➡ !state.boat))
            }
            if ec > 1 {
                    sucs.append(MCState(missionaries: wm, cannibals: wc + 2, boat:
                    ➡ !state.boat))
            }
            if ec > 0 {
                    sucs.append(MCState(missionaries: wm, cannibals: wc + 1, boat:
                    ➡ !state.boat))
            }
            if (ec > 0) && (em > 0){
                    sucs.append(MCState(missionaries: wm + 1, cannibals: wc + 1, boat:
                    ➡ !state.boat))
            }
        }

        return sucs.filter{ isLegalMC(state: $0) }
}
```

2.3.2   *Solving*

We now have all of the ingredients in place to solve the problem. Recall that when we solve a problem using the search functions bfs(), dfs(), and astar(), we get back a Node that ultimately we convert using nodeToPath() into an array of states that leads to a solution. What we still need is a way to convert that array into a comprehensible printed sequence of steps to solve the missionaries and cannibals problem.

The function printMCSolution() converts a solution path into printed output—a human-readable solution to the problem. It works by iterating through all of the states in the solution path while keeping track of the last state as well. It looks at the difference between the last state and the state it is currently iterating on to find how many missionaries and cannibals moved across the river and in what direction.

```
func printMCSolution(path: [MCState]) {
    var oldState = path.first!
    print(oldState)
    for currentState in path[1..<path.count] {
        let wm = currentState.missionaries // west bank missionaries
        let wc = currentState.cannibals // west bank cannibals
        let em = maxNum - wm // east bank missionaries
        let ec = maxNum - wc // east bank cannibals
        if !currentState.boat {
            print("\(oldState.missionaries - wm) missionaries and
            ➡ \(oldState.cannibals - wc) cannibals moved from the west bank
            ➡ to the east bank.")
        } else {
            print("\(maxNum - oldState.missionaries - em) missionaries
            ➡ and \(maxNum - oldState.cannibals - ec) cannibals moved from
```

```
        ➡ the east bank to the west bank.")
        }
        print(currentState)
        oldState = currentState
    }
}
```

The `printMCSolution()` function takes advantage of the fact that `MCState` is `Custom-StringConvertible` to print out a state's description with `print()`.

The last thing we need to do is actually solve the missionaries and cannibals problem. To do so we could use any of our previously implemented search functions. This solution uses `bfs()`.

```
let startMC = MCState(missionaries: 3, cannibals: 3, boat: true)
if let solution = bfs(initialState: startMC, goalTestFn: goalTestMC,
➡ successorFn: successorsMC) {
    let path = nodeToPath(solution)
    printMCSolution(path: path)
}
```

It is great to see how flexible our generic search functions can be. They can easily be adapted for solving a diverse set of problems.

2.4   *Real-world applications*

Search plays some role in all useful software. In some cases it is the central element (Google Search, Spotlight, Lucene); in others it is the basis for using the structures that underlie data storage. Knowing the correct search algorithm to apply to a data structure is essential for performance. For example, it would be very costly to use linear search, instead of binary search, on a sorted data structure.

A* is one of the most widely deployed path-finding algorithms. It is only beaten by algorithms that do precalculation in the search space. For a blind search, A* is yet to be reliably beaten in all scenarios, and this has made it an essential component of everything from route planning to figuring out the shortest way to parse a programming language. Most directions-providing map software (think Google Maps) uses Dijkstra's Algorithm (which A* is a variant of) to navigate (there is more about Dijkstra's Algorithm in chapter 4). Whenever an AI character in a game is finding the shortest-path from one end of the world to the other without human intervention, it is probably using A*.

Breadth-first search and depth-first search are often the basis for more complex search algorithms like uniform-cost search and backtracking search (which you will see in the next chapter). Breadth-first search is often a sufficient technique for finding the shortest path in a fairly small graph. But due to its similarity to A*, it is easy to swap out for A* if a good heuristic exists for a larger graph.

2.5   *Exercises*

1   Show the performance advantage of binary search over linear search by creating an array of one million numbers and timing how long it takes the linear-Contains() and binaryContains() functions defined in this chapter to find various numbers in the array.

2   Add a counter to dfs(), bfs(), and astar() to see how many states each searches through for the same maze. Find the counts for 100 different mazes to get statistically significant results.

3   Find a solution to the missionaries and cannibals problem for a different number of starting missionaries and cannibals.

Constraint-satisfaction problems 3

A large number of problems that computational tools are used to solve can be broadly categorized as constraint-satisfaction problems (CSPs). CSPs are composed of *variables* with possible values that fall into ranges known as *domains. Constraints* between the variables must be satisfied in order for constraint-satisfaction problems to be solved. Those three core concepts—variables, domains, and constraints—are simple to understand, and their generality underlies the wide applicability of constraint-satisfaction problem solving.

Let's consider an example problem. Suppose you are trying to schedule a Friday meeting for Joe, Mary, and Sue. Sue has to be at the meeting with at least one other person. For this scheduling problem, the three people—Joe, Mary, and Sue—may be the variables. The domain for each variable may be their respective hours of availability. For instance, the variable Mary has the domain 2 P.M., 3 P.M., and 4 P.M. This problem also has two constraints. One is that Sue has to be at the meeting. The other is that at least two people must attend the meeting. A constraint-satisfaction problem solver will be provided with the three variables, three domains, and two constraints, and it will then solve the problem without having the user explain exactly *how*. Figure 3.1 illustrates this example.

Programming languages like Prolog and Picat have facilities for solving constraint-satisfaction problems built in. The usual technique in other languages is to build a framework that incorporates a backtracking search and several heuristics to improve the performance of that search. In this chapter we will first build a framework for CSPs that solves them using a simple recursive backtracking search. Then we will use the framework to solve several different example problems.

Friday meeting

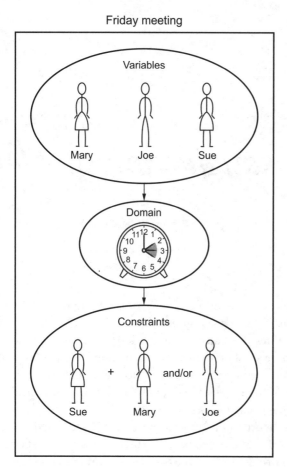

**Figure 3.1   Scheduling problems
are a classic application of
constraint-satisfaction frameworks.**

3.1   *Building a constraint-satisfaction problem framework*

The centerpiece of our constraint-satisfaction framework will be a struct called CSP. CSP
is the gathering point for variables, domains, and constraints. It uses generics to make
itself flexible enough to work with any kind of variables (type V, which must be Hashable
so that the variables can be used as keys in a Dictionary) and domain values (V keys and
D domain values). Within CSP, the definitions of the collections variables, domains, and
constraints are of types that you would expect. The variables collection is an Array
of variables, domains is a Dictionary mapping variables to arrays of possible values (the
domains of those variables), and constraints is a Dictionary that maps each variable
to an Array of the constraints imposed on it.

> **NOTE**   The framework described in this section, and the examples that follow it,
> is largely based on a simplified version of my SwiftCSP open source project
> (https://github.com/davecom/SwiftCSP). SwiftCSP includes a couple of more
> advanced optimization techniques.

```
/// Defines a constraint-satisfaction problem. V is the type of the variables
    ➥ and D is the type of the domains.
public struct CSP <V: Hashable, D> {
    /// The variables in the CSP to be constrained.
    let variables: [V]
    /// The domains - every variable should have an associated domain.
    let domains: [V: [D]]
    /// The constraints on the variables.
    var constraints = Dictionary<V, [Constraint<V, D>]>()

    /// You should create the variables and domains before initializing the
        ➥ CSP.
    public init (variables: [V], domains:[V: [D]]) {
        self.variables = variables
        self.domains = domains
        for variable in variables {
            constraints[variable] = [Constraint]()
            if domains[variable] == nil {
                print("Error: Missing domain for variable \(variable).")
            }
        }
    }

    /// Add a constraint to the CSP. It will automatically be applied to
        ➥ all the variables it includes. It should only include variables
        ➥ actually in the CSP.
    ///
    /// - parameter constraint: The constraint to add.
    public mutating func addConstraint(_ constraint: Constraint<V, D>) {
        for variable in constraint.vars {
            if !variables.contains(variable) {
                print("Error: Could not find variable \(variable)
                    ➥ from constraint \(constraint) in CSP.")
            }
            constraints[variable]?.append(constraint)
        }
    }
}
```

The `init()` initializer creates the `constraintsDictionary`. The `addConstraint()` method goes through all of the variables touched by a given constraint and adds itself to the `constraints` mapping for each of them. Both methods have error-checking in place, but there is no formal failure, other than an error printout, when a `variable` is missing a domain or a `constraint` is on a nonexistent variable. In a more formal system it would make sense to have a failable initializer and an exception-raising `addConstraint()` method.

Constraints are defined using a `Constraint` class. Each `Constraint` consists of the variables it constrains (titled `vars`, so as not to be confused with `variables` on CSP) and a method that checks whether it is satisfied. The determination of whether a constraint is satisfied is the main logic that goes into defining a specific constraint-satisfaction problem. The default implementation should be overridden. It just returns `true`.

```
/// The base class of all constraints.
open class Constraint <V: Hashable, D> {
    /// All subclasses should override this method. It defines whether a
    ➥ constraint has successfully been satisfied
    /// - parameter assignment: Potential domain selections for
    ➥ variables that are part of the constraint.
    /// - returns: Whether the constraint is satisfied.
    func isSatisfied(assignment: Dictionary<V, D>) -> Bool {
        return true
    }
    /// The variables that make up the constraint.
    var vars: [V] { return [] }
}
```

This constraint-satisfaction framework will use a simple backtracking search to find solutions to problems. *Backtracking* is the idea that once you hit a wall in your search, you go back to the last known point where you made a decision before the wall, and choose a different path. If you think that sounds like depth-first search from chapter 2, you are perceptive. The backtracking search implemented in the following backtrackingSearch() function is a kind of recursive depth-first search.

```
public func backtrackingSearch<V, D>(csp: CSP<V, D>, assignment:
➥ Dictionary<V, D> = Dictionary<V, D>()) -> Dictionary<V, D>?
{
    // assignment is complete if it has as many assignments as there
        ➥ are variables
    if assignment.count == csp.variables.count { return assignment } // base
    ➥ case

    // what are the unassigned variables?
    let unassigned = csp.variables.lazy.filter({ assignment[$0] == nil })

    // get the domain of the first unassigned variable
    if let variable: V = unassigned.first, let domain =
    ➥ csp.domains[variable] {
        // try each value in the domain
        for value in domain {
            var localAssignment = assignment
            localAssignment[variable] = value
            // if the value is consistent with the current assignment
                ➥ we continue
            if isConsistent(variable: variable, value: value, assignment:
            ➥ localAssignment, csp: csp) {
                // if as we go down the tree we get a complete assignment,
                    ➥ return it
                if let result = backtrackingSearch(csp: csp, assignment:
                ➥ localAssignment) {
                    return result
                }
            }
        }
    }
    return nil  // no solution
}
```

Let's walk through backtrackingSearch(), line by line.

```
if assignment.count == csp.variables.count { return assignment }
```

The base case for the recursive search is having found a valid assignment for every variable. Once we have, we return the first instance of a solution that was valid (we do not keep searching).

```
let unassigned = csp.variables.lazy.filter({ assignment[$0] == nil })
if let variable: V = unassigned.first, let domain = csp.domains[variable] {
```

To select a new variable whose domain we will explore, we simply go through all of the variables and find the first that does not have an assignment. To do this, we create a lazy version of the array of variables, called unassigned. When unassigned's first property is later accessed, it will only search the array (due to lazy) as far as necessary to find the first value that has no assignment.

```
for value in domain {
    var localAssignment = assignment
    localAssignment[variable] = value
```

We try assigning every possible domain value for that variable, one at a time. The new assignment for each is stored in a local dictionary called localAssignment.

```
if isConsistent(variable: variable, value: value, assignment:
    localAssignment, csp: csp) {
    // if as we go down the tree we get a complete assignment, return it
    if let result = backtrackingSearch(csp: csp, assignment:
    localAssignment) {
        return result
    }
}
```

If the new assignment in localAssignment is consistent with all of the constraints (that is what isConsistent() checks for), we continue recursively searching with the new assignment in place. If the new assignment turns out to be complete (the base case), we return the new assignment up the recursion chain.

```
return nil  // no solution
```

Finally, if we have gone through every possible domain value for a particular variable, and there is no solution utilizing the existing set of assignments, we return nil, indicating no solution. This will lead to backtracking up the recursion chain to the point where a different prior assignment could have been made.

There is one last bit missing. We need to implement the isConsistent() function.

```
/// check if the value assignment is
    ⇒ consistent by checking all constraints of the variable
func isConsistent<V, D>(variable: V, value: D, assignment:
⇒ Dictionary<V, D>, csp: CSP<V,D>) -> Bool {
    for constraint in csp.constraints[variable] ?? [] {
        if !constraint.isSatisfied(assignment: assignment) {
            return false
        }
    }
    return true
}
```

isConsistent() goes through every constraint for a given variable (it will always be the variable that was just added to the assignment) and checks if the constraint is satisfied, given the new assignment. If the assignment satisfies every constraint, true is returned. If any constraint imposed on the variable is not satisfied, false is returned.

> **NOTE** The ?? operator, also known as the *nil coalescing operator*, says "if this thing is nil, then use this other thing instead." A dictionary lookup, as in csp .constraints[variable], can potentially return nil if no value is found in the dictionary for the provided key, and the ?? operator indicates a replacement if a value is nil. In the case of a nil value, if no constraints are found in the dictionary, the loop will be going through an empty array, which means it will not go through any iterations (no constraints, no iterations). An unsafe alternative, if we knew for sure that the csp contained constraints for every variable, would be to force unwrap the constraints, as in csp.constraints [variable]!. But, again, this would be unsafe—what if there were actually no constraints for the given variable?

3.2   *The Australian map-coloring problem*

Imagine you have a map of Australia that you want to color by state/territory (which we will collectively call "regions"). No two adjacent regions should share a color. Can you color the regions with just three different colors?

The answer is yes. Try it out on your own (the easiest way is to print out a map of Australia with a white background). As human beings, we can quickly figure out the solution by inspection and a little trial and error. It is a trivial problem, really, and a great first problem for our backtracking constraint-satisfaction solver. The problem is illustrated in figure 3.2.

To model the problem as a CSP, we need to define the variables, domains, and constraints. The variables are the seven regions of Australia (at least the seven that we will restrict ourselves to): Western Australia, Northern Territory, South Australia, Queensland, New South Wales, Victoria, and Tasmania. In our CSP, they can be modeled with strings. The domain of each variable is the three different colors that can possibly be assigned (we will use red, green, and blue). The constraints are the tricky part. No two adjacent regions can be colored with the same color, so our constraints will be dependent on which regions border one another. We can use what are called binary

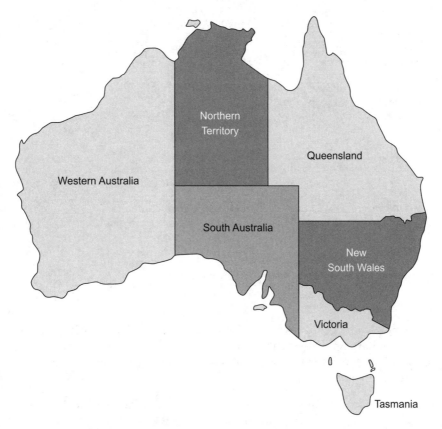

Figure 3.2   In a solution to the Australian map-coloring problem, no two adjacent parts of Australia can be colored with the same color.

constraints (constraints between two variables). Every two regions that share a border will also share a binary constraint indicating they cannot be assigned the same color.

To implement these binary constraints in code, we need to subclass the `Constraint` class. The `MapColoringConstraint` subclass will take two variables in its constructor (therefore being a binary constraint): the two regions that share a border. Its overridden `isSatisfied()` method will check first whether the two regions both have a domain value (color) assigned to them—if either does not, the constraint is trivially satisfied until they do (there cannot be a conflict when one does not yet have a color). Then it will check whether the two regions are assigned the same color (obviously there is a conflict, meaning the constraint is not satisfied, when they are the same).

The class is presented here in its entirety. `MapColoringClass` itself is not generic, but it subclasses a parameterized version of the generic class `Constraint` that indicates both variables and domains are of type `String`.

```
final class MapColoringConstraint: Constraint <String, String> {
    let place1: String
    let place2: String
    final override var vars: [String] { return [place1, place2] }

    init(place1: String, place2: String) {
        self.place1 = place1
        self.place2 = place2
    }

    override func isSatisfied(assignment:
    ➡ Dictionary<String, String>) -> Bool {
        // if either variable is not in the assignment then it must be
        ➡ consistent
        // since they still have their domain
        if assignment[place1] == nil || assignment[place2] == nil {
            return true
        }
        // check that the color of var1 does not equal var2
        return assignment[place1] != assignment[place2]
    }
}
```

TIP MapColoringConstraint is marked as final to let the compiler know that it will have no further subclasses (in fact, marking a class as final explicitly disallows subclasses). This enables the compiler to implement some optimizations at compile time.

Now that we have a way of implementing the constraints between regions, fleshing out the Australian map-coloring problem with our CSP solver is simply a matter of filling in domains and variables, and then adding constraints.

```
let variables: [String] = ["Western
➡ Australia", "Northern Territory", "South Australia",
➡ "Queensland", "New South Wales", "Victoria", "Tasmania"]
var domains = Dictionary<String, [String]>()
for variable in variables {
    domains[variable] = ["r", "g", "b"]
}

var csp = CSP<String, String>(variables: variables, domains: domains)
csp.addConstraint(MapColoringConstraint(place1: "Western Australia", place2:
➡ "Northern Territory"))
csp.addConstraint(MapColoringConstraint(place1: "Western Australia", place2:
➡ "South Australia"))
csp.addConstraint(MapColoringConstraint(place1: "South Australia", place2:
➡ "Northern Territory"))
csp.addConstraint(MapColoringConstraint(place1: "Queensland", place2:
➡ "Northern Territory"))
csp.addConstraint(MapColoringConstraint(place1: "Queensland",
    place2: "South Australia"))
csp.addConstraint(MapColoringConstraint(place1: "Queensland", place2:
➡ "New South Wales"))
```

```
csp.addConstraint(MapColoringConstraint(place1: "New South Wales", place2:
⟹   "South Australia"))
csp.addConstraint(MapColoringConstraint(place1: "Victoria", place2:
⟹   "South Australia"))
csp.addConstraint(MapColoringConstraint(place1: "Victoria",place2:
⟹   "New South Wales"))
```

Finally, `backtrackingSearch()` is called to find a solution.

```
if let solution = backtrackingSearch(csp: csp) {
    print(solution)
} else { print("Couldn't find solution!") }
```

A correct solution will include an assigned color for every region.

```
["Victoria": "r", "Queensland": "r",
⟹   "Northern Territory": "g", "South Australia": "b", "New South
⟹   Wales": "g", "Tasmania": "r", "Western Australia": "r"]
```

3.3 *The eight queens problem*

A chessboard is an eight-by-eight grid of squares. A queen is a chess piece that can move on the chessboard any number of squares along any row, column, or diagonal. A queen is attacking another piece if in a single move it can move to the square the piece is on without jumping over any other piece (in other words, if the other piece is in the line of sight of the queen, then it is attacked by it). The eight queens problem poses the question of how eight queens can be placed on a chessboard without any queen attacking another queen. The problem is illustrated in figure 3.3.

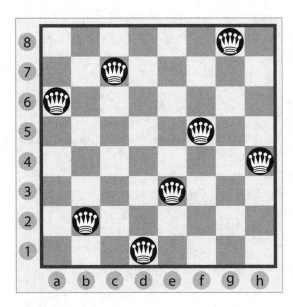

Figure 3.3 In a solution to the eight queens problem (there are many solutions), no two queens can be threatening one another.

To represent squares on the chess board, we will assign each an integer row and an integer column. We can ensure each of the eight queens is not on the same column by simply assigning them sequentially the columns 1 through 8. The variables in our constraint-satisfaction problem can just be the column of the queen in question. The domains can be the possible rows (again 1 through 8).

```
let cols: [Int] = [Int](1...8)
var rows = Dictionary<Int, [Int]>()
for variable in cols {
    rows[variable] = [Int](1...8)
}

var qcsp = CSP<Int, Int>(variables: cols, domains: rows)
```

To solve the problem, we will need a constraint that checks whether any two queens are on the same row or diagonal (they were all assigned different sequential columns to begin with). Checking for the same row is trivial, but checking for the same diagonal requires a little bit of math. If any two queens are on the same diagonal, the difference between their rows will be the same as the difference between their columns. Can you see where these checks take place in QueensConstraint?

```
final class QueensConstraint: Constraint <Int, Int> {
    let columns: [Int]
    final override var vars: [Int] { return columns }

    init(columns: [Int]) {
        self.columns = columns
    }

    override func isSatisfied(assignment: Dictionary<Int, Int>) -> Bool {
        for (q1c, q1r) in assignment { // q1c = queen 1 column, q1r = queen
            1 row
            if (q1c >= vars.count) {
                break
            }
            for q2c in (q1c + 1)...vars.count { // queen 2 column
                if let q2r = assignment[q2c] { // queen 2 row
                    if q1r == q2r { return false } // rows same?
                    if abs(q1r - q2r) == abs(q1c - q2c) { return false }
                    // same diagonal?
                }
            }
        }

        return true
    }
}
```

All that is left is to add the constraint and run the search.

```
qcsp.addConstraint(QueensConstraint(columns: cols))
if let solution = backtrackingSearch(csp: qcsp) {
    print(solution)
} else { print("Couldn't find solution!") }
```

Notice that we were able to reuse the constraint-satisfaction problem-solving framework that we built for map coloring fairly easily for a completely different type of problem. This is the power of writing code generically! Algorithms should be implemented in as broadly applicable a manner as possible, unless a performance optimization for a particular application requires specialization.

A correct solution will assign a column and row to every queen.

```
[2: 5, 4: 6, 5: 3, 6: 7, 7: 2, 3: 8, 1: 1, 8: 4]
```

3.4 Word search

A word search is a grid of letters with hidden words placed along rows, columns, and diagonals. A player of a word-search puzzle attempts to find the hidden words by carefully scanning through the grid. Finding places to put the words so that they all fit on the grid is a kind of constraint-satisfaction problem. The variables are the words, and the domains are the possible locations of those words. The problem is illustrated in figure 3.4.

For the purposes of expediency, our word search will not include words that overlap. You can improve it to allow for overlapping words as an exercise.

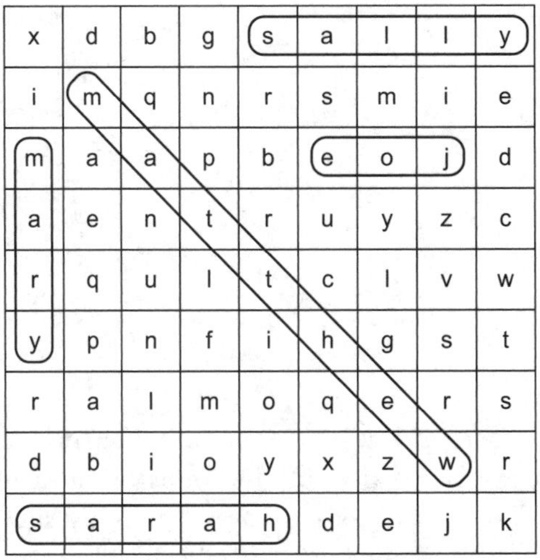

Figure 3.4 A classic word search, such as you might find in a children's puzzle book

The grid of this word-search problem is not entirely dissimilar from the mazes of chapter 2. Some of the following data types should look familiar.

```
// notice not too dissimilar from our Maze code from chapter 2
typealias Grid = [[Character]]

// A point on the grid
struct GridLocation: Hashable {
    let row: Int
    let col: Int
    var hashValue: Int { return row.hashValue ^ col.hashValue }
}
func == (lhs: GridLocation, rhs: GridLocation) -> Bool {
    return lhs.row == rhs.row && lhs.col == rhs.col
}
```

Initially, we will fill the grid with the letters of the English alphabet.

```
// All the letters in our word search
let ALPHABET = "ABCDEFGHIJKLMNOPQRSTUVWXYZ"

// randomly inserted letters
func generateGrid(rows: Int, columns: Int) -> Grid {
    // initialize grid full of empty spaces
    var grid: Grid = Grid(repeating: [Character](repeating: " ",
    ➡ count: columns), count: rows)
    // replace spaces with random letters
    for row in 0..<rows {
        for col in 0..<columns {
            let loc = ALPHABET.index(ALPHABET.startIndex, offsetBy:
            ➡ Int(arc4random_uniform(UInt32(ALPHABET.count))))
            grid[row][col] = ALPHABET[loc]
        }
    }
    return grid
}

func printGrid(_ grid: Grid) {
    for i in 0..<grid.count {
        print(String(grid[i]))
    }
}

var grid = generateGrid(rows: 9, columns: 9)
```

To figure out where words can fit in the grid, we will generate their domains. The domain of a word is an array of arrays of the possible locations of all of its letters (`[[GridLocation]]`). Words cannot just go anywhere, though. They must stay within a row, column, or diagonal that is within the bounds of the grid. In other words, they should not be going off the end of the grid. The purpose of `generateDomain()` is to build these arrays for every word.

```
func generateDomain(word: String, grid: Grid) -> [[GridLocation]] {
    var domain: [[GridLocation]] = [[GridLocation]]()
    let height = grid.count
    let width = grid[0].count
    let wordLength = word.count
    for row in 0..<height {
        for col in 0..<width {
            let columns = col...(col + wordLength)
            let rows = row...(row + wordLength)
            if (col + wordLength <= width) {
                // left to right
                domain.append(columns.map({GridLocation(row: row, col: $0)}))
                // diagonal towards bottom right
                if (row + wordLength <= height) {
                    domain.append(rows.map({GridLocation(row: $0, col:
                    ➥ col + ($0 - row))}))
                }
            }
            if (row + wordLength <= height) {
                // top to bottom
                domain.append(rows.map({GridLocation(row: $0, col: col)}))
                // diagonal towards bottom left
                if (col - wordLength >= 0) {
                    domain.append(rows.map({GridLocation(row: $0, col:
                    ➥ col - ($0 - row))}))
                }
            }
        }
    }
    return domain
}
```

You will notice a slightly clever use of map().[1] For the range of potential locations of a word (along a row, column, or diagonal), map() translates the range into an array of GridLocation by using that struct's constructor. Because generateDomain() loops through every grid location from the top left through to the bottom right for every word, it involves a lot of computation. Can you think of a way to do it more efficiently? What if we looked through all of the words of the same length at once, inside the loop?

To check if a potential solution is valid, we must implement a custom constraint for the word search. The isSatisfied() method of WordSearchConstraint simply checks whether any of the locations proposed for one word are the same as a location proposed for another word. It does this using a Set. Converting an Array into a Set will remove all duplicates. If there are fewer items in a Set converted from an Array than there were in the original Array, that means the original Array contained some duplicates. To prepare the data for this check, we will use flatMap() to combine

---

[1] Thanks goes to an anonymous reviewer of an early version of this chapter who sent in a slightly clearer version of this function than I originally presented.

multiple subarrays of locations for each word in the assignment into a single larger array of locations.

```
final class WordSearchConstraint: Constraint <String, [GridLocation]> {
    let words: [String]
    final override var vars: [String] { return words }

    init(words: [String]) {
        self.words = words
    }

    override func isSatisfied(assignment: Dictionary<String,
    ➡ [GridLocation]>) -> Bool {
        if Set<GridLocation>(assignment.values.flatMap({$0})).count
        ➡ < assignment.values.flatMap({$0}).count {
            return false
        }

        return true
    }
}
```

Finally, we are ready to run. For this example, we have five words in a nine-by-nine grid. The solution we get back should contain mappings between each word and the locations where its letters can fit in the grid.

```
let words: [String] = ["MATTHEW", "JOE", "MARY", "SARAH", "SALLY"]
var locations = Dictionary<String, [[GridLocation]]>()
for word in words {
    locations[word] = generateDomain(word: word, grid: grid)
}

var wordsearch = CSP<String, [GridLocation]>(variables: words, domains:
➡ locations)
wordsearch.addConstraint(WordSearchConstraint(words: words))
if let solution = backtrackingSearch(csp: wordsearch) {
    for (word, gridLocations) in solution {
        let gridLocs = arc4random_uniform(2) > 0 ? gridLocations :
        ➡ gridLocations.reversed() // randomly reverse word half the time
        for (index, letter) in word.enumerated() {
            let (row, col) = (gridLocs[index].row, gridLocations[index].col)
            grid[row][col] = letter
        }
    }
    printGrid(grid)
} else { print("Couldn't find solution!") }
```

There is a finishing touch in the code that fills the grid with words. Some words are randomly chosen to be reversed. This is valid, because this example does not allow overlapping words. Your ultimate output should look something like the following. Can you find Matthew, Joe, Mary, Sarah, and Sally?

```
S A L L Y U S G J
M E P Z E K A Y O
F A C O O A R R E
N P T F J K A A E
D Y T T P G H M N
L R C R H B H F D
K P Z Q I E P Z S
O D N V W F W Y Y
I Y M G R E W E E
```

3.5 *SEND+MORE=MONEY*

SEND+MORE=MONEY is a cryptarithmetic puzzle, meaning it is about finding digits that replace letters to make a mathematical statement true. Each letter in the problem represents one digit (0–9). No two letters can represent the same digit. When a letter repeats, it means a digit repeats in the solution.

To solve this puzzle by hand, it helps to line up the words.

```
 SEND
+MORE
MONEY
```

It is absolutely solvable by hand, with a bit of algebra and intuition. But a fairly simple computer program can solve it faster by brute forcing many possible solutions. Let's represent SEND+MORE=MONEY as a constraint-satisfaction problem.

```swift
final class SendMoreMoneyConstraint: Constraint <Character, Int> {
    let letters: [Character]
    final override var vars: [Character] { return letters }
    init(variables: [Character]) {
        letters = variables
    }

    override func isSatisfied(assignment:
    ➡ Dictionary<Character, Int>) -> Bool {
        // if there are duplicate values then it's not correct
        let d = Set<Int>(assignment.values)
        if d.count < assignment.count {
            return false
        }

        // if all variables have been assigned, check if it adds up correctly
        if assignment.count == letters.count {
            if let s = assignment["S"], let e = assignment["E"], let n =
            ➡ assignment["N"], let d = assignment["D"], let m =
            ➡ assignment["M"], let o = assignment["O"], let r =
            ➡ assignment["R"], let y = assignment["Y"] {
                let send: Int = s * 1000 + e * 100 + n * 10 + d
                let more: Int = m * 1000 + o * 100 + r * 10 + e
                let money: Int = m * 10000 + o * 1000 + n * 100 + e * 10 + y
                if (send + more) == money {
                    return true // answer found
                }
            }
        }
```

```
        }
        return false // this full assignment doesn't work
    }

    // until we have all of the variables assigned, the assignment
    ➡ is valid
    return true
    }
}
```

SendMoreMoneyConstraint's isSatisfied() method does a few things. First, it checks if there are any letters representing the same digits. If there are, that's an invalid solution, and it returns false. Next, it checks if all letters have been assigned. If they have, it checks to see if the formula (SEND+MORE=MONEY) is correct with the given assignment. If it is, a solution has been found, and it returns true. Otherwise, it returns false. Finally, if all letters have not yet been assigned, it returns true. This is to ensure that a partial solution continues to be worked on.

Let's try running it:

```
let letters: [Character] = ["S", "E", "N", "D", "M", "O", "R", "Y"]
var possibleDigits = Dictionary<Character, [Int]>()
for letter in letters {
    possibleDigits[letter] = [0, 1, 2, 3, 4, 5, 6, 7, 8, 9]
}
possibleDigits["S"] = [9]
possibleDigits["M"] = [1]
possibleDigits["O"] = [0]

var smmcsp = CSP<Character, Int>(variables: letters, domains: possibleDigits)
let smmcon = SendMoreMoneyConstraint(variables: letters)
smmcsp.addConstraint(smmcon)

if let solution = backtrackingSearch(csp: smmcsp) {
    print(solution)
} else { print("Couldn't find solution!") }
```

You will notice that we preassigned the answers for the letters S, M, and O. This was to ensure that the program executes in a reasonable amount of time in a Swift Playground. If you are working in a compiled environment, feel free to try it out without those three assignments.

The solution should look something like this:

```
["D": 7, "N": 6, "Y": 2, "R": 8, "O": 0, "M": 1, "S": 9, "E": 5]
```

3.6   *Circuit board layout*

A manufacturer needs to fit certain rectangular chips onto a rectangular circuit board. Essentially, this problem asks, "how can several different-sized rectangles all fit snugly inside of another rectangle?" A constraint-satisfaction problem solver can find the solution. The problem is illustrated in figure 3.5.

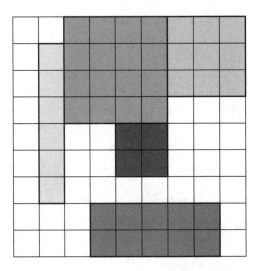

Figure 3.5 The circuit board layout problem is very similar to the word-search problem, but the rectangles are of variable width.

The circuit board layout problem is similar to the word-search problem. Instead of 1xN rectangles (words), the problem presents MxN rectangles. Like in the word-search problem, the rectangles cannot overlap. The rectangles cannot be put on diagonals, so in that sense the problem is actually simpler than the word search.

On your own, try rewriting the word-search solution to accommodate circuit board layout. You can reuse much of the code, including the code for the grid. For an example of a working circuit board layout solution, check out the sample Mac app that comes with SwiftCSP: https://github.com/davecom/SwiftCSP.

3.7 Real-world applications

As was mentioned in the introduction to this chapter, constraint-satisfaction problem solvers are commonly used in scheduling. Several people need to be at a meeting, and they are the variables. The domains consist of the open times on their calendars. The constraints may involve what combinations of people are required at the meeting.

Constraint-satisfaction problem solvers are also used in motion planning. Imagine a robot arm that needs to fit inside of a tube. It has constraints (the walls of the tube), variables (the joints), and domains (possible movements of the joints).

There are also applications in computational biology. You can imagine constraints between molecules required for a chemical reaction. And, of course, as is common with AI, there are applications in games. Writing a Sudoku solver is one of the following exercises, but many logic puzzles can be solved using constraint-satisfaction problem solving.

In this chapter, we built a simple backtracking, depth-first search, problem-solving framework. But it can be greatly improved by adding heuristics (remember A*?)—intuitions that can aid the search process. A newer technique than backtracking, known as *constraint propagation*, is also an efficient avenue for real-world applications.

For more information, check out chapter 6 of Stuart Russell and Peter Norvig's *Artificial Intelligence: A Modern Approach*, third edition (Pearson, 2010).

3.8   *Exercises*

1   Revise `WordSearchConstraint` so that overlapping letters are allowed.

2   Build the circuit board layout problem solver described in section 3.6, if you have not already.

3   Build a program that can solve Sudoku problems using this chapter's constraint-satisfaction problem framework.

Graph problems 4

A *graph* is an abstract mathematical construct that is used for modeling a real-world problem by dividing the problem into a set of connected nodes. We call each of the nodes a *vertex* and each of the connections an *edge*. For instance, a subway map can be thought of as a graph representing a transportation network. Each of the dots represents a station, and each of the lines represents a route between two stations. In graph terminology, we would call the stations "vertices" and the routes "edges."

Why is this useful? Not only do graphs help us abstractly think about a problem, they also let us apply several well-understood and performant search and optimization techniques. For instance, in the subway example, suppose we want to know the shortest route from one station to another. Or, suppose we wanted to know the minimum amount of track needed to connect all of the stations. Graph algorithms that you will learn in this chapter can solve both of those problems. Further, graph algorithms can be applied to any kind of network problem—not just transportation networks. Think of computer networks, distribution networks, and utility networks. Search and optimization problems across all of these spaces can be solved using graph algorithms.

In this chapter, we won't work with a graph of subway stations, but instead cities of the United States and potential routes between them. Figure 4.1 is a map of the continental United States and the fifteen largest metropolitan statistical areas (MSAs) in the country, as estimated by the U.S. Census Bureau.[1]

Famous entrepreneur Elon Musk has suggested building a new high-speed transportation network composed of capsules traveling in pressurized tubes. According to Musk, the capsules would travel at 700 miles per hour and be suitable

---

[1] Data from the United States Census Bureau's American Fact Finder, https://factfinder.census.gov/.

Figure 4.1   A map of the 15 largest MSAs in the United States

for cost-effective transportation between cities less than 900 miles apart.[2] He calls this new transportation system the "Hyperloop." In this chapter we will explore classic graph problems in the context of building out this transportation network.

Musk initially proposed the Hyperloop idea for connecting Los Angeles and San Francisco. If one were to build a national Hyperloop network, it would make sense to do so between America's largest metropolitan areas. In figure 4.2 the state outlines from figure 4.1 are removed. In addition, each of the MSAs is connected with some of its neighbors (not always its nearest neighbors, to make the graph a little more interesting).

Figure 4.2 is a graph with vertices representing the 15 largest MSAs in the United States and edges representing potential Hyperloop routes between cities. The routes were chosen for illustrative purposes. Certainly other potential routes could be part of a new Hyperloop network.

This abstract representation of a real-world problem highlights the power of graphs. Now that we have an abstraction to work with, we can ignore the geography of the United States and concentrate on thinking about the potential Hyperloop network simply in the context of connecting cities. In fact, as long as we keep the edges the same, we can think about the problem with a different looking graph. In figure 4.3, the location of Miami has moved. The graph in figure 4.3, being an abstract representation, can still address the same fundamental computational problems as the graph in figure 4.2, even if Miami is not where we would expect it. But for our sanity, we will stick with the representation in figure 4.2.

---

[2] Elon Musk, "Hyperloop Alpha," http://mng.bz/chmu.

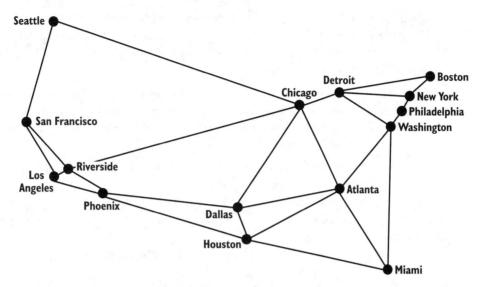

Figure 4.2 A graph with the vertices representing the 15 largest MSAs in the United States and the edges representing potential Hyperloop routes between them

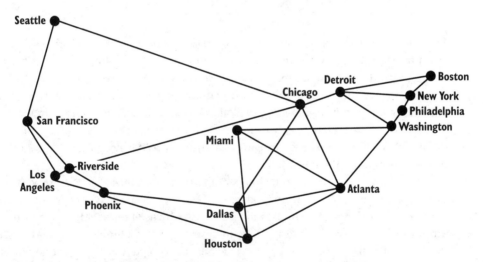

Figure 4.3 An equivalent graph to that in figure 4.2, with the location of Miami moved

4.1 Building a graph framework

Swift has been promoted as enabling a protocol-oriented style of programming (as opposed to the traditional object-oriented or functional paradigms).[3] Although the orthodoxy of this new paradigm is still being fleshed-out, what is clear is that it puts interfaces and composition ahead of inheritance. Whereas the class is the fundamental

---

[3] Dave Abrahams, "Protocol-Oriented Programming in Swift," WWDC 2015, Session 408, Apple Inc., http://mng.bz/zWP3.

building block in the object-oriented paradigm, and the function is the fundamental building block in functional programming, the protocol is the fundamental building block in protocol-oriented programming. In that light, we will try building a graph framework in a protocol-first style.

> **NOTE** The framework described in this section, and the examples that follow it, are largely based on a simplified version of my SwiftGraph open source project (https://github.com/davecom/SwiftGraph). SwiftGraph includes several features that go beyond the scope of this book.

We want this graph framework to be as flexible as possible, so that it can represent as many different problems as possible. To achieve this goal, we will use generics to abstract away the type of the vertices, and we will define an easy-to-adopt protocol for edges. Every vertex will ultimately be assigned an integer index, but it will be stored as the user-defined generic type.

Let's start work on the framework by defining the Edge protocol.

```
public protocol Edge: CustomStringConvertible {
    var u: Int { get set } // index of the "from" vertex
    var v: Int { get set } // index of the "to" vertex
    var reversed: Edge { get }
}
```

An Edge is defined as a connection between two vertices, each of which is represented by an integer index. By convention, u is used to refer to the first vertex, and v is used to represent the second vertex. You can also think of u as "from" and v as "to." In this chapter, we are only working with bidirectional edges (edges that can be travelled in both directions), but in *directed graphs*, also known as *digraphs*, edges can also be one-way, and the reversed property is meant to return an Edge that travels in the opposite direction. All Edge adoptees must implement CustomStringConvertible so they can be easily printed to the console.

The Graph protocol is about the essential role of a graph: associating vertices with edges. Again, we want to let the actual types of the vertices and edges be whatever the user of the framework desires. This lets the framework be used for a wide range of problems without needing to make intermediate data structures that glue everything together. In this light, we will use the Swift keyword associatedtype to define types that adopters of Graph can configure. For example, in a graph like the one for Hyperloop routes, we might define VertexType to be String, because we would use strings like "New York" and "Los Angeles" as the vertices. The only requirement of a potential VertexType is that it implements Equatable. String implements Equatable, so it is a valid VertexType.

```
protocol Graph: class, CustomStringConvertible {
    associatedtype VertexType: Equatable
    associatedtype EdgeType: Edge
    var vertices: [VertexType] { get set }
    var edges: [[EdgeType]] { get set }
}
```

The `vertices` array can be an array of any type that adopts `Equatable`. Each vertex will be stored in the array, but we will later refer to them by their integer index in the array. The vertex itself may be a complex data type, but its index will always be an `Int`, which is easy to work with. On another level, by putting this index between graph algorithms and the `vertices` array, it allows us to have two vertices that are equal in the same graph (imagine a graph with a country's cities as vertices, where the country has more than one city named "Springfield"). Even though they are the same, they will have different integer indexes.

There are many ways to implement a graph data structure, but the two most common are to use a *vertex matrix* or *adjacency lists.* In a vertex matrix, each cell of the matrix represents the intersection of two vertices in the graph, and the value of that cell indicates the connection (or lack thereof) between them. Our graph data structure uses adjacency lists. In this graph representation, every vertex has an array (or list) of vertices that it is connected to. Our specific representation uses an array of arrays of edges, so for every vertex there is an array of edges via which the vertex is connected to other vertices. `edges` is this two-dimensional array.

Notice, as well, that anything that adopts `Graph` must also adopt `class` and `CustomStringConvertible`. We want graph data structures to be reference types for memory-management purposes. It will also be slightly easier to write some of the protocol extensions if we know the adopters will be classes. `class` ensures that all graphs adopters are classes. `CustomStringConvertible` forces adopters of the protocol to be printable.

Introduced in Swift 2, protocol extensions allow fully fleshed out functions to be a part of a protocol. Amazingly, this will allow us to implement most of the functionality a graph needs before we actually define a concrete adopter of `Graph`. The following code shows the entirety of the protocol extension that adds this basic functionality, with in-source comments describing each of the functions.

```
extension Graph {
    /// How many vertices are in the graph?
    public var vertexCount: Int { return vertices.count }

    /// How many edges are in the graph?
    public var edgeCount: Int { return edges.joined().count }

    /// Get a vertex by its index.
    ///
    /// - parameter index: The index of the vertex.
    /// - returns: The vertex at i.
    public func vertexAtIndex(_ index: Int) -> VertexType {
        return vertices[index]
    }

    /// Find the first occurrence of a vertex if it exists.
    ///
    /// - parameter vertex: The vertex you are looking for.
    /// - returns: The index of the vertex. Return nil if it can't find it.
    public func indexOfVertex(_ vertex: VertexType) -> Int? {
```

```
        if let i = vertices.index(of: vertex) {
            return i
        }
        return nil
    }


    /// Find all of the neighbors of a vertex at a given index.
    ///
    /// - parameter index: The index for the vertex to find the neighbors of.
    /// - returns: An array of the neighbor vertices.
    public func neighborsForIndex(_ index: Int) -> [VertexType] {
        return edges[index].map({self.vertices[$0.v]})
    }


    /// Find all of the neighbors of a given Vertex.
    ///
    /// - parameter vertex: The vertex to find the neighbors of.
    /// - returns: An optional array of the neighbor vertices.
    public func neighborsForVertex(_ vertex: VertexType) -> [VertexType]? {
        if let i = indexOfVertex(vertex) {
            return neighborsForIndex(i)
        }
        return nil
    }


    /// Find all of the edges of a vertex at a given index.
    ///
    /// - parameter index: The index for the vertex to find the children of.
    public func edgesForIndex(_ index: Int) -> [EdgeType] {
        return edges[index]
    }


    /// Find all of the edges of a given vertex.
    ///
    /// - parameter vertex: The vertex to find the edges of.
    public func edgesForVertex(_ vertex: VertexType) -> [EdgeType]? {
        if let i = indexOfVertex(vertex) {
            return edgesForIndex(i)
        }
        return nil
    }


    /// Add a vertex to the graph.
    ///
    /// - parameter v: The vertex to be added.
    /// - returns: The index where the vertex was added.
    public func addVertex(_ v: VertexType) -> Int {
        vertices.append(v)
        edges.append([EdgeType]())
        return vertices.count - 1
    }


    /// Add an edge to the graph.
```

```
    ///
    /// - parameter e: The edge to add.
    public func addEdge(_ e: EdgeType) {
        edges[e.u].append(e)
        edges[e.v].append(e.reversed as! EdgeType)
    }
}
```

Let's step back for a moment and consider why this protocol has two versions of most of its functions. We know from the protocol definition that the array `vertices` is an array of elements of type `VertexType`, which can be anything that implements `Equatable`. So we have vertices of type `VertexType` that are stored in the `vertices` array. But if we want to retrieve or manipulate them later, we need to know where they are stored in that array. Hence, every vertex has an index in the array (an integer) associated with it. If we don't know a vertex's index, we need to look it up by searching through `vertices`. That is why there are two versions of every function. One operates on `Int` indexes, and one operates on `VertexType` itself. The functions that operate on `VertexType` look up the relevant indices and call the index-based function.

Most of the functions are fairly self-explanatory, but `neighborsForIndex()` deserves a little unpacking. It returns the *neighbors* of a vertex. A vertex's neighbors are all of the other vertices that are directly connected to it by an edge. For example, in figure 4.2, New York and Washington are neighbors (the only neighbors) of Philadelphia. We find the neighbors for a vertex by looking at the ends (the vs) of all of the edges going out from it.

```
public func neighborsForIndex(_ index: Int) -> [VertexType] {
    return edges[index].map({self.vertices[$0.v]})
}
```

`edges[index]` is the adjacency list, the list of edges through which the vertex in question is connected to other vertices. In the closure of the map call, `$0` represents one particular edge, and `$0.v` represents the neighbor that the edge is connected to. `map()` will return all of the vertices (as opposed to just their indices), because `$0.v` is passed as an index into the `vertices` array.

Another important thing to note is the way `addEdge()` works. `addEdge()` first adds an edge to the adjacency list of the "from" vertex (`u`), and then adds a reversed version of itself to the adjacency list of the "to" vertex (`v`). The second step is necessary because this graph is not directed. We want every edge added to be bidirectional—that means that `u` will be a neighbor of `v` in the same way that `v` is a neighbor of `u`.

```
public func addEdge(_ e: EdgeType) {
    edges[e.u].append(e)
    edges[e.v].append(e.reversed as! EdgeType)
}
```

4.1.1 A concrete implementation of Edge

As was mentioned earlier, we are only dealing with bidirectional edges in this chapter. Beyond being bidirectional or unidirectional, edges can also be *unweighted* or *weighted*. A weighted edge is one that has some comparable value (usually numeric, but not always) associated with it. We could think of the weights in our potential Hyperloop network as being the distances between the stations. For now, though, we will deal with an unweighted version of the graph. An unweighted edge is simply a connection between two vertices. Another way of putting it is that in an unweighted graph we know which vertices are connected, whereas in a weighted graph we know which vertices are connected and we know something about those connections.

Our implementation of an unweighted edge, UnweightedEdge, will of course implement the Edge protocol. It must have a place for a "from" vertex (u), a place for a "to" vertex (v), and a way to reverse itself. It also must implement CustomString-Convertible, as required by Edge, which means having a description property.

```
open class UnweightedEdge: Edge {
    public var u: Int // "from" vertex
    public var v: Int // "to" vertex
    public var reversed: Edge {
        return UnweightedEdge(u: v, v: u)
    }

    public init(u: Int, v: Int) {
        self.u = u
        self.v = v
    }

    //MARK: CustomStringConvertable
    public var description: String {
        return "\(u) <-> \(v)"
    }
}
```

4.1.2 A concrete implementation of Graph

UnweightedEdge is pretty simple. Surprisingly, so is our concrete implementation of Graph. An UnweightedGraph is a Graph whose vertices can be any Equatable type (as per the Graph protocol) and whose edges are of type UnweightedEdge. By defining the types of the vertices and edges arrays, we are implicitly filling in the associated types VertexType and EdgeType in the Graph protocol.

```
open class UnweightedGraph<V: Equatable>: Graph {
    var vertices: [V] = [V]()
    var edges: [[UnweightedEdge]] = [[UnweightedEdge]]() //adjacency lists

    public init() {
    }

    public init(vertices: [V]) {
```

```
        for vertex in vertices {
            _ = self.addVertex(vertex)
        }
    }

    /// This is a convenience method that adds an unweighted edge.
    ///
    /// - parameter from: The starting vertex's index.
    /// - parameter to: The ending vertex's index.
    public func addEdge(from: Int, to: Int) {
        addEdge(UnweightedEdge(u: from, v: to))
    }

    /// This is a convenience method that adds an unweighted, undirected
    ➥    edge between the first occurrence of two vertices.
    ///
    /// - parameter from: The starting vertex.
    /// - parameter to: The ending vertex.
    public func addEdge(from: V, to: V) {
        if let u = indexOfVertex(from) {
            if let v = indexOfVertex(to) {
                addEdge(UnweightedEdge(u: u, v: v))
            }
        }
    }

    /// MARK: Implement CustomStringConvertible
    public var description: String {
        var d: String = ""
        for i in 0..<vertices.count {
            d += "\(vertices[i]) -> \(neighborsForIndex(i))\n"
        }
        return d
    }
}
```

The new abilities in UnweightedGraph are init methods, convenience methods for adding UnweightedEdges to the graph, and the property description for conformance with CustomStringConvertible.

Now that we have concrete implementations of Edge and Graph we can actually create a representation of the potential Hyperloop network. The vertices and edges in cityGraph correspond to the vertices and edges represented in figure 4.2.

```
var cityGraph: UnweightedGraph<String>
➥    = UnweightedGraph<String>(vertices: ["Seattle", "San
➥    Francisco", "Los Angeles", "Riverside", "Phoenix", "Chicago",
➥    "Boston", "New York", "Atlanta", "Miami", "Dallas", "Houston",
➥    "Detroit", "Philadelphia", "Washington"])

cityGraph.addEdge(from: "Seattle", to: "Chicago")
cityGraph.addEdge(from: "Seattle", to: "San Francisco")
cityGraph.addEdge(from: "San Francisco", to: "Riverside")
cityGraph.addEdge(from: "San Francisco", to: "Los Angeles")
```

```
cityGraph.addEdge(from: "Los Angeles", to: "Riverside")
cityGraph.addEdge(from: "Los Angeles", to: "Phoenix")
cityGraph.addEdge(from: "Riverside", to: "Phoenix")
cityGraph.addEdge(from: "Riverside", to: "Chicago")
cityGraph.addEdge(from: "Phoenix", to: "Dallas")
cityGraph.addEdge(from: "Phoenix", to: "Houston")
cityGraph.addEdge(from: "Dallas", to: "Chicago")
cityGraph.addEdge(from: "Dallas", to: "Atlanta")
cityGraph.addEdge(from: "Dallas", to: "Houston")
cityGraph.addEdge(from: "Houston", to: "Atlanta")
cityGraph.addEdge(from: "Houston", to: "Miami")
cityGraph.addEdge(from: "Atlanta", to: "Chicago")
cityGraph.addEdge(from: "Atlanta", to: "Washington")
cityGraph.addEdge(from: "Atlanta", to: "Miami")
cityGraph.addEdge(from: "Miami", to: "Washington")
cityGraph.addEdge(from: "Chicago", to: "Detroit")
cityGraph.addEdge(from: "Detroit", to: "Boston")
cityGraph.addEdge(from: "Detroit", to: "Washington")
cityGraph.addEdge(from: "Detroit", to: "New York")
cityGraph.addEdge(from: "Boston", to: "New York")
cityGraph.addEdge(from: "New York", to: "Philadelphia")
cityGraph.addEdge(from: "Philadelphia", to: "Washington")
```

cityGraph has vertices of type String, and we indicate each vertex with the name of
the MSA that it represents. It is irrelevant in what order we add the edges to city-
Graph. Because we implemented CustomStringConvertible in UnweightedGraph with
a nicely printed description of the graph, we can now pretty-print (that's a real term!)
the graph.

```
print(cityGraph)
```

You should get output similar to the following:

```
Seattle -> ["Chicago", "San Francisco"]
San Francisco -> ["Seattle", "Riverside", "Los Angeles"]
Los Angeles -> ["San Francisco", "Riverside", "Phoenix"]
Riverside -> ["San Francisco", "Los Angeles", "Phoenix", "Chicago"]
Phoenix -> ["Los Angeles", "Riverside", "Dallas", "Houston"]
Chicago -> ["Seattle", "Riverside", "Dallas", "Atlanta", "Detroit"]
Boston -> ["Detroit", "New York"]
New York -> ["Detroit", "Boston", "Philadelphia"]
Atlanta -> ["Dallas", "Houston", "Chicago", "Washington", "Miami"]
Miami -> ["Houston", "Atlanta", "Washington"]
Dallas -> ["Phoenix", "Chicago", "Atlanta", "Houston"]
Houston -> ["Phoenix", "Dallas", "Atlanta", "Miami"]
Detroit -> ["Chicago", "Boston", "Washington", "New York"]
Philadelphia -> ["New York", "Washington"]
Washington -> ["Atlanta", "Miami", "Detroit", "Philadelphia"]
```

4.2 Finding the shortest path

The Hyperloop is so fast that, for optimizing travel time from one station to another, it probably matters less how long the distances are between the stations and more how many hops it takes (how many stations need to be visited) to get from one station to another. Each station may involve a layover, so just like with flights, the fewer stops the better.

In graph theory, a set of edges that connects two vertices is known as a *path*. In other words, a path is a way of getting from one vertex to another vertex. In the context of the Hyperloop network, a set of tubes (edges) represents the path from one city (vertex) to another (vertex). Finding optimal paths between vertices is one of the most common problems that graphs are used for.

4.2.1 Defining a path

In our graphs, a path can simply be thought of as an array of edges.

```
public typealias Path = [Edge]
```

Every Edge knows the index of its "from" vertex (u) and its "to" vertex (v), so given a Graph, it is easy to deduce the vertices that it connects. There's a method in Graph for that, vertexAtIndex(). It would be nice to have a method to pretty-print a Path within a Graph. We can do that in a short extension to Graph.

```
extension Graph {
    /// Prints a path in a readable format
    public func printPath(_ path: Path) {
        for edge in path {
            print("\(vertexAtIndex(edge.u)) > \(vertexAtIndex(edge.v))")
        }
    }
}
```

4.2.2 Revisiting breadth-first search (BFS)

In an unweighted graph, finding the shortest path means finding the path that has the fewest edges between the starting vertex and the destination vertex. To build out the Hyperloop network, it might make sense to first connect the furthest cities on the highly populated seaboards. That raises the question, "what is the shortest path between Boston and Miami?"

Luckily, we already know an algorithm for finding shortest paths, and we can reuse it to answer this question. Breadth-first search, introduced in chapter 2, is just as viable for graphs as it is for mazes. In fact, the mazes we worked with in chapter 2 really are graphs. The vertices are the locations in the maze, and the edges are the moves that can be made from one location to another. In an unweighted graph, a breadth-first search will find the shortest path between any two vertices.

We can rewrite the breadth-first search implementation from chapter 2 to suit working with Graph. We can even reuse the same Queue class, unchanged.

```
public class Queue<T> {
    private var container: [T] = [T]()
    public var isEmpty: Bool { return container.isEmpty }
    public func push(_ thing: T) { container.append(thing) }
    public func pop() -> T { return container.removeFirst() }
}
```

The new version of bfs() will be an extension to Graph. It will no longer operate on Nodes, as in chapter 2, but instead on vertices, referred to by their indices (Ints). Recall from chapter 2 that we used the Node class to keep track of the parent of each new Node we found. There was also a function, nodeToPath(), that used the parent property of each node to generate a path from the goal back to the start node (but reversed to start at the start). We will use a similar function, pathDictToPath(), to generate a Path from our starting vertex to the destination vertex.

```
/// Takes a dictionary of edges to reach each node and returns an array
    ➡ of edges
/// that goes from `from` to `to`
public func pathDictToPath(from: Int, to: Int, pathDict:
➡ [Int: Edge]) -> Path {
    if pathDict.count == 0 {
        return []
    }
    var edgePath: Path = Path()
    var e: Edge = pathDict[to]!
    edgePath.append(e)
    while (e.u != from) {
        e = pathDict[e.u]!
        edgePath.append(e)
    }
    return Array(edgePath.reversed())
}
```

In the new version of bfs(), in lieu of having access to the parent property on Node, we will use a dictionary associating each vertex index with the Edge that got us to it. This is what we will call pathDict. pathDictToPath() extrapolates from this dictionary the Path that connects the from vertex to the to vertex by looking at every Edge between to and from in pathDict.

As you study the implementation of bfs() on Graph, it may be helpful to flip back to the implementation of bfs() you are already familiar with from chapter 2. How has it changed? What has stayed the same? All of the basic machinery, aside from path-Dict, is essentially the same, but several of the parameter types and generic types have been modified.

```
extension Graph {
    //returns a path to the goal vertex
    func bfs(initialVertex: VertexType, goalTestFn:
    ➡ (VertexType) -> Bool) -> Path? {
```

```
        guard let startIndex = indexOfVertex(initialVertex)
    ➡ else { return nil }
        // frontier is where we've yet to go
        let frontier: Queue<Int> = Queue<Int>()
        frontier.push(startIndex)
        // explored is where we've been
        var explored: Set<Int> = Set<Int>()
        explored.insert(startIndex)
        // how did we get to each vertex
        var pathDict: [Int: EdgeType] = [Int: EdgeType]()
        // keep going while there is more to explore
        while !frontier.isEmpty {
            let currentIndex = frontier.pop()
            let currentVertex = vertexAtIndex(currentIndex)
            // if we found the goal, we're done
            if goalTestFn(currentVertex) {
                return pathDictToPath(from: startIndex, to: currentIndex,
                ➡ pathDict: pathDict)
            }
            // check where we can go next and haven't explored
            for edge in edgesForIndex(currentIndex)
            ➡ where !explored.contains(edge.v) {
                explored.insert(edge.v)
                frontier.push(edge.v)
                pathDict[edge.v] = edge
            }
        }
        return nil // never found the goal
    }
}
```

The new bfs() takes a starting vertex, initialVertex, a function that will determine if the goal is reached, goalTestFn(), and returns an optional Path. The returned optional Path will be nil if initialVertex is not actually in the Graph (this is determined by the guard statement). It will also return nil if goalTestFn() never returns true for any of the searched vertices in the graph. frontier and explored are much the same as they were in chapter 2, except that now the generic type of each is set to Int—the index of a vertex in a Graph. This version of bfs() has no successorFn(). Instead, edgesForIndex() brings the next unexplored vertices onto the frontier. Finally, the last main difference between this version and the prior one is the use of pathDict, which gets updated when a new vertex is added to the queue, and which is used to return the final Path when the goal is found by calling pathDictToPath().

We are now ready to find the shortest path (in terms of number of edges) between Boston and Miami. We can pass a closure to bfs() that tests for a goal of a vertex equivalent to the String "Miami". If a Path is found, we can print it using the printPath() method introduced earlier as a protocol extension to Graph.

```
if let bostonToMiami = cityGraph.bfs(initialVertex: "Boston",
➡ goalTestFn: { $0 == "Miami" }) {
    cityGraph.printPath(bostonToMiami)
}
```

The output should look something like this:

```
Boston > Detroit
Detroit > Washington
Washington > Miami
```

Boston to Detroit to Washington to Miami, composed of three edges, is the shortest route between Boston and Miami in terms of number of edges. Figure 4.4 highlights this route.

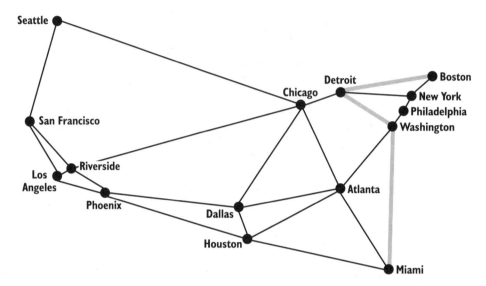

Figure 4.4   The shortest route between Boston and Miami, in terms of number of edges, is highlighted.

4.3   *Minimizing the cost of building the network*

Imagine we want to connect all 15 of the largest MSAs to the Hyperloop network. Our goal is to minimize the cost of rolling out the network, so that means using a minimum of track. The question is then, "how can we connect all of the MSAs using the minimum amount of track?"

4.3.1   *Workings with weights*

To understand the amount of track that a particular edge may require, we need to know the distance that the edge represents. This is an opportunity to re-introduce the concept of weights. In the Hyperloop network, the weight of an edge is the distance between the two MSAs that it connects. Figure 4.5 is the same as figure 4.2, except it has a weight added to each edge, representing the distance in miles between the two vertices that the edge connects.

To handle weights, we will need a new implementation of Edge and a new implementation of Graph. Once again, we want to design our framework in as flexible a way

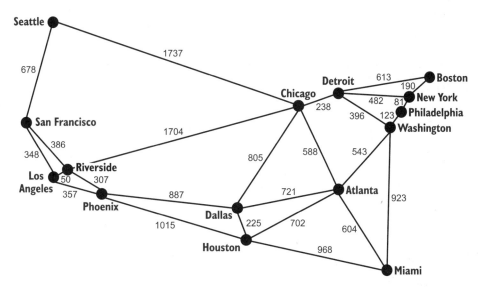

Figure 4.5   A weighted graph of the 15 largest MSAs in the United States, where each of the weights represents the distance between two MSAs in miles

as possible. To this end, we will allow the type of the weights associated with edges in our new `WeightedEdge` and `WeightedGraph` to be generic and therefore determined at creation time. But in order to execute several algorithms on weighted graphs, we do need the weights to have two properties: It must be possible to compare them, and it must be possible to add them together.

Any type that implements `Comparable` can be compared using operators like `==` and `<`. There is no built-in protocol in Swift for specifying that a type can be added, so we will create our own.

```
public protocol Summable {
    static func +(lhs: Self, rhs: Self) -> Self
}
```

If a type implements `Summable`, it means that instances of it can be added together. All of our weights must be `Summable`, meaning it must be possible to add them together, so they must implement the + operator. Of course, one category of types that can be added is numbers. Because the built-in number types in Swift already implement the + operator, it is possible to add `Summable` support to them without any work.

```
extension Int: Summable {}
extension Double: Summable {}
extension Float: Summable {}
```

A `WeightedEdge` will have a generic type, `W`, representing the type of its weight. It will also implement the protocols `Edge` and `Comparable`. Why does it implement `Comparable`?

The reason is that Jarnik's algorithm, which we will cover shortly, requires the ability to compare one edge with another.

```
open class WeightedEdge<W: Comparable & Summable>: Edge, Comparable {
    public var u: Int
    public var v: Int
    public let weight: W

    public var reversed: Edge {
        return WeightedEdge(u: v, v: u, weight: weight)
    }

    public init(u: Int, v: Int, weight: W) {
        self.weight = weight
        self.u = u
        self.v = v
    }

    //Implement CustomStringConvertible protocol
    public var description: String {
        return "\(u) <\(weight)> \(v)"
    }

    //MARK: Operator Overloads for Comparable
    static public func == <W>(lhs: WeightedEdge<W>,
➡  rhs: WeightedEdge<W>) -> Bool {
        return lhs.u == rhs.u && lhs.v == rhs.v && lhs.weight == rhs.weight
    }

    static public func < <W>(lhs: WeightedEdge<W>, rhs:
➡  WeightedEdge<W>) -> Bool {
        return lhs.weight < rhs.weight
    }
}
```

The implementation of `WeightedEdge` is not immensely different from the implementation of `UnweightedEdge`. It just has a new `weight` property and the implementation of `Comparable` via the == and < operators. The < operator is only interested in looking at weights, because Jarnik's algorithm is interested in finding the smallest edge by weight.

A `WeightedGraph` is a lot like an `UnweightedGraph`: It has init methods, it has convenience methods for adding `WeightedEdges`, and it implements `Custom-StringConvertible` via a `description` property. Where it differs is in the new generic type, `W`, that matches the type its weighted edges take. There is also a new method, `neighborsForIndexWithWeights()`, that returns not only each neighbor but also the weight of the edge that got to it. This method is useful for the new version of `description`.

```
open class WeightedGraph<V: Equatable & Hashable, W: Comparable & Summable>:
➡  Graph {
    var vertices: [V] = [V]()
    var edges: [[WeightedEdge<W>]] = [[WeightedEdge<W>]]() //adjacency lists
```

```
    public init() {
    }

    public init(vertices: [V]) {
        for vertex in vertices {
            _ = self.addVertex(vertex)
        }
    }

    /// Find all of the neighbors of a vertex at a given index.
    ///
    /// - parameter index: The index for the vertex to find the neighbors of.
    /// - returns: An array of tuples including the vertices as the first
    ➡   element and the weights as the second element.
    public func neighborsForIndexWithWeights(_ index: Int) -> [(V, W)] {
        var distanceTuples: [(V, W)] = [(V, W)]()
        for edge in edges[index] {
            distanceTuples += [(vertices[edge.v], edge.weight)]
        }
        return distanceTuples
    }

    /// This is a convenience method that adds a weighted edge.
    ///
    /// - parameter from: The starting vertex's index.
    /// - parameter to: The ending vertex's index.
    /// - parameter weight: the Weight of the edge to add.
    public func addEdge(from: Int, to: Int, weight:W) {
        addEdge(WeightedEdge<W>(u: from, v: to, weight: weight))
    }

    /// This is a convenience method that adds a weighted edge between the
    ➡   first occurrence of two vertices. It takes O(n) time.
    ///
    /// - parameter from: The starting vertex.
    /// - parameter to: The ending vertex.
    /// - parameter weight: the Weight of the edge to add.
    public func addEdge(from: V, to: V, weight: W) {
        if let u = indexOfVertex(from) {
            if let v = indexOfVertex(to) {
                addEdge(WeightedEdge<W>(u: u, v: v, weight:weight))
            }
        }
    }

    //Implement Printable protocol
    public var description: String {
        var d: String = ""
        for i in 0..<vertices.count {
            d += "\(vertices[i]) -> \(neighborsForIndexWithWeights(i))\n"
        }
        return d
    }
}
```

It is now possible to actually define a weighted graph. The weighted graph we will work with is a representation of figure 4.5, called cityGraph2.

```
let cityGraph2: WeightedGraph<String,
➡ Int> = WeightedGraph<String, Int>(vertices:
➡ ["Seattle", "San Francisco", "Los Angeles", "Riverside",
➡ "Phoenix", "Chicago", "Boston", "New York", "Atlanta",
➡ "Miami", "Dallas", "Houston", "Detroit", "Philadelphia", "Washington"])

cityGraph2.addEdge(from: "Seattle", to: "Chicago", weight: 1737)
cityGraph2.addEdge(from: "Seattle", to: "San Francisco", weight: 678)
cityGraph2.addEdge(from: "San Francisco", to: "Riverside", weight: 386)
cityGraph2.addEdge(from: "San Francisco", to: "Los Angeles", weight: 348)
cityGraph2.addEdge(from: "Los Angeles", to: "Riverside", weight: 50)
cityGraph2.addEdge(from: "Los Angeles", to: "Phoenix", weight: 357)
cityGraph2.addEdge(from: "Riverside", to: "Phoenix", weight: 307)
cityGraph2.addEdge(from: "Riverside", to: "Chicago", weight: 1704)
cityGraph2.addEdge(from: "Phoenix", to: "Dallas", weight: 887)
cityGraph2.addEdge(from: "Phoenix", to: "Houston", weight: 1015)
cityGraph2.addEdge(from: "Dallas", to: "Chicago", weight: 805)
cityGraph2.addEdge(from: "Dallas", to: "Atlanta", weight: 721)
cityGraph2.addEdge(from: "Dallas", to: "Houston", weight: 225)
cityGraph2.addEdge(from: "Houston", to: "Atlanta", weight: 702)
cityGraph2.addEdge(from: "Houston", to: "Miami", weight: 968)
cityGraph2.addEdge(from: "Atlanta", to: "Chicago", weight: 588)
cityGraph2.addEdge(from: "Atlanta", to: "Washington", weight: 543)
cityGraph2.addEdge(from: "Atlanta", to: "Miami", weight: 604)
cityGraph2.addEdge(from: "Miami", to: "Washington", weight: 923)
cityGraph2.addEdge(from: "Chicago", to: "Detroit", weight: 238)
cityGraph2.addEdge(from: "Detroit", to: "Boston", weight: 613)
cityGraph2.addEdge(from: "Detroit", to: "Washington", weight: 396)
cityGraph2.addEdge(from: "Detroit", to: "New York", weight: 482)
cityGraph2.addEdge(from: "Boston", to: "New York", weight: 190)
cityGraph2.addEdge(from: "New York", to: "Philadelphia", weight: 81)
cityGraph2.addEdge(from: "Philadelphia", to: "Washington", weight: 123)
```

Because WeightedGraph implements CustomStringConvertible, we can print out cityGraph2.

```
print(cityGraph2)
```

In the output, you will see both the vertices each vertex is connected to and the weight of those connections.

```
Seattle -> [("Chicago", 1737), ("San Francisco", 678)]
San Francisco -> [("Seattle", 678), ("Riverside", 386), ("Los Angeles", 348)]
Los Angeles -> [("San Francisco", 348), ("Riverside", 50), ("Phoenix", 357)]
Riverside -> [("San Francisco", 386), ("Los Angeles", 50), ("Phoenix", 307),
➡ ("Chicago", 1704)]
Phoenix -> [("Los Angeles", 357), ("Riverside", 307), ("Dallas", 887),
➡ ("Houston", 1015)]
Chicago -> [("Seattle", 1737), ("Riverside", 1704), ("Dallas", 805),
➡ ("Atlanta", 588), ("Detroit", 238)]
Boston -> [("Detroit", 613), ("New York", 190)]
```

```
New York -> [("Detroit", 482), ("Boston", 190), ("Philadelphia", 81)]
Atlanta -> [("Dallas", 721), ("Houston", 702), ("Chicago", 588),
➥ ("Washington", 543), ("Miami", 604)]
Miami -> [("Houston", 968), ("Atlanta", 604), ("Washington", 923)]
Dallas -> [("Phoenix", 887), ("Chicago", 805), ("Atlanta", 721),
➥ ("Houston", 225)]
Houston -> [("Phoenix", 1015), ("Dallas", 225), ("Atlanta", 702),
➥ ("Miami", 968)]
Detroit -> [("Chicago", 238), ("Boston", 613), ("Washington", 396),
➥ ("New York", 482)]
Philadelphia -> [("New York", 81), ("Washington", 123)]
Washington -> [("Atlanta", 543), ("Miami", 923), ("Detroit", 396),
➥ ("Philadelphia", 123)]
```

4.3.2   *Finding the minimum spanning tree*

A *tree* is a special kind of graph that has one, and only one, path between any two vertices. This implies that there are no *cycles* in a tree (which is sometimes called being *acyclic*). A cycle can be thought of as a circle (in the common sense, not the geometrical sense): If it is possible to traverse a graph from a starting vertex, never repeat any edges, and get back to the same starting vertex, then it has a cycle. Any graph that is not a tree can become a tree by pruning edges. Figure 4.6 illustrates pruning an edge to turn a graph into a tree.

A *connected* graph is a graph that has some way of getting from any vertex to any other vertex (all of the graphs we are looking at in this chapter are connected). A *spanning tree* is a tree that connects every vertex in a graph. A *minimum spanning tree* is a tree that connects every vertex in a weighted graph with the minimum total weight (compared to other spanning trees). For every weighted graph, it is possible to efficiently find its minimum spanning tree.

Whew, that was a lot of terminology! The point is that finding a minimum spanning tree is the same as finding a way to connect every vertex in a weighted graph with the minimum weight. This is an important and practical problem for anyone designing a network (transportation network, computer network, and so on)—how can every node in the network be connected for the minimum cost? That cost may be in terms of wire, track, road, or anything else. For instance, for a telephone network, another way of posing the problem is, "what is the minimum length of cable one needs to connect every phone?"

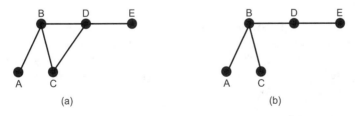

Figure 4.6   In (a), a cycle exists between vertices B, C, and D, so it is not a tree. In (b), the edge connecting C and D has been pruned, so the graph is a tree.

CALCULATING THE TOTAL WEIGHT OF A WEIGHTED PATH

Before we develop a method for finding a minimum spanning tree, we will develop a function we can use to test our future development. The solution to the minimum spanning tree problem will consist of an array of weighted edges that compose the tree. The function `totalWeight()` takes an array of `WeightedEdge<W>` and finds the total weight, W, that results from adding all of its edges' weights together.

```
public func totalWeight<W>(_ edges: [WeightedEdge<W>]) -> W? {
    guard let firstWeight = edges.first?.weight else { return nil }
    return edges.dropFirst().reduce(firstWeight) { (result, next) -> W in
        return result + next.weight
    }
}
```

`reduce()` is a higher-order function built in to most programming languages that can be programmed in a functional style. It takes a sequence of values and combines them via a closure. The closure is passed the result of each prior combination (the parameter `result` here) and the next value to be combined (`next` here). There's one problem—`reduce()` also requires a starting value. For most numbers, this would be 0, but because we don't know if W actually represents a number, we pull the first element out of `edges` and use it as the starting value. Because we do not want to re-add the first element after using it as the starting value, we call `dropFirst()` to ensure it is not added twice.

TIP   `reduce()` is also known as "fold" in many other programming languages.

JARNIK'S ALGORITHM

Jarnik's algorithm for finding a minimum spanning tree works by dividing a graph into two parts: the vertices in the still-being-assembled minimum spanning tree, and the vertices not yet in the minimum spanning tree. It takes the following steps:

1   Pick an arbitrary vertex to be in the minimum spanning tree.
2   Find the lowest-weight edge connecting the minimum spanning tree to the vertices not yet in the minimum spanning tree.
3   Add the vertex at the end of that minimum edge to the minimum spanning tree.
4   Repeat steps 2 and 3 until every vertex in the graph is in the minimum spanning tree.

NOTE   Jarnik's algorithm is commonly referred to as Prim's algorithm. Two Czech mathematicians, Otakar Borůvka and Vojtěch Jarník, interested in minimizing the cost of laying electric lines in the late 1920s, came up with algorithms to solve the problem of finding a minimum spanning tree. Their algorithms were "rediscovered" decades later by others.[4]

---

[4]   Helena Durnova, "Otakar Boruvka (1899-1995) and the Minimum Spanning Tree" (Institute of Mathematics of the Czech Academy of Sciences, 2006), https://dml.cz/handle/10338.dmlcz/500001.

To run Jarnik's algorithm efficiently, a priority queue is used. Every time a new vertex is added to the minimum spanning tree, all of its outgoing edges that link to vertices outside the tree are added to the priority queue. The lowest-weight edge is always popped off the priority queue, and the algorithm keeps executing until the priority queue is empty. This ensures that the lowest-weight edges are always added to the tree first. Edges that connect to vertices already in the tree are ignored when they are popped.

The following code for `mst()` is the full implementation of Jarnik's algorithm,[5] along with a utility function for printing a `WeightedPath` and a new type defined in this extension of `WeightedGraph`.

> **WARNING** Jarnik's algorithm will not necessarily work correctly in a graph with directed edges. It also will not work in a graph that is not connected.

```
/// Extensions to WeightedGraph for building a Minimum-Spanning Tree (MST)
public extension WeightedGraph {
    typealias WeightedPath = [WeightedEdge<W>]

    /// Find the minimum spanning tree in a weighted graph. This is the set
    ➥ of edges
    /// that touches every vertex in the graph and is of minimal combined
    ➥ weight. This function
    /// uses Jarnik's algorithm (aka Prim's algorithm) and so assumes the
    ➥ graph has
    /// undirected edges. For a graph with directed edges, the result may
    ➥ be incorrect. Also,
    /// if the graph is not fully connected, the tree will only span the
    ➥ connected component from which
    /// the starting vertex belongs.
    ///
    /// - parameter start: The index of the vertex to start creating
    ➥ the MST from.
    /// - returns: An array of WeightedEdges containing the minimum
    ➥ spanning tree, or nil if the starting vertex is invalid. If
    ➥ there are is only one vertex connected to the starting vertex,
    ➥ an empty list is returned.
    public func mst(start: Int = 0) -> WeightedPath? {
        if start > (vertexCount - 1) || start < 0 { return nil }
        var result: [WeightedEdge<W>] = [WeightedEdge<W>]() // the final
        ➥ MST goes in here
        var pq: PriorityQueue<WeightedEdge<W>> =
        ➥ PriorityQueue<WeightedEdge<W>>(ascending: true) // minPQ
        var visited: [Bool] = Array<Bool>(repeating: false, count:
        ➥ vertexCount) // already been to these

        func visit(_ index: Int) {
            visited[index] = true // mark as visited
            for edge in edgesForIndex(index) { // add all edges coming from
            ➥ here to pq
                if !visited[edge.v] { pq.push(edge) }
            }
```

---

5 Robert Sedgewick and Kevin Wayne, *Algorithms*, 4th Edition (Addison-Wesley Professional, 2011), p. 619.

```
        }

        visit(start) // the first vertex is where everything begins

        while let edge = pq.pop() { // keep going as long as there are
        ➡ edges to process
            if visited[edge.v] { continue } // if we've been both places,
            ➡ ignore
            result.append(edge) // otherwise this is the current smallest
            ➡ so add it to the result set
            visit(edge.v) // visit where this connects
        }

        return result
    }

    /// Pretty-print an edge list returned from an MST
    /// - parameter edges The edge array representing the MST
    public func printWeightedPath(_ weightedPath: WeightedPath) {
        for edge in weightedPath {
            print("\(vertexAtIndex(edge.u)) \(edge.weight)>
            ➡ \(vertexAtIndex(edge.v))")
        }
        if let tw = totalWeight(weightedPath) {
            print("Total Weight: \(tw)")
        }
    }
}
```

Let's walk through mst(), line by line.

```
public func mst(start: Int = 0) -> WeightedPath? {
    if start > (vertexCount - 1) || start < 0 { return nil }
```

The algorithm returns an optional WeightedPath representing the minimum spanning tree. It does not matter where the algorithm starts (assuming the graph is connected and undirected), so the default is set to vertex index 0. If it so happens that the start is invalid, mst() returns nil.

```
var result: [WeightedEdge<W>] = [WeightedEdge<W>]() // the final MST goes
➡ in here
var pq: PriorityQueue<WeightedEdge<W>> =
➡ PriorityQueue<WeightedEdge<W>>(ascending: true) // minPQ
var visited: [Bool] = Array<Bool>(repeating: false, count: vertexCount)
➡ // already been to these
```

result will ultimately hold the weighted path containing the minimum spanning tree. This is where we will add WeightedEdges, as the lowest-weight edge is popped off and takes us to a new part of the graph. Jarnik's algorithm is considered a *greedy algorithm* because it always selects the lowest-weight edge. pq is where newly discovered edges are stored and the next-lowest-weight edge is popped. visited keeps track of vertex indices that we have already been to. This could also have been accomplished with a Set, similar to explored in bfs().

```
func visit(_ index: Int) {
    visited[index] = true // mark as visited
    for edge in edgesForIndex(index) { // add all edges coming from here
    ⇥ to pq
        if !visited[edge.v] { pq.push(edge) }
    }
}
```

visit() is an inner convenience function that marks a vertex as visited and adds all of its edges that connect to vertices not yet visited to pq. Note how easy the adjacency-list model makes finding edges belonging to a particular vertex.

```
visit(start) // the first vertex is where everything begins
```

It does not matter which vertex is visited first, unless the graph is not connected. If the graph is not connected, but is instead made up of disconnected *components*, mst() will return a tree that spans the particular component that the starting vertex belongs to.

```
while let edge = pq.pop() { // keep going as long as there are edges to
    process
    if visited[edge.v] { continue } // if we've been both places, ignore
    result.append(edge) // otherwise this is the current smallest so add
    ⇥ it to the result set
    visit(edge.v) // visit where this connects
}
return result
```

While there are still edges on the priority queue, we pop them off and check if they lead to vertices not yet in the tree. Because the priority queue is ascending, it pops the lowest-weight edges first. This ensures that the result is indeed of minimum total weight. Any edge popped that does not lead to an unexplored vertex is ignored. Otherwise, because the edge is the lowest seen so far, it is added to the result set, and the new vertex it leads to is explored. When there are no edges left to explore, the result is returned.

Let's finally return to the problem of connecting all 15 of the largest MSAs in the United States by Hyperloop, using a minimum amount of track. The route that accomplishes this is simply the minimum spanning tree of cityGraph2. Let's try running mst() on cityGraph2.

```
if let mst = cityGraph2.mst() {
    cityGraph2.printWeightedPath(mst)
}
```

Thanks to the pretty-printing printWeightedPath() method, the minimum spanning tree is easy to read.

```
Seattle 678> San Francisco
San Francisco 348> Los Angeles
Los Angeles 50> Riverside
Riverside 307> Phoenix
Phoenix 887> Dallas
Dallas 225> Houston
Houston 702> Atlanta
Atlanta 543> Washington
Washington 123> Philadelphia
Philadelphia 81> New York
New York 190> Boston
Washington 396> Detroit
Detroit 238> Chicago
Atlanta 604> Miami
Total Weight: 5372
```

In other words, this is the cumulatively shortest collection of edges that connects all of the MSAs in the weighted graph. The minimum length of track needed to connect all of them is 5372 miles. Figure 4.7 illustrates the minimum spanning tree.

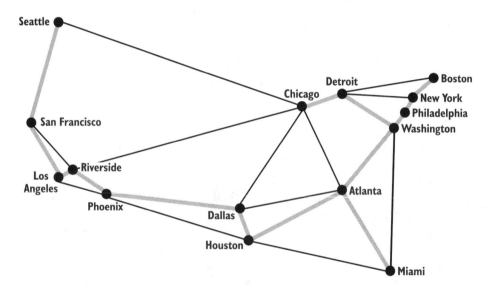

Figure 4.7   The highlighted edges represent a minimum spanning tree that connects all 15 MSAs.

4.4   *Finding shortest paths in a weighted graph*

As the Hyperloop network gets built, it is unlikely the builders will have the ambition to connect the whole country at once. Instead, it is likely the builders will want to minimize the cost to lay track between key cities. The cost to extend the network to particular cities will obviously depend on where the builders start.

Finding the cost to any city from some starting city is a version of the "single-source shortest path" problem. That problem asks, "what is the shortest path (in terms of total edge weight) from some vertex to every other vertex in a weighted graph?"

4.4.1 *Dijkstra's algorithm*

Dijkstra's algorithm solves the single-source shortest path problem. It is provided a starting vertex, and it returns the lowest-weight path to any other vertex on a weighted graph. It also returns the minimum total weight to every other vertex from the starting vertex. Dijkstra's algorithm starts at the single-source vertex, and then continually explores the closest vertices to the start vertex. For this reason, like Jarnik's algorithm, Dijkstra's algorithm is greedy. When Dijkstra's algorithm encounters a new vertex, it keeps track of how far it is from the start vertex, and updates this value if it ever finds a shorter path. It also keeps track of what edge got it to each vertex, like a breadth-first search.

Here are all of the algorithm's steps:

1 Add the start vertex to a priority queue.

2 Pop the closest vertex from the priority queue (at the beginning this is just the start vertex)—we'll call it the current vertex.

3 Look at all of the neighbors connected to the current vertex. If they have not previously been recorded, or the edge offers a new shortest path to them, then for each of them record its distance from the start, record the edge that produced this distance, and add the new vertex to the priority queue.

4 Repeat steps 2 and 3 until the priority queue is empty.

5 Return the shortest distance to every vertex from the start vertex and the path to get to each of them.

The extension to `WeightedGraph` for Dijkstra's algorithm includes `DijkstraNode`, a simple data structure for keeping track of costs associated with each vertex explored so far and for comparing them. This is not dissimilar to the `Node` class in chapter 2. It also includes utility functions for converting the returned array of distances to something easier to use for looking up by vertex, and for calling `dijkstra()` without vertex indices.

Without further ado, here is the code for the extension. We will go over it line by line after.

```
public extension WeightedGraph {

    /// Represents a node in the priority queue used
    /// for selecting the next
    struct DijkstraNode: Comparable, Equatable {
        let vertex: Int
        let distance: W

        public static func < (lhs: DijkstraNode, rhs: DijkstraNode) -> Bool {
            return lhs.distance < rhs.distance
        }

        public static func == (lhs: DijkstraNode, rhs: DijkstraNode)
        -> Bool {
            return lhs.distance == rhs.distance
        }
```

```
}

/// Finds the shortest paths from some route vertex to every other
    ➡ vertex in the graph.
///
/// - parameter graph: The WeightedGraph to look within.
/// - parameter root: The index of the root node to build the shortest
    ➡ paths from.
/// - parameter startDistance: The distance to get to the root node
    ➡ (typically 0).
/// - returns: Returns a tuple of two things: the first, an array
    ➡ containing the distances, the second, a dictionary containing
    ➡ the edge to reach each vertex. Use the function
    ➡ pathDictToPath() to convert the dictionary into something
    ➡ useful for a specific point.
public func dijkstra(root: Int, startDistance: W) -> ([W?],
    ➡ [Int: WeightedEdge<W>]) {
    var distances: [W?] = [W?](repeating: nil, count: vertexCount)
        ➡ // how far each vertex is from start
    distances[root] = startDistance // the start vertex is
        ➡ startDistance away
    var pq: PriorityQueue<DijkstraNode> =
        ➡ PriorityQueue<DijkstraNode>(ascending: true)
    var pathDict: [Int: WeightedEdge<W>] = [Int: WeightedEdge<W>]()
        ➡ // how we got to each vertex
    pq.push(DijkstraNode(vertex: root, distance: startDistance))

    while let u = pq.pop()?.vertex { // explore the next closest vertex
        guard let distU = distances[u] else { continue } // should
            ➡ already have seen it
        for we in edgesForIndex(u) { // look at every edge/vertex
            ➡ from the vertex in question
            let distV = distances[we.v] // the old distance to
                ➡ this vertex
            if distV == nil || distV! > we.weight + distU { // if
                ➡ we have no old distance or we found a shorter path
                distances[we.v] = we.weight + distU
                    ➡ // update the distance to this vertex
                pathDict[we.v] = we // update the edge on the shortest
                    ➡ path to this vertex
                pq.push(DijkstraNode(vertex: we.v, distance:
                    ➡ we.weight + distU)) // explore it soon
            }
        }
    }

    return (distances, pathDict)
}


/// A convenience version of dijkstra() that allows the supply of
    ➡ the root
/// vertex instead of the index of the root vertex.
public func dijkstra(root: V, startDistance: W)
    ➡ -> ([W?], [Int: WeightedEdge<W>]) {
```

```
            if let u = indexOfVertex(root) {
                return dijkstra(root: u, startDistance: startDistance)
            }
            return ([], [:])
        }

        /// Helper function to get easier access to Dijkstra results.
        public func distanceArrayToVertexDict(distances: [W?]) -> [V : W?] {
            var distanceDict: [V: W?] = [V: W?]()
            for i in 0..<distances.count {
                distanceDict[vertexAtIndex(i)] = distances[i]
            }
            return distanceDict
        }
    }
```

The first few lines of dijkstra() use data structures you have become familiar with, except for distances, which is a placeholder for the distances to every vertex in the graph from the root. Initially all of these distances are nil, because we do not yet know how far each of them is—that is what we are using Dijkstra's algorithm to figure out!

```
public func dijkstra(root: Int, startDistance: W) -> ([W?],
➡ [Int: WeightedEdge<W>]) {
    var distances: [W?] = [W?](repeating: nil, count: vertexCount)
    ➡ // how far each vertex is from start
    distances[root] = startDistance // the start vertex is startDistance away
    var pq: PriorityQueue<DijkstraNode> =
    ➡ PriorityQueue<DijkstraNode>(ascending: true)
    var pathDict: [Int: WeightedEdge<W>] = [Int: WeightedEdge<W>]()
    ➡ // how we got to each vertex
    pq.push(DijkstraNode(vertex: root, distance: startDistance))
```

The first node pushed onto the priority queue contains the root vertex.

```
while let u = pq.pop()?.vertex { // explore the next closest vertex
    guard let distU = distances[u] else { continue } // should already have
    ➡ seen it
```

We keep running Dijkstra's algorithm until the priority queue is empty. u is the current vertex we are searching from, and distU is the stored distance for getting to u along known routes. Every vertex explored at this stage has already been found, so it must have a known distance. If it doesn't, something is wrong, hence the guard statement.

```
for we in edgesForIndex(u) { // look at every edge/vertex from the vertex
➡ in question
    let distV = distances[we.v] // the old distance to this vertex
```

Next, every edge connected to u is explored. distV is the distance to any known vertex attached by an edge to u.

```
if distV == nil || distV! >
➥ we.weight + distU { // if we have no old distance or we found a
➥ shorter path
    distances[we.v] = we.weight + distU // update the distance to this vertex
    pathDict[we.v] = we // update the edge on the shortest path to
    ➥ this vertex
    pq.push(DijkstraNode(vertex: we.v, distance: we.weight + distU))
    ➥ // explore it soon
}
```

If we have found a vertex that has not yet been explored (distV == nil), or we have found a new, shorter path to it, we record that new shortest distance to v and the edge that got us there. It is okay to force unwrap distV here, because the second part of the "or" operator (||) is short-circuited, and we know if we get to it that distV is not nil. Finally, we push any vertices that have new paths to them to the priority queue.

```
return (distances, pathDict)
```

dijkstra() returns both the distances to every vertex in the weighted graph from the root vertex, and the pathDict that can unlock the shortest paths to them. It is safe to run Dijkstra's algorithm now. Let's start by finding the distance from Los Angeles to every other MSA in the graph.

```
let (distances, pathDict) = cityGraph2.dijkstra(root: "Los Angeles",
➥ startDistance: 0)
var nameDistance: [String: Int?] =
➥ cityGraph2.distanceArrayToVertexDict(distances: distances)
for (key, value) in nameDistance {
    print("\(key) : \(String(describing: value!))")
}
```

Your output should look something like this:

```
Phoenix : 357
Detroit : 1992
Houston : 1372
Washington : 2388
Riverside : 50
Chicago : 1754
Dallas : 1244
Atlanta : 1965
New York : 2474
Philadelphia : 2511
Boston : 2605
San Francisco : 348
Seattle : 1026
Los Angeles : 0
Miami : 2340
```

We can use our old friend, `pathDictToPath()`, to find the shortest path between Los Angeles and a specific other MSA—say Boston. Finally, we can use `printWeighted-Path()` to pretty-print the result.

```
let path = pathDictToPath(from:
➥ cityGraph2.indexOfVertex("Los Angeles")!, to:
➥ cityGraph2.indexOfVertex("Boston")!, pathDict: pathDict)
cityGraph2.printWeightedPath(path as! [WeightedEdge<Int>])
```

The shortest path from Los Angeles to Boston is

```
Los Angeles 50> Riverside
Riverside 1704> Chicago
Chicago 238> Detroit
Detroit 613> Boston
Total Weight: 2605
```

You may have noticed that Dijkstra's algorithm has some resemblance to Jarnik's algorithm. They are both greedy, and it is possible to implement them using quite similar code if one is sufficiently motivated. Another algorithm that Dijkstra's algorithm resembles is A* from chapter 2. A* can be thought of as a modification of Dijkstra's algorithm. Add a heuristic and restrict Dijkstra's algorithm to finding a single destination, and the two algorithms are the same.

4.5 *Real-world applications*

A huge amount of our world can be represented using graphs. You have seen in this chapter how effective they are for working with transportation networks, but many other kinds of networks have the same essential optimization problems: telephone networks, computer networks, utility networks (electricity, plumbing, and so on). As a result, graph algorithms are essential for efficiency in the telecommunications, shipping, transportation, and utility industries.

Retailers must handle complex distribution problems. Stores and warehouses can be thought of as vertices and the distances between them as edges. The algorithms are the same. The internet itself is a giant graph, with each connected device a vertex and each wired or wireless connection being an edge. Whether a business is saving fuel or wire, minimum spanning tree and shortest path problem-solving are useful for more than just games. Some of the world's most famous brands became successful by optimizing graph problems: think of Walmart building out an efficient distribution network, Google indexing the web (a giant graph), and FedEx finding the right set of hubs to connect the world's addresses.

Some obvious applications of graph algorithms are social networks and map applications. In a social network, people are vertices, and connections (friendships on Facebook, for instance) are edges. In fact, one of Facebook's most prominent developer tools is known as the "Graph API" (https://developers.facebook.com/docs/graph-api). In map applications like Apple Maps and Google Maps, graph algorithms are used to provide directions and calculate trip times.

Several popular video games also make explicit use of graph algorithms. MiniMetro and Ticket to Ride are two examples of games that closely mimic the problems solved in this chapter.

4.6 *Exercises*

1 Add support to the graph framework for removing edges and vertices.

2 Add support to the graph framework for directed graphs (digraphs).

3 Add an extension to `Graph` for depth-first search (see chapter 2).

4 Use this chapter's graph framework to prove or disprove the classic Bridges of Konigsberg problem.

Genetic algorithms

Genetic algorithms are not used for everyday programmatic problems. They are called upon when traditional algorithmic approaches are insufficient for arriving at a solution to a problem in a reasonable amount of time. In other words, genetic algorithms are usually reserved for complex problems without easy solutions. If you need a sense of what some of these complex problems might be, feel free to read ahead in section 5.7 before proceeding.

5.1 *Biological background*

In biology, the theory of evolution is an explanation of how genetic mutation coupled with the constraints of an environment leads to changes in organisms over time (including speciation—the creation of new species). The mechanism by which the well-adapted organisms succeed and the less well-adapted organisms fail is known as *natural selection*. Each generation of a species will include individuals with different (and sometimes new) traits that come about through genetic mutation. All individuals compete for limited resources to survive, and because there are more individuals than there are resources, some individuals must die.

An individual with a mutation that makes it better adapted for survival in its environment will have a higher probability of living and reproducing. Over time, the better-adapted individuals in an environment will have more children, and through inheritance will pass on their mutations to those children. Therefore, a mutation that benefits survival is likely to eventually proliferate amongst a population.

For example, if bacteria are being killed by a specific antibiotic, and one individual bacterium in the population has a mutation in a gene that makes it more resistant to the antibiotic, it is more likely to survive and reproduce. If the antibiotic is continually applied over time, the children who have inherited the gene for antibiotic resistance will also be more likely to reproduce and have children of their own.

Eventually the whole population may gain the mutation, as continued assault by the antibiotic kills off the individuals without the mutation. The antibiotic does not cause the mutation to develop, but it does lead to the proliferation of individuals with the mutation.

Natural selection has been applied in spheres beyond biology. Social Darwinism is natural selection applied to the sphere of social theory. In computer science, genetic algorithms are a simulation of natural selection to solve computational challenges.

A genetic algorithm includes a *population* (group) of individuals known as *chromosomes*. The chromosomes, each composed of *genes* that specify their traits, are competing to solve some problem. How well a chromosome solves a problem is defined by a *fitness function*.

The genetic algorithm goes through *generations*. In each generation, the chromosomes that are more fit are more likely to be *selected* to reproduce. There is also a probability in each generation that two chromosomes will have their genes merged. This is known as *crossover*. And finally, there is the important possibility in each generation that a gene in a chromosome may *mutate* (randomly change).

After the fitness function of some individual in the population crosses some specified threshold, or the algorithm runs through some specified maximum number of generations, the best individual (the one that scored highest in the fitness function) is returned.

Genetic algorithms are not a good solution for all problems. They depend on three partially or fully *stochastic* (randomly determined) operations: selection, crossover, and mutation. Therefore, they may not find an optimal solution in a reasonable amount of time. For most problems, more deterministic algorithms exist with better guarantees. But there are problems for which no fast deterministic algorithm exists. In these cases, genetic algorithms are a good choice.

5.2   *Preliminaries*

Genetic algorithms require a lot of random number generation. The Swift standard library does not include a facility for random number generation, but both macOS and Linux do. When you `import Foundation`, by extension you import the system libraries that random number generation relies on. This includes `Darwin` on macOS and `Glibc` on Linux. These libraries include two pseudo-random number generation functions ("pseudo" because they are generated by an algorithm, not random from nature) that we already used in chapters 1 and 2: `arc4random_uniform()` and `drand48()`.

> **TIP** `arc4random_uniform()` is not available on Linux. If you are working on Linux, you can approximate its functionality with your own function that multiplies the result of `drand48()` by some maximum parameter and converts the result to an integer.

arc4random_uniform() finds a pseudo-random UInt32 between 0 (inclusive) and a provided upper bound (exclusive). drand48() finds a pseudo-random Double between 0 (inclusive) and 1 (exclusive). drand48() requires a seed—a beginning value used at the startup of the pseudo-random number generation algorithm. The seed function is srand48(). If the same seed is used, drand48() will return the same sequence of numbers. Generally, the current time is used, because it is always different and therefore will not result in the same sequence of numbers during subsequent runs of the program. This can be accomplished using the time() function.

Hence, this is the first preliminary code we need:

```
import Foundation // for arc4random_uniform() and drand48()

srand48(time(nil)) // seed random number generator for drand48()
```

It will also be helpful in this chapter to have a way of randomly shuffling values in an Array. Many programming language standard libraries offer a shuffle() method on their built-in list or array types. Unfortunately, Swift does not, so we will create our own. The naive algorithm for shuffling is to go through every item in the array, generate a random location, and swap it with the item at the random location. Unfortunately, for mathematical reasons beyond the scope of this chapter, the naive approach does not result in randomly distributed items. An algorithm called the Fisher-Yates shuffle does. Here it is implemented as an extension to Array.

```
extension Array {
    public func shuffled() -> Array<Element> {
        var shuffledArray = self // value semantics (Array is Struct)
        ⇒ makes this a copy
        if count < 2 { return shuffledArray } // already shuffled
        for i in (1..<count).reversed() { // count backwards
            let position = Int(arc4random_uniform(UInt32(i + 1)))
            ⇒ // random to swap
            if i != position { // swap with the end, don't bother with
            ⇒ self swaps
                shuffledArray.swapAt(i, position)
            }
        }
        return shuffledArray
    }
}
```

shuffledArray is a duplicate of the array that shuffled() is called on. An array that is of length 0 or 1 is considered already shuffled. The algorithm runs through locations backward from the end of the array. At each iteration, it swaps the element at the current location with the element at a randomly selected location between 0 and the current location. This is the key difference between Fisher-Yates and the naive approach. The naive approach swaps every element with any other element in the array. Fisher-Yates will only swap an element with another at a location below it numerically (notice the argument passed to `arc4random_uniform()`, and recall that it is a non-inclusive maximum; hence the + 1).

5.3   *A generic genetic algorithm*

Genetic algorithms are often highly specialized and tuned for a particular application. In this chapter, we will define a generic genetic algorithm that can be used with multiple problems, while not being particularly well tuned for any of them. It will include some configurable options, but the goal is to show the algorithm's fundamentals instead of its tunability.

We will start by defining an interface for the individuals that the generic algorithm can operate on. The protocol `Chromosome` defines six essential components. A chromosome must be able to do the following:

- Determine its own fitness
- Copy itself
- Create a random instance of itself (for use in filling the first generation)
- Implement crossover (combine itself with another of the same type to create children)—in other words, mix itself with another chromosome
- Mutate—make a small, fairly random change in itself
- Print itself for human digestion

Here is the code for `Chromosome`, codifying these six needs.

```
public protocol Chromosome {
    var fitness: Double { get } // how well does this individual solve
    ➡ the problem?
    init(from: Self) // must be able to copy itself
    static func randomInstance() -> Self
    func crossover(other: Self)
    ➡ -> (child1: Self, child2: Self) // combine with other to form children
    func mutate() // make a small change somewhere
    func prettyPrint()
}
```

> **WARNING** You may wonder why `prettyPrint()` is a requirement of `Chromosome` instead of conformance to `CustomStringConvertible`, the Swift standard library protocol for making something printable. The reason is for performance in Playgrounds. This code is meant to run in an Xcode Playground, and the behavior of Xcode Playgrounds (at the time of writing) is to call `description()` on `CustomStringConvertible` items every time they are manipulated internally. This massively degrades performance, and the genetic algorithm problems in this chapter need significant performance to run in a reasonable amount of time.

We will implement the algorithm itself (the code that will manipulate chromosomes) as a generic class that is open to subclassing for future specialized applications. Before we do so, though, let's revisit the description of a genetic algorithm from the beginning of the chapter, and clearly define the steps that a generic algorithm takes:

1 Create an initial population of random chromosomes that represents the first generation of the algorithm.
2 Measure the fitness of each chromosome in this generation of the population. If any exceeds the threshold, return it and the algorithm ends.
3 Select some individuals to reproduce, with a higher probability of selecting those with the highest fitness.
4 Crossover (combine), with some probability, some of the selected chromosomes to create children that represent the population of the next generation.
5 Mutate, usually with a low probability, some of those chromosomes. The population of the new generation is now complete, and it replaces the population of the last generation.
6 Return to step 2 unless the maximum number of generations has been reached. If that is the case, return the best chromosome found so far.

This general outline of a genetic algorithm (illustrated in figure 5.1) is missing a lot of important details. How many chromosomes should be in the population? What is the threshold that stops the algorithm? How should the chromosomes be selected for reproduction? How should they be combined (crossover) and at what probability? At what probability should mutations occur? How many generations should be run?

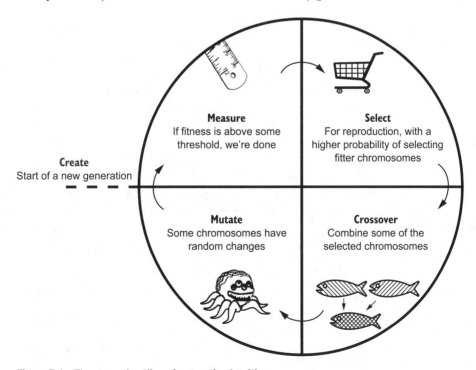

Figure 5.1   The general outline of a genetic algorithm

All of these points will be configurable in our GeneticAlgorithm class. We will define it piece by piece so we can talk about each piece separately.

```
open class GeneticAlgorithm<ChromosomeType: Chromosome> {
    enum SelectionType {
        case roulette
        case tournament(UInt) // the UInt is the number of participants
        ➡ in the tournament
    }
```

GeneticAlgorithm takes a generic type that conforms to Chromosome, and in its init method, it will create a population of this type. The enum SelectionType is an internal type used for specifying the selection method used by the algorithm. The two most common genetic algorithm selection methods are known as *roulette-wheel selection* (sometimes called "fitness proportionate selection") and *tournament selection*. The former gives every chromosome a chance of being picked, proportionate to its fitness. In tournament selection, a certain number of random chromosomes are challenged against one another, and the one with the best fitness is selected. In this enum, the associated value of type UInt that goes with tournament is the number of random chromosomes that should participate in the tournament.

```
    private let threshold: Double // at what fitness level to stop running
    private let maxGenerations: UInt // number of generations to run
    private let mutationChance: Double // probability of mutation for each
    ➡ individual in each generation
    private let crossoverChance: Double // probability of any two children
    ➡ being crossed each generation
    private let selectionType: SelectionType // which selection method?
```

The preceding are all properties of the genetic algorithm that will be configured at the time of creation, through init. threshold is the fitness level that indicates that a solution has been found for the problem the genetic algorithm is trying to solve. maxGenerations is the maximum number of generations to run. If we have run that many generations and no solution with a fitness level beyond threshold has been found, the best solution that has been found will be returned. mutationChance is the probability of each chromosome in each generation mutating. crossoverChance is the probability that two parents selected to reproduce have children that are a mixture of their genes; otherwise the children are just duplicates of the parents. Finally, selectionType is the type of selection method to use, as delineated by the enum SelectionType.

```
    private var population: [ChromosomeType] // all of the individuals in
    ➡ a generation
    private var fitnessCache: [Double] // the fitness of each individual
    ➡ in the current generation
    private var fitnessSum: Double = -Double.greatestFiniteMagnitude
    ➡ // summed generation fitness
```

The preceding three instance variables represent the chromosomes and their fitness in any generation. population is the actual chromosomes. fitnessCache is an array of fitnesses that correspond to the chromosomes in population. It is useful to cache these values so that they do not need to be recalculated in various other methods multiple times per generation. fitnessSum is what it sounds like—the sum of the fitnesses of all of the chromosomes in a given generation.

```
init(size: UInt, threshold: Double,
    maxGenerations: UInt = 100, mutationChance: Double = 0.01,
    crossoverChance: Double = 0.7, selectionType:
    SelectionType = SelectionType.tournament(4)) {
        self.threshold = threshold
        self.maxGenerations = maxGenerations
        self.mutationChance = mutationChance
        self.crossoverChance = crossoverChance
        self.selectionType = selectionType

        population = [ChromosomeType]() // initialize the population with
            random chromosomes
        for _ in 0..<size {
            population.append(ChromosomeType.randomInstance())
        }
        fitnessCache = [Double](repeating: -Double.greatestFiniteMagnitude,
            count: Int(size))
}
```

The preceding init method takes a long list of parameters, most of which have default values. They set up the configurable properties we just discussed. population is initialized with a random set of chromosomes using the Chromosome protocol's randomInstance() static method. In other words, the first generation of chromosomes is just composed of random individuals. This is a point of potential optimization for a more sophisticated genetic algorithm. Instead of starting with purely random individuals, the first generation could contain individuals that are closer to the solution, through some knowledge of the problem.

Now we will examine the two selection methods that our class supports.

```
// pick based on the proportion of summed total fitness that each
    individual represents
private func pickRoulette(wheel: [Double]) -> ChromosomeType {
    var pick = drand48() // chance of picking a particular one
    for (index, chance) in wheel.enumerated() {
        pick -= chance
        if pick <= 0 { // we had one that took us over, leads to a pick
            return population[index]
        }
    }
    return population[0]
}
```

Roulette-wheel selection is based on each chromosome's proportion of fitness of the sum of all fitnesses in a generation. The chromosomes with the highest fitness have a better chance of being picked. The values that represent each chromosome's percentage of total fitness are provided in the parameter `wheel`. These percentages are represented by floating-point values between 0 and 1. A random number (`pick`) between 0 and 1 is used to figure out which chromosome to select. The algorithm works by decreasing `pick` by each chromosome's proportional fitness value sequentially. When it crosses 0, that's the chromosome to select.

Does it make sense to you why this process results in each chromosome being pickable by its proportion? If not, think about it on pencil and paper. Consider drawing a proportional roulette wheel, as in figure 5.2.

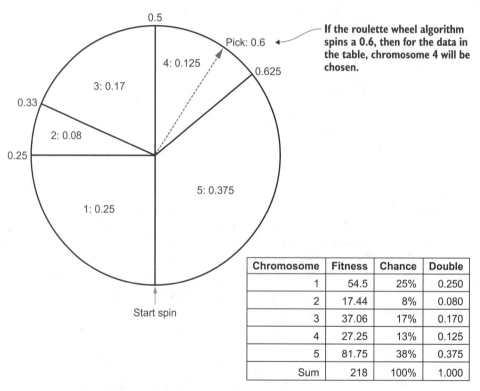

Chromosome	Fitness	Chance	Double
1	54.5	25%	0.250
2	17.44	8%	0.080
3	37.06	17%	0.170
4	27.25	13%	0.125
5	81.75	38%	0.375
Sum	218	100%	1.000

Figure 5.2   An example of roulette-wheel selection in action

The most basic form of tournament selection is simpler than roulette-wheel selection. Instead of figuring out proportions, we simply pick k chromosomes from the whole population at random. The chromosome with the best fitness wins.

```
// find k random individuals in the population and pick the best one
private func pickTournament(numParticipants: UInt) -> ChromosomeType {
    var best: ChromosomeType = ChromosomeType.randomInstance()
    var bestFitness: Double = best.fitness
```

```
    for _ in 0..<numParticipants { // find the best participant
        let test = Int(arc4random_uniform(UInt32(population.count)))
        if fitnessCache[test] > bestFitness {
            bestFitness = fitnessCache[test]
            best = population[test]
        }
    }
    return best
}
```

The code for `pickTournament()` is self-explanatory. What is the right number for `numParticipants`? Like many parameters in a genetic algorithm, trial and error may be the best way to determine it. One thing to keep in mind is that a higher number of participants in the tournament leads to less diversity in the population (because chromosomes with poor fitness are more likely to be eliminated in matchups).[1] More sophisticated forms of tournament selection may pick individuals that are not the best, but second- or third-best, based on some kind of decreasing probability model.

These two methods, `pickRoulette()` and `pickTournament()`, are used for selection, which occurs during reproduction. Reproduction is implemented in `reproduceAndReplace()`, and it also takes care of ensuring a new population of an equal number of chromosomes replaces the chromosomes in the last generation.

```
private func reproduceAndReplace() {
    var newPopulation: [ChromosomeType] = [ChromosomeType]()
    ⇒ // replacement population
    var chanceEach: [Double] = [Double]() // used for pickRoulette,
    ⇒ chance of each individual being picked
    if case .roulette = selectionType {
        chanceEach = fitnessCache.map({return $0/fitnessSum})
    }
    while newPopulation.count < population.count {
        var parents: (parent1: ChromosomeType, parent2: ChromosomeType)
        switch selectionType { // how to pick parents
        case let .tournament(k):
            parents = (parent1: pickTournament(numParticipants: k),
            ⇒ parent2: pickTournament(numParticipants: k))
        default: // don't have a case for roulette because no other option
            parents = (parent1: pickRoulette(wheel: chanceEach), parent2:
            ⇒ pickRoulette(wheel: chanceEach))
        }
        if drand48() < crossoverChance { // if crossover, produce children
            let children = parents.parent1.crossover(other:
            ⇒ parents.parent2)
            newPopulation.append(children.child1)
            newPopulation.append(children.child2)
        } else { // no crossover, just use parents
            newPopulation.append(parents.parent1)
            newPopulation.append(parents.parent2)
```

---

[1] Artem Sokolov and Darrell Whitley, "Unbiased Tournament Selection," GECCO'05 (June 25–29, 2005, Washington, D.C., U.S.A.), http://mng.bz/S7l6.

```
            }
        }
        if newPopulation.count > population.count { // in case we had an
        ➡ odd population
            newPopulation.removeLast()
        }
        population = newPopulation
    }
```

In reproduceAndReplace(), the following steps occur in broad strokes:

1 Two chromosomes, called parents, are selected for reproduction using one of the two selection methods.

2 There is crossoverChance that the two parents will be combined to produce two new chromosomes, children, in which case children are added to new-Population. If there are no children, the two parents are just added to newPopulation.

3 If newPopulation has as many chromosomes as population, it replaces it. Otherwise, we return to step 1.

The method that implements mutation, mutate(), is very simple, with the details of how to perform a mutation being left to individual chromosomes.

```
private func mutate() {
    for individual in population { // every individual could possibly
    ➡ be mutated each generation
        if drand48() < mutationChance {
            individual.mutate()
        }
    }
}
```

We now have all of the building blocks needed to run the genetic algorithm. run() coordinates the measurement, reproduction (which includes selection), and mutation steps that bring the population from one generation to another. It also keeps track of the best (fittest) chromosome found at any point in the search.

```
public func run() -> ChromosomeType {
    var best: ChromosomeType = ChromosomeType.randomInstance()
    ➡ // best in any run so far
    var bestFitness: Double = best.fitness
    for generation in 1...maxGenerations { // try maxGenerations of
    ➡ the genetic algorithm
        print("generation \(generation) best \(best.fitness) avg
        ➡ \(fitnessSum / Double(fitnessCache.count))")
        for (index, individual) in population.enumerated() {
            fitnessCache[index] = individual.fitness
            if fitnessCache[index] >= threshold { // early end;
            ➡ found something great
                return individual
            }
```

```
                if fitnessCache[index] > bestFitness {
            ➥    // best so far in any iteration
                    bestFitness = fitnessCache[index]
                    best = ChromosomeType(from: individual)
                }
            }
            fitnessSum = fitnessCache.reduce(0, +)
            reproduceAndReplace()
            mutate()
        }
        return best
    }
}
```

best and bestFitness keep track of the best chromosome (and its fitness) found so far.
The main loop executes maxGenerations times. At the beginning of the loop, it calcu-
lates, and caches, the fitness of every chromosome. If any chromosome exceeds
threshold in fitness, it is returned and the method ends. Otherwise, it calls reproduce-
AndReplace() as well as mutate() to create the next generation and run the loop again.
If maxGenerations is reached, the best chromosome found so far is returned.

5.4   *A naive test*

The generic genetic algorithm, GeneticAlgorithm, will work with any type that
implements Chromosome. As a test, we will start by implementing a simple problem
that can be easily solved using traditional methods. We will try to maximize the
equation $6x - x^2 + 4y - y^2$. In other words, what values for x and y in that equation will
yield the largest number? The maximizing values can be found, using calculus, by
taking partial derivatives and setting each equal to zero. The result is x = 3 and y = 2.
Can our genetic algorithm, using no calculus, find the same result? Let's dig in.

```
final class SimpleEquation: Chromosome {
    var x: Int = Int(arc4random_uniform(100))
    var y: Int = Int(arc4random_uniform(100))

    var fitness: Double { // 6x - x^2 + 4y - y^2
        return Double(6 * x - x * x + 4 * y - y * y)
    }

    init(from: SimpleEquation) { // like making a copy
        x = from.x
        y = from.y
    }

    init() {}

    static func randomInstance() -> SimpleEquation {
        return SimpleEquation()
    }

    func crossover(other: SimpleEquation)
    ➥    -> (child1: SimpleEquation, child2: SimpleEquation) {
```

```
            let child1 = SimpleEquation(from: self)
            let child2 = SimpleEquation(from: other)
            child1.y = other.y
            child2.y = self.y
            return (child1: child1, child2: child2)
        }

        func mutate() {
            if drand48() > 0.5 { // mutate x
                if drand48() > 0.5 {
                    x += 1
                } else {
                    x -= 1
                }
            } else { // otherwise mutate y
                if drand48() > 0.5 {
                    y += 1
                } else {
                    y -= 1
                }
            }
        }

        func prettyPrint() {
            print("x:\(x) y:\(y) fitness:\(fitness)")
        }
    }
```

SimpleEquation conforms to Chromosome, and, true to its name, it does so as simply as possible. The genes of a SimpleEquation chromosome can be thought of as x and y. The property fitness evaluates x and y using the equation $6x - x^2 + 4y - y^2$. The higher the value, the more fit the individual chromosome is, according to GeneticAlgorithm. x and y are initially set to be random integers between 0 and 100, so randomInstance() does not need to do anything other than instantiate a new SimpleEquation. To combine one SimpleEquation with another in crossover(), the y values of the two instances are simply swapped to create the two children. mutate() randomly increments or decrements x or y. And that is pretty much it.

Because SimpleEquation conforms to Chromosome, we can already plug it into GeneticAlgorithm.

```
let se = GeneticAlgorithm<SimpleEquation>(size: 10, threshold: 13.0,
➡ maxGenerations: 100, mutationChance: 0.1, crossoverChance: 0.7)
let result1 = se.run()
result1.prettyPrint()
```

The parameters used here were derived through guess-and-check. You can try others. threshold is set to 13.0 because we already know the correct answer. When x = 3 and y = 2, the equation evaluates to 13.

If you did not previously know the answer, you might want to see the best result that could be found in a certain number of generations. In that case, you would set threshold to some arbitrarily large number. Remember, because genetic algorithms are stochastic, every run will be different.

Here is some sample output from a run in which the genetic algorithm solved the equation in 18 generations.

```
generation 1 best -8080.0 avg -1.79769313486232e+307
generation 2 best -892.0 avg -5699.1
generation 3 best -52.0 avg -1626.3
generation 4 best -51.0 avg -187.1
generation 5 best -37.0 avg -70.2
generation 6 best -37.0 avg -37.0
generation 7 best -24.0 avg -35.6
generation 8 best -13.0 avg -31.9
generation 9 best 11.0 avg -19.6
generation 10 best 11.0 avg -6.1
generation 11 best 11.0 avg 8.6
generation 12 best 11.0 avg 10.1
generation 13 best 11.0 avg 10.7
generation 14 best 11.0 avg 11.0
generation 15 best 11.0 avg 11.0
generation 16 best 11.0 avg 11.0
generation 17 best 12.0 avg 11.3
generation 18 best 12.0 avg 11.7
x:3 y:2 fitness:13.0
```

As you can see, it came to the proper solution derived earlier with calculus, x = 3 and y = 2. You may also note that almost every generation, it got closer to the right answer. Take into consideration that the genetic algorithm took more computational power than other methods would have to find the solution. In the real world, such a simple maximization problem would not be a good use of a genetic algorithm. But its simple implementation at least suffices to prove that our genetic algorithm works.

5.5 *SEND+MORE=MONEY revisited*

In chapter 3, we solved the classic cryptarithmetic problem SEND+MORE=MONEY using a constraint-satisfaction framework. (For a refresher on what the problem is all about, please look back to the description in chapter 3.) However, we cheated a bit in that earlier solution. Because the fairly naive backtracking search would take an incredibly long time to execute in a Swift Playground, we presupplied the answers to the letters S, M, and O. The problem can be solved in a reasonable amount of time in a Swift Playground, without any cheating, using a genetic algorithm.

One of the largest difficulties in formulating a problem for a genetic algorithm solution is determining how to represent it. A convenient representation for crypt-arithmetic problems is to use array indices as digits.[2] Hence, to represent the 10 possible digits (0, 1, 2, 3, 4, 5, 6, 7, 8, 9), a 10-element array is required. The characters to

---

[2] Reza Abbasian and Masoud Mazloom, "Solving Cryptarithmetic Problems Using Parallel Genetic Algorithm," 2009 Second International Conference on Computer and Electrical Engineering, http://mng.bz/RQ7V.

be searched within the problem can then be shifted around from place to place. For example, if it is suspected that the solution to a problem includes the character "E" representing the digit 4, then array[4] = "E". SEND+MORE=MONEY has 8 distinct letters (S, E, N, D, M, O, R, Y), leaving two slots in the array empty. They can be filled with spaces indicating no letter.

A chromosome that represents the SEND+MORE=MONEY problem is represented in SendMoreMoney. Note how the fitness property is strikingly similar to isSatisfied() from SendMoreMoneyConstraint in chapter 3.

```
final class SendMoreMoney: Chromosome {
    var genes: [Character]
    static let letters: [Character] = ["S", "E", "N", "D", "M", "O", "R",
     "Y", " ", " "]

    var fitness: Double {
        if let s = genes.index(of: "S"), let e = genes.index(of: "E"), let
         n = genes.index(of: "N"), let d = genes.index(of: "D"),
         let m =  genes.index(of: "M"), let o = genes.index(of: "O"),
         let r =  genes.index(of: "R"), let y = genes.index(of: "Y") {
            let send: Int = s * 1000 + e * 100 + n * 10 + d
            let more: Int = m * 1000 + o * 100 + r * 10 + e
            let money: Int = m * 10000 + o * 1000 + n * 100 + e * 10 + y
            let difference = abs(money - (send + more))
            return 1 / Double(difference + 1)
        }
        return 0
    }

    init(from: SendMoreMoney) {
        genes = from.genes
    }

    init(genes: [Character]) {
        self.genes = genes
    }

    static func randomInstance() -> SendMoreMoney {
        return SendMoreMoney(genes: letters.shuffled())
    }

    func crossover(other: SendMoreMoney)
     -> (child1: SendMoreMoney, child2: SendMoreMoney) {
        let crossingPoint = Int(arc4random_uniform(UInt32(genes.count)))
        let childGenes1 = genes[0..<crossingPoint] +
         other.genes[crossingPoint..<other.genes.count]
        let childGenes2 = other.genes[0..<crossingPoint] +
         genes[crossingPoint..<genes.count]
        return (child1: SendMoreMoney(genes: Array(childGenes1)), child2:
         SendMoreMoney(genes: Array(childGenes2)))
    }

    func mutate() {
        // put a random letter in a random place
```

```
        let position1 =
    ➡ Int(arc4random_uniform(UInt32(SendMoreMoney.letters.count)))
        let position2 = Int(arc4random_uniform(UInt32(genes.count)))
        if drand48() < 0.5 { // half the time random letter
            genes[position2] = SendMoreMoney.letters[position1]
        } else { // half the time random swap
            if position1 != position2 { genes.swapAt(position1, position2) }
        }
    }

    func prettyPrint() {
        if let s = genes.index(of: "S"), let e = genes.index(of: "E"),
    ➡ let n = genes.index(of: "N"), let d = genes.index(of: "D"),
    ➡ let m =  genes.index(of: "M"), let o = genes.index(of: "O"),
    ➡ let r =  genes.index(of: "R"), let y = genes.index(of: "Y") {
            let send: Int = s * 1000 + e * 100 + n * 10 + d
            let more: Int = m * 1000 + o * 100 + r * 10 + e
            let money: Int = m * 10000 + o * 1000 + n * 100 + e * 10 + y
            print("\(send) + \(more) =
            ➡ \(money) difference:\(money - (send + more))")
        } else {
            print("Missing some letters")
        }
    }
}
```

There is, however, a major difference between isSatisfied() in chapter 3 and fitness here. Look at the final return values. At the very end, we return 0 if a letter is missing. That is not fit at all! If we do have all of the letters, though, we return 1 / Double(difference + 1). difference is the absolute value of the difference between MONEY and SEND+MORE. This represents how far off the chromosome is from solving the problem. If we were trying to minimize the fitness this would be a fine number to return. But because GeneticAlgorithm tries to maximize the value of fitness, it needs to be flipped (so smaller values look like larger values), and that is why 1 is divided by difference. 1 is added to difference first, so that a difference of 0 does not yield a fitness of 0 but instead of 1. Table 5.1 should help.

Table 5.1 How the equation 1 / (difference + 1) yields fitnesses for maximization

difference	difference + 1	fitness (1/(difference + 1))
0	1	1
1	2	0.5
2	3	0.25
3	4	0.125

Remember, lower differences are better and higher fitnesses are better. Because this formula causes those two facts to line up, it works well. Dividing 1 by a fitness value is a simple way to convert a minimization problem into a maximization problem. It does introduce some biases, though, so it is not foolproof.

randomInstance() makes use of the shuffled() extension to Array introduced at the beginning of the chapter. crossover() selects a random point in the genes array of both chromosomes, and divides both at that point. It swaps the pieces of the two arrays so that the children are a combination. For example, if crossingPoint is 4, it takes the first 4 elements of the first parent and merges that with the latter 6 elements of the second parent to create the first child. It then takes the first 4 elements of the second parent and merges that with the latter 6 elements of the first parent to create the second child. mutate() either swaps two random locations in a genes array or puts a random letter into a random slot in the array.

We can plug SendMoreMoney into GeneticAlgorithm just as easily as we plugged in SimpleEquation. But be forewarned: this is a fairly tough problem, and it will take a long time to execute in a Swift Playground if the population size is set to about 100 or greater. The problem may be solved in a few seconds or a few minutes. Unfortunately, that is the nature of genetic algorithms!

```
let smm: GeneticAlgorithm<SendMoreMoney> =
➡ GeneticAlgorithm<SendMoreMoney>(size: 100, threshold: 1.0,
➡ maxGenerations: 1000, mutationChance: 0.3, crossoverChance: 0.7,
➡ selectionType: .tournament(5))
let result2 = smm.run()
result2.prettyPrint()
```

The following output is from a run that solved the problem in 38 generations. See if you can mess around with the configurable parameters of GeneticAlgorithm to get this number down.

```
generation 1 best 4.40606274233345e-05 avg -1.79769313486232e+306
generation 2 best 0.00662251655629139 avg 0.000149274918883093
generation 3 best 0.00662251655629139 avg 7.54324207922214e-05
generation 4 best 0.00662251655629139 avg 0.000179701356382686
generation 5 best 0.00662251655629139 avg 0.000191508227007907
generation 6 best 0.00662251655629139 avg 0.000427770153261289
generation 7 best 0.00662251655629139 avg 0.000451925157998017
generation 8 best 0.00662251655629139 avg 0.000773980169008364
generation 9 best 0.00662251655629139 avg 0.00127997518255647
...
generation 32 best 0.2 avg 0.0551205015837618
generation 33 best 0.25 avg 0.0902090428070604
generation 34 best 0.5 avg 0.12896873861678
generation 35 best 0.5 avg 0.160618496435873
generation 36 best 0.5 avg 0.150776355741466
generation 37 best 0.5 avg 0.181086928014186
6419 + 724 = 7143 difference:0
```

This solution indicates that SEND = 6419, MORE = 724, and MONEY = 7143. How is that possible? It looks like letters are missing from the solution. In fact, if M = 0, there are several solutions to the problem not possible in the version from chapter 2. MORE is actually 0724 here, and MONEY is 07143. The 0 is just ignored.

5.6 Challenges for genetic algorithms

Genetic algorithms are not a panacea. In fact, they are not suitable for most problems. For any problem in which a fast deterministic algorithm exists, a genetic algorithm approach does not make sense. Their inherently stochastic nature makes their run-times unpredictable. To solve this problem, they can be cut off after a certain number of generations. But then it is not clear if a truly optimal solution has been found.

Steven Skiena, author of one of the most popular texts on algorithms, even went so far as to write this:

> *I have never encountered any problem where genetic algorithms seemed to me the right way to attack it. Further, I have never seen any computational results reported using genetic algorithms that have favorably impressed me.*[3]

Skiena's view is a little extreme, but it is indicative of the fact that genetic algorithms should only be chosen when you are reasonably confidant that a better solution does not exist. Another issue with genetic algorithms is determining how to represent a potential solution to a problem as a chromosome. The traditional practice is to represent most problems as binary strings (sequences of 1's and 0's, raw bits). This is often optimal in terms of space usage, and it lends itself to easy crossover functions. But most complex problems are not easily represented as divisible bit strings.

In short, for most problems large enough to warrant using them, genetic algorithms cannot guarantee the discovery of an optimal solution in a predictable amount of time. For this reason, they are best utilized in situations that do not call for an optimal solution, but instead a "good enough" solution. They are fairly easy to implement, but tweaking their configurable parameters can take a lot of trial and error.

5.7 Real-world applications

Despite what Skiena wrote, genetic algorithms are frequently and effectively applied in a myriad of problem spaces. They are often used on hard problems that do not require perfectly optimal solutions, such as constraint-satisfaction problems too large to be solved using traditional methods. One example is complex scheduling problems.

Genetic algorithms have found many applications in computational biology. They have been used successfully for protein-ligand docking, which is a search for the configuration of a small molecule when it is bound to a receptor. This is used in pharmaceutical research and to better understand mechanisms in nature.

The Traveling Salesman problem is one of the most famous problems in computer science. A traveling salesman wants to find the shortest route on a map that visits every city exactly once and brings him back to his starting location. It may sound like minimum spanning trees in chapter 4, but it is different. In the Traveling Salesman, the

---

[3] Steven Skiena, *The Algorithm Design Manual*, 2nd edition (Springer, 2009), p. 267

solution is a giant cycle that minimizes the cost to traverse it, whereas a minimum spanning tree minimizes the cost to connect every city. A person traveling a minimum spanning tree of cities may have to visit the same city twice to reach every city. Even though they sound similar, there is no reasonably timed algorithm for finding a solution to the Traveling Salesman problem for an arbitrary number of cities. Genetic algorithms have been shown to find suboptimal, but pretty good, solutions in short periods of time. The problem is widely applicable to the efficient distribution of goods. For example, dispatchers of FedEx and UPS trucks use software to solve the Traveling Salesman problem every day. Algorithms that help solve the problem can cut costs in a large variety of industries.

In computer-generated art, genetic algorithms are sometimes used to mimic photographs using stochastic methods. Imagine fifty polygons placed randomly on a screen and gradually twisted, turned, moved, resized, and changed in color until they match a photograph as closely as possible. The result looks like the work of an abstract artist, or if more angular shapes are used, a stained glass window.

Genetic algorithms are part of a larger field called evolutionary computation. One area of evolutionary computation closely related to genetic algorithms is *genetic programming*, in which programs use the selection, crossover, and mutation operations to modify themselves to find non-obvious solutions to programming problems. Genetic programming is not a widely used technique, but imagine a future where programs write themselves.

A benefit of genetic algorithms is that they lend themselves to easy parallelization. In the most obvious form, each population can be simulated on a separate processor. In the most granular form, each individual can be mutated, crossed, and have its fitness calculated in a separate thread. There are also many possibilities in between.

5.8   *Exercises*

1   Add support to `GeneticAlgorithm` for an advanced form of tournament selection that may sometimes choose the second or third best chromosome, based on a diminishing probability.

2   Add a new function to the constraint-satisfaction framework from chapter 3 that solves any arbitrary CSP using a genetic algorithm. A possible measure of fitness is the number of constraints that are resolved by a chromosome.

3   Create a struct, `BitString`, that implements `Chromosome`.

K-means clustering

Humanity has never had more data about more facets of society than it does today. Computers are great for storing data sets, but they need humans to draw meaning through their analysis. *Clustering* is a computational technique that divides the points in a data set into groups. A successful clustering results in groups that contain points that are related to one another, and whether those relationships are meaningful generally requires human verification.

In clustering, the group (a.k.a. *cluster*) that a data point belongs to is not predetermined, but instead is decided during the run of the clustering algorithm. In fact, the algorithm is not guided to place any particular data point in any particular cluster by presupposed information. For this reason, clustering is sometimes considered an *unsupervised* method within the realm of machine learning. You can think of "unsupervised" as meaning "not guided by foreknowledge."

Clustering is a useful technique when you want to learn about the structure of a data set, but you do not know ahead of time its constituent parts. For example, imagine you own a grocery store, and you collect data about customers and their transactions. You want to run mobile advertisements of specials at relevant times of the week to bring customers into your store. You could try clustering your data by day of the week and demographic information. Perhaps you will find a cluster that indicates younger shoppers prefer to shop on Tuesdays, and you could use that information to run an ad specifically targeting them on that day.

6.1 Preliminaries

Clustering algorithms require some statistical primitives (mean, standard deviation, and so on). The Swift standard library does not provide these primitives, but it is not unheard of for standard libraries to do so (Python since version 3.4 and Java since version 8 do, for instance). We will implement these primitives from scratch, but in a production system it would make sense to use a well-tested open source library instead of rolling your own, because their performance is critical for any sizable data set.

For simplicity's sake, the data points in this chapter consist exclusively of dimensions defined by type `Double`, so there will be many operations on arrays of `Doubles`. The statistical primitives `sum`, `mean`, `variance`, `std`, and `zscored` are defined in this context. Their definitions follow directly from the formulas you would find in a statistics textbook.

```swift
import Foundation // for pow(), srand48(), drand48()

extension Array where Element == Double {
    var sum: Double {
        return self.reduce(0.0, +)
    }

    // Find the average (mean)
    var mean: Double {
        return sum / Double(self.count)
    }

    // Find the variance sum((Xi - mean)^2) / N
    var variance: Double {
        let mean = self.mean // cache so not recalculated for every element
        return self.map { pow(($0 - mean), 2) }.mean
    }

    // Find the standard deviation sqrt(variance)
    var std: Double {
        return sqrt(variance)
    }

    // Convert elements to respective z-scores (formula z-score =
    //    (x - mean) / std)
    var zscored: [Double] {
        let mean = self.mean
        let std = self.std
        return self.map{ std != 0 ? (($0 -
    mean) / std) : 0.0 } // avoid divide by zero
    }
}
```

TIP Swift has no built-in operator for calculating arbitrary powers. `pow()`, like random-number generation functions, is actually defined in the `Darwin` module (`Glibc` on Linux). The import of `Foundation` takes care of the import of `Darwin` or `Glibc`.

Because these primitives are implemented as an extension of `Array`, they will work with any array of `Doubles`. Notice how they build on one another. `mean` uses `sum`, `variance` uses `mean`, `std` uses `variance`, and `zscored` uses `std` and `mean`. By breaking up the properties into small parts, it makes them easier to test and reason about. All of the properties return a single Double except zscored, which returns a copy of the whole array converted into z-scores. There will be more about z-scores later in the chapter.

NOTE It is beyond the purview of this book to teach elementary statistics, but you do not need more than a rudimentary understanding of mean and standard deviation to follow the rest of the chapter. If it has been a while, and you need a refresher, or you never previously learned these terms, it may be worthwhile to quickly peruse a statistics resource that explains these two fundamental concepts.

It is worth quickly testing the fundamentals.

```
let test: [Double] = [600, 470, 170, 430, 300]
test.sum
test.mean
test.variance
test.std
test.zscored
```

If you use the preceding test data, you should get the following results:

- sum: 1970
- mean: 394
- variance: 21704
- std: 147.3227748856232
- zscored: [1.398290251863176, 0.5158740735029193, -1.520470953482288, 0.2443614032382249, -0.6380547751220317]

The most basic form of the k-means algorithm uses random guesses to seed the centers of each cluster (more on the algorithm itself shortly). Therefore, we again need pseudorandom number generators, but for this chapter we need floating-point pseudorandom numbers that fall within a certain range. Instead of using drand48() directly, here we will define a more convenient means of access.

```
struct Random {
    private static var seeded = false

    // a random Double between *from* and *to*, assumes *from* < *to*
    static func double(from: Double, to: Double) -> Double {
        if !Random.seeded {
            srand48(time(nil))
            Random.seeded = true
        }

        return (drand48() * (to - from)) + from
    }
}
```

In prior chapters, we placed a call to srand48() seemingly randomly near the top of an example. By using a static Boolean variable, seeded, that will be "remembered" between calls to the static function Random.double(), we can accomplish seeding in the first call of Random.double(). The rest of the code in Random.double() uses some simple arithmetic to ensure a random number falls within a certain range. Recall that drand48() returns a Double between 0 and 1. This method will always work as long as to is greater than from.

All clustering algorithms work with points of data, and our implementation of k-means will be no exception. We will define a common interface called DataPoint.

```
public protocol DataPoint: CustomStringConvertible, Equatable {
    static var numDimensions: UInt { get }
    var dimensions: [Double] { get set }
    init(values: [Double])
}
```

Every data point must be comparable to other data points of the same type (Equatable), and human-readable for printing (CustomStringConvertible). Every data point type has a certain number of dimensions (numDimensions), and this property is static because data points of the same type will always have the same number of dimensions. The array dimensions stores the actual values for each of those dimensions as Doubles. Finally, an init() method that takes an array of values for the dimensions is required, because we will need a way of initializing random DataPoints within a certain range in the initialization of k-means.

One final preliminary we need, before we can dig into k-means, is a way of calculating the distance between any two data points of the same type. There are many ways to calculate distance, but the form most commonly used with k-means is Euclidean distance. This is the distance formula familiar to most from a grade school course in geometry, derivable from the Pythagorean theorem. In fact, we already discussed the formula and derived a version of it for two-dimensional spaces in chapter 2, where we used it to find the distance between any two locations within a maze. Our version for DataPoint needs to be more sophisticated, because a DataPoint can involve any number of dimensions.

```
extension DataPoint {
    // Euclidean distance
    func distance<PointType: DataPoint>(to: PointType) -> Double {
        return sqrt(zip(dimensions, to.dimensions).map({
            pow(($0.1 - $0.0), 2) }).sum)
    }
}
```

This version of distance() is especially compact and will work with DataPoint types with any number of dimensions. The zip() call creates tuples filled with pairs of each dimension of the two points, combined into a sequence. The map() call finds the difference between each point at each dimension, and squares that value, storing the squares in a new sequence. `sum` adds all of these values together, and the final value returned by `distance()` is the square root of this sum.

To test `distance()`, let's define a generic implementation of `DataPoint` that will work for any three-dimensional problem. `Point3D` can represent a point in a 3D space. It refers to each of the dimensions using the classic variables x, y, and z.

```swift
public struct Point3D: DataPoint {
    public static let numDimensions: UInt = 3
    public let x: Double
    public let y: Double
    public let z: Double
    public var dimensions: [Double]

    public init(x: Double, y: Double, z: Double) {
        self.x = x
        self.y = y
        self.z = z
        dimensions = [x, y, z]
    }

    public init(values: [Double]) {
        self.x = values[0]
        self.y = values[1]
        self.z = values[2]
        dimensions = values
    }

    // Implement Equatable
    public static func == (lhs: Point3D, rhs: Point3D) -> Bool {
        return lhs.x == rhs.x && lhs.y == rhs.y && lhs.z == rhs.z
    }

    // Implement CustomStringConvertible
    public var description: String {
        return "(\(x), \(y), \(z))"
    }
}
```

It is time for a quick test of `distance()`.

```swift
let j = Point3D(x: 2.0, y: 1.0, z: 1.0)
let k = Point3D(x: 2.0, y: 2.0, z: 5.0)
j.distance(to: k)
```

The distance should be ~4.123

6.2 *The k-means clustering algorithm*

K-means is a clustering algorithm that attempts to group data points into a certain predefined number of clusters, based on each point's relative distance to the center of the cluster. In every round of k-means, the distance between every data point and every center of a cluster (a point known as a *centroid*) is calculated. Points are assigned to the cluster whose centroid they are closest to. Then the algorithm recalculates all of the centroids, finding the mean of each cluster's assigned points and replacing the old centroid with the new mean. The process of assigning points and recalculating centroids continues until the centroids stop moving or a certain number of iterations occurs.

Each dimension of the initial points provided to k-means needs to be comparable in magnitude. If they are not, k-means will skew toward clustering based on dimensions with the largest differences. The process of making different types of data (in our case, different dimensions) comparable is known as *normalization*. One common way of normalizing data is to evaluate each value based on its *z-score* (also known as *standard score*) relative to the other values of the same type. A z-score is calculated by taking a value, subtracting the mean of all of the values from it, and dividing that result by the standard deviation of all of the values. The `zscored` property devised near the beginning of the previous section does exactly this for every value in an array of `Double`.

The main difficulty with k-means is choosing how to assign the initial centroids. In the most basic form of the algorithm, which is what we will be implementing, the initial centroids are placed randomly within the range of the data. Another difficulty is deciding how many clusters to divide the data into (the "k" in k-means). In the classical algorithm, that number is determined by the user, but the user may not know the right number, and this will require some experimentation. We will let the user define "k."

Putting all of these steps and considerations together, here is our k-means clustering algorithm:

1 Initialize all of the data points and "k" empty clusters.
2 Normalize all of the data points.
3 Create random centroids associated with each cluster.
4 Assign each data point to the cluster of the centroid it is closest to.
5 Recalculate each centroid so it is the center (mean) of the cluster it is associated with.
6 Repeat steps 4 and 5 until a maximum number of iterations is reached or the centroids stop moving (convergence).

Conceptually, k-means is actually quite simple: In each iteration, every data point is associated with the cluster that it is closest to in terms of the cluster's center. That center moves as new points are associated with the cluster.

We will implement a class for maintaining state and running the algorithm, similar to `GeneticAlgorithm` in chapter 5.

```
public final class KMeans<PointType: DataPoint> {
    public final class Cluster {
        var points: [PointType] = [PointType]()
        var centroid: PointType
```

```
        init(centroid: PointType) {
            self.centroid = centroid
        }
    }
```

KMeans is a generic class. It works with any type that implements DataPoint. It has an internal type, Cluster, that keeps track of the individual clusters in the operation. Each Cluster has data points and a centroid associated with it.

```
    private var points: [PointType]
    private var clusters: [Cluster]

    private var centroids: [PointType] {
        return clusters.map{ $0.centroid }
    }
```

KMeans has an array, points, associated with it. This is all of the points in the data set. The points are further divided between the clusters, which are stored in the appropriately titled clusters variable. The computed centroids property returns all of the centroids associated with the clusters that are associated with the algorithm.

```
    init(k: UInt, points: [PointType]) {
        self.points = points
        clusters = [Cluster]()
        zscoreNormalize()
        for _ in 0..<k { // initialize a random centroid for each cluster
            let randPoint = randomPoint()
            clusters.append(Cluster(centroid: randPoint))
        }
    }
```

When KMeans is instantiated, it needs to know how many clusters it will be trying to divide the data into (k). Every cluster initially has a random centroid. All of the data points that will be used in the algorithm are normalized by z-score.

```
    private func dimensionSlice(_ index: Int) -> [Double] {
        return points.map{ $0.dimensions[index] }
    }
```

dimensionSlice() is a convenience method that can be thought of as returning a column of data. It will return an array composed of every value at a particular index in every data point. For instance, if the data points were of type Point3D, then dimensionSlice[0] would return an array of every x value of every data point in the points array.

```
    private func zscoreNormalize() {
        for dimension in 0..<Int(PointType.numDimensions) {
            for (index, zscore)
            ➡ in dimensionSlice(dimension).zscored.enumerated() {
```

```
                    points[index].dimensions[dimension] = zscore
                }
            }
        }
```

zscoreNormalize() replaces the values in the dimensions array of every data point with its z-scored equivalent. This uses the zscored property that we defined for arrays of Double earlier. Although the values in the dimensions array are replaced, individual properties not specified in the DataPoint protocol are not. If, for example, an array of points composed of Point3D was zscoreNormalized(), the values in its dimensions array would change, but the values of its properties x, y, and z would not. This is useful—the user of the algorithm can still retrieve the original values of the dimensions before normalization after the algorithm runs if they are stored in both places.

```
    private func randomPoint() -> PointType {
        var randDimensions = [Double]()
        for dimension in 0..<Int(PointType.numDimensions) {
            let values = dimensionSlice(dimension)
            let randValue = Random.double(from: values.min()!,
                to:values.max()!)
            randDimensions.append(randValue)
        }
        return PointType(values: randDimensions)
    }
```

The preceding randomPoint() function is used in the init() method to create the initial random centroids for each cluster. It constrains the random values of each point to be within the range of the existing data points' values. It uses the constructor we specified earlier on DataPoint to create a new point from an array of values.

```
    // Find the closest cluster centroid to each point and assign the point
        to that cluster
    private func assignClusters() {
        for point in points {
            var lowestDistance = Double.greatestFiniteMagnitude // temporary
            var closestCluster = clusters.first!
            for (index, centroid) in centroids.enumerated() {
                if centroid.distance(to: point) < lowestDistance {
                    lowestDistance = centroid.distance(to: point)
                    closestCluster = clusters[index]
                }
            }
            closestCluster.points.append(point)
        }
    }
```

Throughout the book, we have created several functions that find the minimum or find the maximum in an array. This one is not dissimilar. In this case we are looking for the cluster centroid that has the minimum distance to each individual point. The point is then assigned to that cluster.

```
    // find the center of each cluster and move the centroid to there
    private func generateCentroids() {
        for cluster in clusters {
            var means: [Double] = [Double]()
            for dimension in 0..<Int(PointType.numDimensions) {
                means.append(cluster.points.map({
                    ➥ $0.dimensions[dimension] }).mean)
            }
            cluster.centroid = PointType(values: means)
        }
    }
```

After every point is assigned to a cluster, the new centroids are calculated. This involves calculating the mean of each dimension of every point in the cluster. The means of each dimension are then combined to find the "mean point" in the cluster, which becomes the new centroid. Note that we cannot use dimensionSlice() here, because the points in question are a subset of all of the points (just those belonging to a particular cluster). How could dimensionSlice() be rewritten to be more generic?

Now, let's look at the method that will actually execute the algorithm.

```
    public func run(maxIterations: UInt = 100) -> [Cluster] {
        for iteration in 0..<maxIterations {
            clusters.forEach{ $0.points.removeAll() } // clear all clusters
            assignClusters() // find clusters each is closest to - assign
            let lastCentroids = centroids // record centroids
            generateCentroids() // find new centroids
            if lastCentroids == centroids { // have centroids moved?
                print("Converged after \(iteration) iterations.")
                return clusters // they haven't moved, so we've converged
            }
        }

        return clusters
    }
}
```

Finally, there is run(), which is the most pure expression of the original algorithm. The only change to the algorithm you may find unexpected is the removal of all points at the beginning of each iteration. If this were not to occur, the assignClusters() method, as written, would end up putting duplicate points in each cluster.

You can perform a quick test using the test Point3Ds from before and k set to 1. You should see a single cluster containing both points.

```
let kmeansTest = KMeans<Point3D>(k: 1, points: [j, k])
let testClusters = kmeansTest.run()
for (index, cluster) in testClusters.enumerated() {
    print("Cluster \(index): \(cluster.points)")
}
```

This is the expected result:

```
Converged after 1 iterations.
Cluster 0: [(2.0, 1.0, 1.0), (2.0, 2.0, 5.0)]
```

6.3   *Clustering governors by age and longitude*

Every American state has a governor. In June 2017, those governors ranged in age from 42 to 79. If we take the United States from east to west, looking at each state by its longitude, perhaps we can find clusters of states with similar longitudes and similar age governors. Figure 6.1 is a scatter plot of all 50 governors. The x-axis is state longitude and the y-axis is governor age.

Are there any obvious clusters in figure 6.1? In this figure, the axes are not normalized. Instead, we are looking at raw data. If clusters were always obvious, there would be no need for clustering algorithms.

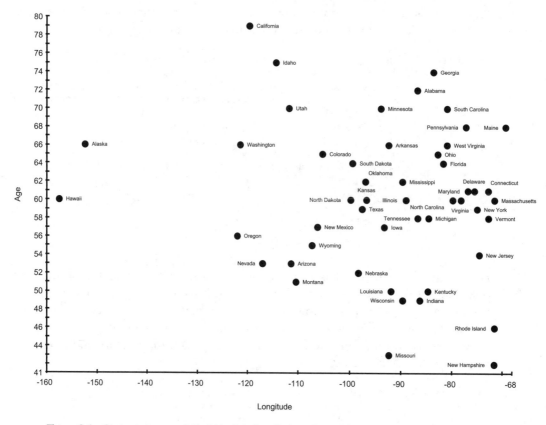

Figure 6.1   State governors plotted by state longitude and governor age

Let's try running this data set through k-means. First, we will need a way of representing an individual data point.

```
struct Governor: DataPoint {
    public static let numDimensions: UInt = 2
    public let longitude: Double
    public let age: Double
    public var dimensions: [Double]
    public let state: String

    public init(longitude: Double, age: Double, state: String) {
        self.longitude = longitude
        self.age = age
        self.state = state
        dimensions = [longitude, age]
    }

    public init(values: [Double]) {
        self.longitude = values[0]
        self.age = values[1]
        self.state = ""
        dimensions = values
    }

    // Implement Equatable
    public static func == (lhs: Governor, rhs: Governor) -> Bool {
        return lhs.longitude == rhs.longitude && lhs.age == rhs.age &&
            ⮕ lhs.state == rhs.state
    }

    // Implement CustomStringConvertible
    public var description: String {
        return "\(state): (longitude: \(longitude), age: \(age))"
    }
}
```

A `Governor` has two dimensions—`longitude` and `age`—rather than the three in `Point3D`. Other than that, `Governor` is almost identical to `Point3D` in implementation. It would be pretty unreasonable to enter the following data manually, so check out the Playground that accompanies this book.

```
let governors = [Governor(longitude: -86.79113, age: 72, state: "Alabama"),
Governor(longitude: -152.404419, age: 66, state: "Alaska"),
Governor(longitude: -111.431221, age: 53, state: "Arizona"),
Governor(longitude: -92.373123, age: 66, state: "Arkansas"),
Governor(longitude: -119.681564, age: 79, state: "California"),
Governor(longitude: -105.311104, age: 65, state: "Colorado"),
Governor(longitude: -72.755371, age: 61, state: "Connecticut"),
Governor(longitude: -75.507141, age: 61, state: "Delaware"),
Governor(longitude: -81.686783, age: 64, state: "Florida"),
```

```
Governor(longitude: -83.643074, age: 74, state: "Georgia"),
Governor(longitude: -157.498337, age: 60, state: "Hawaii"),
Governor(longitude: -114.478828, age: 75, state: "Idaho"),
Governor(longitude: -88.986137, age: 60, state: "Illinois"),
Governor(longitude: -86.258278, age: 49, state: "Indiana"),
Governor(longitude: -93.210526, age: 57, state: "Iowa"),
Governor(longitude: -96.726486, age: 60, state: "Kansas"),
Governor(longitude: -84.670067, age: 50, state: "Kentucky"),
Governor(longitude: -91.867805, age: 50, state: "Louisiana"),
Governor(longitude: -69.381927, age: 68, state: "Maine"),
Governor(longitude: -76.802101, age: 61, state: "Maryland"),
Governor(longitude: -71.530106, age: 60, state: "Massachusetts"),
Governor(longitude: -84.536095, age: 58, state: "Michigan"),
Governor(longitude: -93.900192, age: 70, state: "Minnesota"),
Governor(longitude: -89.678696, age: 62, state: "Mississippi"),
Governor(longitude: -92.288368, age: 43, state: "Missouri"),
Governor(longitude: -110.454353, age: 51, state: "Montana"),
Governor(longitude: -98.268082, age: 52, state: "Nebraska"),
Governor(longitude: -117.055374, age: 53, state: "Nevada"),
Governor(longitude: -71.563896, age: 42, state: "New Hampshire"),
Governor(longitude: -74.521011, age: 54, state: "New Jersey"),
Governor(longitude: -106.248482, age: 57, state: "New Mexico"),
Governor(longitude: -74.948051, age: 59, state: "New York"),
Governor(longitude: -79.806419, age: 60, state: "North Carolina"),
Governor(longitude: -99.784012, age: 60, state: "North Dakota"),
Governor(longitude: -82.764915, age: 65, state: "Ohio"),
Governor(longitude: -96.928917, age: 62, state: "Oklahoma"),
Governor(longitude: -122.070938, age: 56, state: "Oregon"),
Governor(longitude: -77.209755, age: 68, state: "Pennsylvania"),
Governor(longitude: -71.51178, age: 46, state: "Rhode Island"),
Governor(longitude: -80.945007, age: 70, state: "South Carolina"),
Governor(longitude: -99.438828, age: 64, state: "South Dakota"),
Governor(longitude: -86.692345, age: 58, state: "Tennessee"),
Governor(longitude: -97.563461, age: 59, state: "Texas"),
Governor(longitude: -111.862434, age: 70, state: "Utah"),
Governor(longitude: -72.710686, age: 58, state: "Vermont"),
Governor(longitude: -78.169968, age: 60, state: "Virginia"),
Governor(longitude: -121.490494, age: 66, state: "Washington"),
Governor(longitude: -80.954453, age: 66, state: "West Virginia"),
Governor(longitude: -89.616508, age: 49, state: "Wisconsin"),
Governor(longitude: -107.30249, age: 55, state: "Wyoming")]
```

We will run k-means with k set to 2.

```
let kmeans = KMeans<Governor>(k: 2, points: governors)
let govClusters = kmeans.run()
for (index, cluster) in govClusters.enumerated() {
    print("Cluster \(index): \(cluster.points)")
}
```

Because it starts with randomized centroids, every run of KMeans may potentially return different clusters. It takes some human analysis to see if the clusters are actually relevant. The following result is from a run that did have an interesting cluster.

```
Converged after 2 iterations.
Cluster 0: [Alabama: (longitude: -86.79113, age: 72.0), Arizona:
(longitude: -111.431221, age: 53.0), Arkansas: (longitude: -92.373123,
age: 66.0), Colorado: (longitude: -105.311104, age: 65.0), Connecticut:
(longitude: -72.755371, age: 61.0), Delaware: (longitude: -75.507141, age:
61.0), Florida: (longitude: -81.686783, age: 64.0), Georgia: (longitude:
-83.643074, age: 74.0), Illinois: (longitude: -88.986137, age: 60.0),
Indiana: (longitude: -86.258278, age: 49.0), Iowa: (longitude: -93.210526,
age: 57.0), Kansas: (longitude: -96.726486, age: 60.0), Kentucky:
(longitude: -84.670067, age: 50.0), Louisiana: (longitude: -91.867805,
age: 50.0), Maine: (longitude: -69.381927, age: 68.0), Maryland:
(longitude: -76.802101, age: 61.0), Massachusetts: (longitude: -71.530106,
age: 60.0), Michigan: (longitude: -84.536095, age: 58.0), Minnesota:
(longitude: -93.900192, age: 70.0), Mississippi: (longitude: -89.678696,
age: 62.0), Missouri: (longitude: -92.288368, age: 43.0), Montana:
(longitude: -110.454353, age: 51.0), Nebraska: (longitude: -98.268082,
age: 52.0), Nevada: (longitude: -117.055374, age: 53.0), New Hampshire:
(longitude: -71.563896, age: 42.0), New Jersey: (longitude: -74.521011,
age: 54.0), New Mexico: (longitude: -106.248482, age: 57.0), New York:
(longitude: -74.948051, age: 59.0), North Carolina: (longitude: -79.806419,
age: 60.0), North Dakota: (longitude: -99.784012, age: 60.0), Ohio:
(longitude: -82.764915, age: 65.0), Oklahoma: (longitude: -96.928917,
age: 62.0), Pennsylvania: (longitude: -77.209755, age: 68.0), Rhode Island:
(longitude: -71.51178, age: 46.0), South Carolina: (longitude: -80.945007,
age: 70.0), South Dakota: (longitude: -99.438828, age: 64.0), Tennessee:
(longitude: -86.692345, age: 58.0), Texas: (longitude: -97.563461, age:
59.0), Vermont: (longitude: -72.710686, age: 58.0), Virginia: (longitude:
-78.169968, age: 60.0), West Virginia: (longitude: -80.954453, age: 66.0),
Wisconsin: (longitude: -89.616508, age: 49.0), Wyoming: (longitude:
-107.30249, age: 55.0)]
Cluster 1: [Alaska: (longitude: -152.404419, age: 66.0), California:
(longitude: -119.681564, age: 79.0), Hawaii: (longitude: -157.498337, age:
60.0), Idaho: (longitude: -114.478828, age: 75.0), Oregon: (longitude:
-122.070938, age: 56.0), Utah: (longitude: -111.862434, age: 70.0),
Washington: (longitude: -121.490494, age: 66.0)]
```

Cluster 1 represents the extreme Western states, all geographically next to each other (if you consider Alaska and Hawaii next to the Pacific coast states). They all have relatively old governors and hence formed an interesting cluster. Do folks on the Pacific rim like older governors? We cannot determine anything conclusive from these clusters beyond a correlation. Figure 6.2 illustrates the result. Squares are cluster 1 and circles are cluster 0.

> **TIP** It cannot be emphasized enough that your results with k-means using random initialization of centroids will vary. Be sure to try running k-means multiple times with any data set.

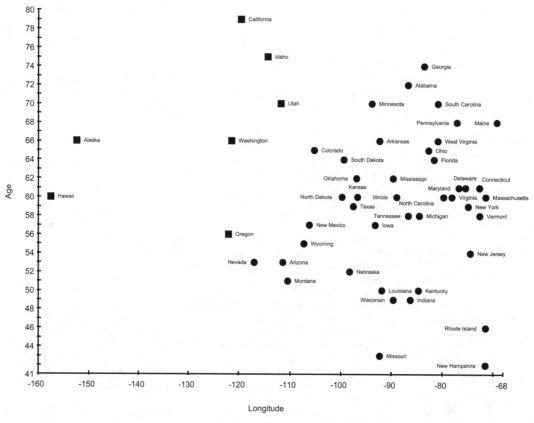

Figure 6.2   Data points in cluster 0 are designated by circles, and data points in cluster 1 are designated by squares.

6.4   *K-means clustering problems and extensions*

When k-means clustering is implemented using random starting points, it may completely miss useful points of division within the data. This often results in a lot of trial and error for the operator. Figuring out the right value for "k" (the number of clusters) is also difficult and error prone if the operator does not have good insight into how many groups of data should exist.

There are more sophisticated versions of k-means that can try to make educated guesses or do automatic trial and error regarding these problematic variables. One popular variant is k-means++, which attempts to solve the initialization problem by choosing centroids based on a probability distribution of distance to every point, instead of pure randomness. An even better option for many applications is to choose good starting regions for each of the centroids based on information about the data that is known ahead of time. In other words, a version of k-means where the user of the algorithm chooses the initial centroids.

The runtime for k-means clustering is proportional to the number of data points, the number of clusters, and the number of dimensions of the data points. It can become unusable in its basic form when there are a high number of points that have a large number of dimensions. There are extensions that try to not do as much calculation between every point and every center by evaluating whether a point really has the potential to move to another cluster before doing the calculation. Another option for numerous-point or high-dimension data sets is to run just a sampling of the data points through k-means. This will approximate the clusters that the full k-means algorithm may find.

Outliers in a data set may result in strange results for k-means. If an initial centroid happens to fall near an outlier, it could form a cluster of one. K-means may run better with outliers removed.[1]

Finally, the mean is not always considered a good measure of the center. K-medians looks at the median of each dimension and k-medoids uses an actual point in the data set as the middle of each cluster. There are statistical reasons beyond the scope of this book for choosing each of these centering methods, but common sense dictates that for a tricky problem it may be worth trying each of them and sampling the results. The implementations of each are not that different.

6.5   *Real-world applications*

Clustering is often the purview of data scientists and statistical analysts. It is used widely as a way to interpret data in a variety of fields. K-means clustering, in particular, is a useful technique when little is known about the structure of the data set.

In data analysis, clustering is an essential technique. Imagine a police department that wants to know where to put cops on patrol. Imagine a fast food franchise that wants to figure out where its best customers are, to send promotions. Imagine a boat rental operator that wants to minimize accidents by analyzing when they occur and who causes them. Now, imagine how they could solve their problems using clustering.

Clustering helps with pattern recognition. A clustering algorithm may detect a pattern that the human eye misses. For instance, in biology clustering is sometimes used to identify groups of discongruous cells.

In image recognition, clustering helps to identify non-obvious features. Individual pixels can be treated as data points with their relationship to one another being defined by distance and color difference.

In political science, clustering is sometimes used to find voters to target. Can a political party find disenfranchised voters concentrated in a single district that they should focus their campaign dollars on? What issues are similar voters likely to be concerned about?

---

[1] Hantao Zhang, "Unsupervised Learning," The University of Iowa, http://mng.bz/W0pn.

6.6   *Exercises*

1 Create a function that can import data from a CSV file into `DataPoints`.
2 Create a graphical program that plots the results of k-means on a chart.
3 Create a new initializer for `KMeans` that takes initial centroid positions instead of assigning them randomly.
4 Research and implement the k-means++ algorithm.

Fairly simple
neural networks

In the late 2010s, when we hear about advances in artificial intelligence, they generally concern a particular subdiscipline known as *machine learning* (computers learning some new information without being explicitly told it). More often than not those advances are being driven by a particular machine-learning technique known as *neural networks*. Although invented decades ago, neural networks have been going through a kind of renaissance as improved hardware and newly discovered research-driven software techniques enable a new paradigm known as *deep learning*.

Deep learning has turned out to be a broadly applicable technique. It has been found useful in everything from hedge fund algorithms to bioinformatics. Two deep-learning applications that consumers have become familiar with are image recognition and speech recognition. If you have ever asked your digital assistant what the weather is, or had a photo program recognize your face, there was probably some deep learning going on.

Deep-learning techniques utilize the same building blocks as simpler neural networks. In this chapter we will explore those blocks by building a simple neural network. It will not be state of the art, but it will give you a basis for understanding deep learning (which is based on more complex neural networks than we will build). Most practitioners of machine learning do not build neural networks from scratch. Instead, they use popular, highly optimized, off-the-shelf frameworks that do the heavy lifting. Although this chapter will not help you learn how to use any specific framework, and the network we will build will not be useful for an actual application, it will help you understand how those frameworks work at a low level.

7.1   *Biological basis?*

The human brain is the most incredible computational device in existence. It cannot crunch numbers as fast as a microprocessor, but its ability to adapt to new situations, learn new skills, and be creative is unsurpassed by any known machine. Since the dawn of computers, scientists have been interested in modeling the brain's machinery. Each nerve cell in the brain is known as a *neuron*. Neurons in the brain are networked to one another via connections known as *synapses*. Electricity passes through synapses to power these networks of neurons—also known as *neural networks*.

> **NOTE** The preceding description of biological neurons is a gross oversimplification for analogy's sake. In fact, biological neurons have parts like axons, dendrites, and nuclei that you may remember from high school biology. And synapses are actually spaces where neurotransmitters are secreted to enable those electrical signals to pass.

Although scientists have identified the parts and functions of neurons, the details of how biological neural networks form complex thought patterns are still not well understood. How do they process information? How do they form original thoughts? Most of our knowledge of how the brain works comes from looking at it on a macro level. Functional magnetic resonance imaging (fMRI) scans of the brain show where blood flows when a human is doing a particular activity or thinking a particular thought (illustrated in figure 7.1). This and other macro-techniques can lead to inferences about how the various parts are connected, but they do not explain the mysteries of how individual neurons aid in the development of new thoughts.

Teams of scientists are racing around the globe to unlock the brain's secrets, but consider this: The human brain has approximately 100,000,000,000 neurons, and each of them may have connections with as many as tens of thousands of other neurons. Even for a computer with billions of logic gates and terabytes of memory, a single human brain would be impossible to model using today's technology. Humans will still likely be the most advanced general-purpose learning entities for the foreseeable future.

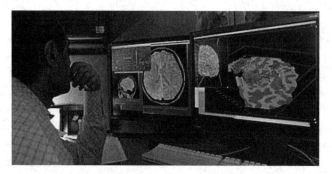

Figure 7.1   A researcher studies fMRI images of the brain. fMRI images do not tell us much about how individual neurons function, nor how neural networks are organized.[1]

---

[1] Public Domain. U.S. National Institute for Mental Health

> **NOTE** A general-purpose learning machine that is equivalent to human beings in abilities is the goal of so-called "strong AI" (also known as "artificial general intelligence"). At this point in history, it is still the stuff of science fiction. "Weak AI" is the type of AI you see every day—computers intelligently solving specific tasks they were preconfigured to accomplish.

If biological neural networks are not fully understood, then how has modeling them been an effective computational technique? Although digital neural networks, known as *artificial neural networks,* are inspired by biological neural networks, inspiration is where the similarities end. Modern artificial neural networks do not claim to work like their biological counterparts. In fact, that would be impossible, since we do not completely understand how biological neural networks work to begin with.

7.2 Artificial neural networks

In this section we will look at what is arguably the most common type of neural network, a *feed-forward* network with *backpropagation*—the same type we will later be developing. "Feed-forward" means the signal is generally moving in one direction through the network. "Backpropagation" means we will determine errors at the end of each signal's traversal through the network, and try to distribute fixes for those errors back through the network, especially affecting the neurons that were most responsible for them. There are many other types of artificial neural networks, and hopefully this chapter will pique your interest in exploring further.

7.2.1 Neurons

The smallest unit in an artificial neural network is a neuron. It holds a vector of weights, which are just floating-point numbers. A vector of inputs (also just floating-point numbers) is passed to the neuron. It combines those inputs with its weights using a dot product. It then runs an *activation function* on that product and spits the result out as its output.

An activation function is a transformer of the neuron's output. The activation function is almost always nonlinear, which allows neural networks to represent solutions to nonlinear problems. If there were no activation functions, the entire neural network would just be a linear transformation. Figure 7.2 shows a single neuron and its operation.

> **NOTE** There are some math terms in this section that you may not have seen since a precalculus or linear algebra class. Explaining what vectors or dot products are is beyond the scope of this chapter, but you will likely get an intuition of what a neural network does by following along in this chapter, even if you do not understand all of the math. Later in the chapter there will be some calculus, including a discussion of derivatives and partial derivatives, but even if you do not understand all of the math, you should be able to follow the code. In fact, this chapter will not explain how to derive the formulas using calculus. Instead, it will focus on using the derivations.

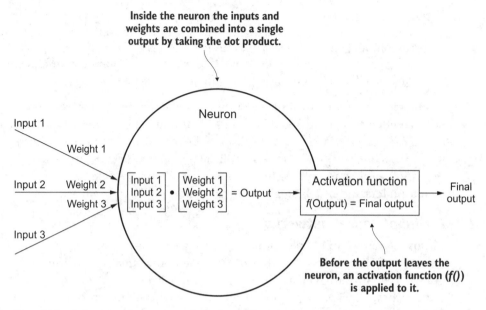

Figure 7.2   A single neuron combines its weights with input signals to produce an output signal that is modified by an activation function.

7.2.2   *Layers*

In a typical feed-forward artificial neural network, neurons are organized in layers. Each layer consists of a certain number of neurons lined up in a row or column (depending on the diagram—the two are equivalent). In a feed-forward network, which is what we will be building, signals always pass in a single direction from one layer to the next. The neurons in each layer send their output signal to be used as input to the neurons in the next layer. Every neuron in each layer is connected to every neuron in the next layer.

The first layer is known as the *input layer,* and it receives its signals from some external entity. The last layer is known as the *output layer,* and its output typically must be interpreted by an external actor to get an intelligent result. The layers between the input and output layers are known as *hidden layers.* In simple neural networks, like the one we will be building in this chapter, there is just one hidden layer, but deep-learning networks have many. Figure 7.3 shows the layers working together in a simple network. Note how the outputs from one layer are used as the inputs to every neuron in the next layer.

These layers are just manipulating floating-point numbers. The inputs to the input layer are floating-point numbers, and the outputs from the output layer are floating-point numbers.

Obviously, these numbers must represent something meaningful. Imagine that the network was designed to classify small black and white images of animals. Perhaps the input layer has 100 neurons representing the grayscale intensity of each pixel in a 10x10

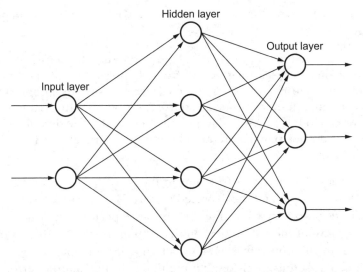

Figure 7.3   A simple neural network with one input layer of two neurons, one hidden layer of four neurons, and one output layer of three neurons. The number of neurons in each layer in this figure is arbitrary.

pixel animal image, and the output layer has 5 neurons representing the likelihood that the image is of a mammal, reptile, amphibian, fish, or bird. The final classification could be determined by the output neuron with the highest floating-point output. If the output numbers were 0.24, 0.65, 0.70, 0.12, and 0.21 respectively, the image would be determined to be an amphibian.

7.2.3   *Backpropagation*

The last piece of the puzzle, and the part that is most confusing, is backpropagation. Backpropagation finds the error in a neural network's output and uses it to modify the weights of neurons. The neurons most responsible for the error are most heavily modified. But where does the error come from? How can we know the error? The error comes from a phase in the use of a neural network known as *training*.

> **TIP**   There are steps written out (in English) for several mathematical formulas in this section. Pseudo formulas (not using proper notation) are in the accompanying figures. This approach will make the formulas readable for those uninitiated in (or out of practice with) mathematical notation. If the more formal notation (and the derivation of the formulas) interests you, check out chapter 18 of Norvig and Russell's *Artificial Intelligence.*[2]

Before they can be used, most neural networks must be trained. We must know the right outputs for some inputs so that we can use the difference between expected outputs and actual outputs to find errors and modify weights. In other words, neural networks know nothing until they are told the right answers for a certain set of inputs, so

---

[2]   Stuart Russell and Peter Norvig, *Artificial Intelligence: A Modern Approach,* third edition (Pearson, 2010).

that they can prepare themselves for other inputs. Backpropagation only occurs during training.

> **NOTE** Because most neural networks must be trained, they are considered a type of *supervised* machine learning. Recall from chapter 6 that the k-means algorithm and other cluster algorithms are considered a form of *unsupervised* machine learning because once they are started, no outside intervention is required. There are other types of neural networks than the one described in this chapter that do not require pretraining and are considered a form of unsupervised learning.

The first step in backpropagation is to calculate the error between the neural network's output for some input and the expected output. This error is spread across all of the neurons in the output layer (each neuron has an expected output and its actual output). The derivative of the output neuron's activation function is then applied to what was output by the neuron before its activation function was applied (we cache its pre-activation function output). This result is multiplied by the neuron's error to find its *delta*. This formula for finding the delta uses a partial derivative, and its calculus derivation is beyond the scope of this book, but we are basically figuring out how much of the error each output neuron was responsible for. See figure 7.4 for a diagram of this calculation.

Deltas must then be calculated for every neuron in the hidden layer(s) in the network. We must determine how much each neuron was responsible for the incorrect output in the output layer. The deltas in the output layer are used to calculate the deltas in the hidden layer(s). For each previous layer, the deltas are calculated by taking the dot product of the next layer's weights with respect to the particular neuron in

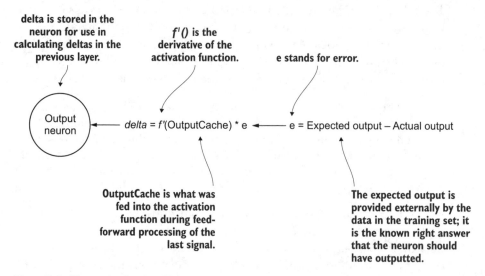

Figure 7.4   The mechanism by which an output neuron's delta is calculated during the backpropagation phase of training

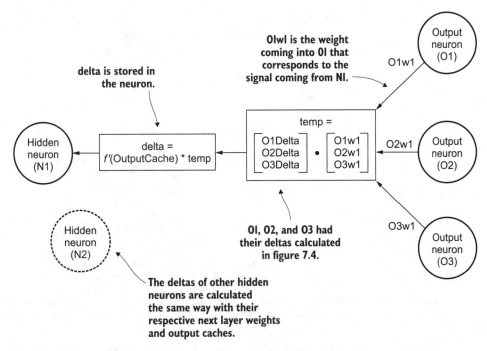

Figure 7.5 How a delta is calculated for a neuron in a hidden layer

question and the deltas already calculated in the next layer. This value is multiplied by the derivative of the activation function applied to a neuron's last output (cached before the activation function was applied) to get the neuron's delta. Again, this formula is derived using a partial derivative, which you can read about in more mathematically focused texts. Figure 7.5 shows the actual calculation of deltas for neurons in hidden layers. In a network with multiple hidden layers, neurons O1, O2, and O3 could be neurons in the next hidden layer instead of in the output layer.

Last, but most importantly, all of the weights for every neuron in the network must be updated by multiplying each individual weight's last input with the delta of the neuron and something called a *learning rate*, and adding that to the existing weight. This method of modifying the weight of a neuron is known as *gradient descent*. It is like climbing down a hill representing the error function of the neuron toward a point of minimal error. The delta represents the direction we want to climb, and the learning rate affects how fast we climb. It is hard to determine a good learning rate for an unknown problem without trial and error. Figure 7.6 shows how every weight in the hidden layer and output layer is updated.

Once the weights are updated, the neural network is ready to be trained again with another input and expected output. This process repeats until the network is deemed well trained by the neural network's user. This can be determined by testing it against inputs with known correct outputs.

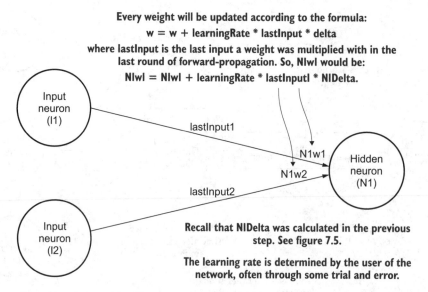

Every weight will be updated according to the formula:

w = w + learningRate * lastInput * delta

where lastInput is the last input a weight was multiplied with in the last round of forward-propagation. So, N1w1 would be:

N1w1 = N1w1 + learningRate * lastInput1 * N1Delta.

Recall that N1Delta was calculated in the previous step. See figure 7.5.

The learning rate is determined by the user of the network, often through some trial and error.

Figure 7.6   The weights of every hidden layer and output layer neuron are updated using the deltas calculated in the previous steps, the prior weights, the prior inputs, and a user-determined learning rate.

The explanation in this section may not give you enough information to understand why backpropagation works, but it does tell you how. As we implement our neural network and backpropagation, keep in mind this overarching theme: Backpropagation is a way of adjusting each individual weight in the network according to its responsibility for an incorrect output.

7.2.4   *The big picture*

We covered a lot of ground in this section. Even if the details do not yet make sense, it is important to keep the main themes in mind for a feed-forward network with backpropagation:

- Signals (floating-point numbers) move through neurons organized in layers in one direction. Every neuron in each layer is connected to every neuron in the next layer.
- Each neuron (except in the input layer) processes the signals it receives by combining them with weights (also floating-point numbers) and applying an activation function.
- During a process called training, network outputs are compared with expected outputs to calculate errors.
- Errors are backpropagated through the network (back toward where they came from) to modify weights, so that they are more likely to create correct outputs.

There are more methods for training neural networks than the one explained here. There are also many other ways for signals to move within neural networks. The method explained here, and that we will be implementing, is just a particularly common form that serves as a decent introduction. Appendix B lists further resources for learning more about neural networks (including other types) and more about the math.

7.3 *Preliminaries*

Neural networks utilize mathematical mechanisms that require a lot of fast floating-point operations. Before we develop the actual structures of our simple neural network, we will need some mathematical primitives. You have seen a couple of these in previous chapters. To build new primitives, we will use Apple's Accelerate framework to speed up some floating-point arithmetic. We will also need some utility methods offered in Foundation.

> **NOTE** The source code examples in this chapter are based on my SwiftSimple-NeuralNetwork open source project (https://github.com/davecom/Swift-SimpleNeuralNetwork).

> **WARNING** The complexity of the code in this chapter is arguably greater than any other in the book. There is a lot of build-up, with actual results seen only at the very end. There are many resources about neural networks that help you build one in very few lines of code, but this example is aimed at exploring the machinery and how the different components work together in a readable and extensible fashion. That is our goal, even if the code is a little longer and more expressive.

We will start by importing Foundation and Accelerate.

```
import Foundation
import Accelerate
```

7.3.1 *Help with randomization*

In chapter 5 we discussed how to shuffle an `Array` using the Fisher-Yates method. We will shuffle arrays later in this chapter too, when we want to randomize the order of our input data. We will use that code verbatim from chapter 5.

```
// A derivative of the
Fisher-Yates algorithm to shuffle an array
extension Array {
    public func shuffled() -> Array<Element> {
        var shuffledArray = self // value semantics (Array is Struct) makes
        ➡ this a copy
        if count < 2 { return shuffledArray } // already shuffled
        for i in (1..<count).reversed() { // count backwards
            let position = Int(arc4random_uniform(UInt32(i + 1))) // random
            ➡ to swap
            if i != position { // swap with the end, don't bother with self
            ➡ swaps
                shuffledArray.swapAt(i, position)
            }
```

```
    }
        return shuffledArray
    }
}
```

In chapter 6 we built a little convenience struct for generating random Doubles. We will need random Doubles to seed our neural network, so we will reuse that snippet too.

```
struct Random {
    private static var seeded = false

    // a random Double between *from* and *to*, assumes *from* < *to*
    static func double(from: Double, to: Double) -> Double {
        if !Random.seeded {
            srand48(time(nil))
            Random.seeded = true
        }

        return (drand48() * (to - from)) + from
    }
}
```

Specifically, seeding our neural network will require an Array of random Doubles between 0.0 and 1.0. This short function will do just that:

```
/// Create *number* of random Doubles between 0.0 and 1.0
func randomWeights(number: Int) -> [Double] {
    return (0..<number).map{ _ in Random.double(from: 0.0, to: 1.0) }
}
```

That one-liner is dense. It takes a range of integers (0..<number) and maps it to the same number of random Doubles. If it does not make sense to you, try coding an equivalent iterative solution and work through the elements of the iterative approach that map to this more functional approach.

7.3.2   *Fast arithmetic*

Neural networks require a lot of vector/matrix math. Essentially, this means taking a list of numbers, such as an array, and doing an operation on all of them at once. Libraries for optimized, performant vector/matrix math are increasingly important as machine learning continues to permeate our society. Many of these libraries take advantage of GPUs, because GPUs are somewhat optimized for this role (vectors/matrices are at the heart of computer graphics). An older library specification you may have heard of is BLAS (Basic Linear Algebra Subprograms). A BLAS implementation is included with Apple's Accelerate framework.

WARNING The code in this chapter is the only code in the book that will not run on Linux with minor modifications. Unfortunately, the Accelerate framework is macOS only (as is the assumption that the CSV files mentioned at the end of the chapter are in the Playground's `Bundle`). You might find an equivalent library on Linux and replace the arithmetic functions presented in this chapter. You can also just use the Swift standard library's arithmetic and suffer a performance hit.

Beyond the GPU, CPUs also have extensions that can speed up vector/matrix processing. Accelerate includes functions that make use of *single instruction, multiple data* (SIMD) instructions. SIMD instructions are special microprocessor instructions that allow multiple pieces of data to be processed at once. They are sometimes known as *vector instructions.*

Different microprocessors include different SIMD instructions. For example, the SIMD extension to the G4 (a PowerPC architecture processor found in early '00s Macs) was known as AltiVec. ARM microprocessors, like those found in iPhones, have an extension known as NEON. And modern Intel microprocessors include SIMD extensions known as MMX, SSE, SSE2, and SSE3. Luckily, you do not need to know the differences. A library like Accelerate will automatically choose the right instructions for the underlying architecture that your program is compiled for.

NOTE The following four short functions are based on examples originally presented in the Surge open source project by Mattt Thompson (https://github.com/mattt/Surge).

We will need to do one thing particularly fast with vectors: dot products. As you will recall, dot products are required both for the feed-forward phase and for the backpropagation phase. Luckily, there is a built-in function for computing dot products in Accelerate. The function we are adding to our source just makes using it a little friendlier.

```
/// Find the dot product of two vectors
/// assuming that they are of the same length
/// using SIMD instructions to speed computation
func dotProduct(_ xs: [Double], _ ys: [Double]) -> Double {
    var answer: Double = 0.0
    vDSP_dotprD(xs, 1, ys, 1, &answer, vDSP_Length(xs.count))
    return answer
}
```

We will not explicitly use the next three SIMD accelerated functions in our code unless we are printing error rates, in which case they are useful for quickly summarizing total error across the entire output layer.

```
/// Subtract one vector from another
public func sub(_ x: [Double], _ y: [Double]) -> [Double] {
    var results = [Double](y)
    catlas_daxpby(Int32(x.count), 1.0, x, 1, -1, &results, 1)
    return results
}

/// Multiply two vectors together
public func mul(_ x: [Double], _ y: [Double]) -> [Double] {
    var results = [Double](repeating: 0.0, count: x.count)
    vDSP_vmulD(x, 1, y, 1, &results, 1, vDSP_Length(x.count))
    return results
}

/// Sum a vector
public func sum(_ x: [Double]) -> Double {
    var result: Double = 0.0
    vDSP_sveD(x, 1, &result, vDSP_Length(x.count))
    return result
}
```

7.4   *The activation function*

Recall that the activation function transforms the output of a neuron before the signal passes to the next layer (see figure 7.2). The activation function has two purposes: It allows the neural network to represent solutions that are not just linear transformations (as long as the activation function itself is not just a linear transformation) and it can keep the output of each neuron within a certain range. An activation function should have a computable derivative, so that it can be used for backpropagation.

A popular set of activation functions are known as *sigmoid* functions. One particularly popular sigmoid function (often just referred to as "the sigmoid function") is illustrated in figure 7.7 (referred to in the figure as S(x)), along with its equation and derivative (S'(x)). The result of the sigmoid function will always be a value between 0 and 1. Having this consistency is useful for the network.

There are other activation functions, but we will use the sigmoid function. Here is a straightforward conversion of the formulas in figure 7.7 into code.

```
/// the classic sigmoid activation function
func sigmoid(_ x: Double) -> Double {
    return 1.0 / (1.0 + exp(-x))
}

// as derived at http://www.ai.mit.edu/courses/6.892/lecture8-html/sld015.htm
func derivativeSigmoid(_ x: Double) -> Double {
    return sigmoid(x) * (1 - sigmoid(x))
}
```

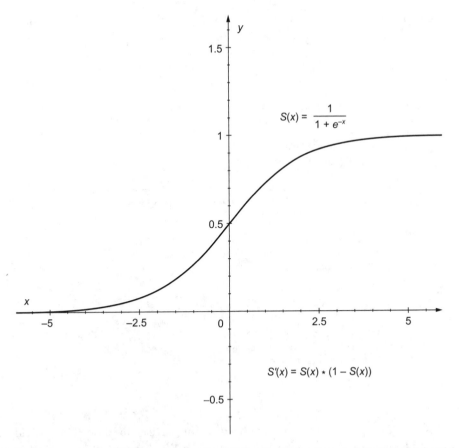

Figure 7.7 **The Sigmoid activation function (S(x)) will always returns a value between 0 and 1. Note that its derivative is easy to compute as well (S'(x)).**

7.5 *Building the network*

We will create classes to model all three organizational units in the network: neurons, layers, and the network itself. For the sake of simplicity, we will start from the smallest (neurons), move to the central organizing component (layers), and build up to the largest (the whole network). As we go from smallest component to largest component, we will encapsulate the previous level. Neurons only know about themselves. Layers know about the neurons they contain and other layers. And the network knows about all of the layers.

7.5.1 *Implementing neurons*

Let's start with a neuron. An individual neuron will store many pieces of state, including its weights, its delta, its learning rate, a cache of its last output, and its activation function, along with the derivative of that activation function. Some of these elements could be more efficiently stored up a level (in the future Layer class), but they are included in the following Neuron class for illustrative purposes.

```
/// An individual node in a layer
class Neuron {
    var weights: [Double]
    var activationFunction: (Double) -> Double
    var derivativeActivationFunction: (Double) -> Double
    var outputCache: Double = 0.0
    var delta: Double = 0.0
    var learningRate: Double

    init(weights: [Double], activationFunction: @escaping (Double) ->
    Double, derivativeActivationFunction: @escaping (Double) -> Double,
    learningRate: Double) {
      self.weights = weights
      self.activationFunction = activationFunction
      self.derivativeActivationFunction = derivativeActivationFunction
      self.learningRate = learningRate
    }

    /// The output that will be going to the next layer
    /// or the final output if this is an output layer
    func output(inputs: [Double]) -> Double {
      outputCache = dotProduct(inputs, weights)
      return activationFunction(outputCache)
    }

}
```

Most of these parameters are initialized in the init() method. Because delta and outputCache are not known when a Neuron is first created, they are just initialized to 0. All of these variables are marked as var instead of let. In the life of the neuron (as we will be using it) their values may never change, but there is still a reason to make them mutable—flexibility. If this Neuron class were to be used with other types of neural networks, it is possible that some of these values might change on the fly. There are neural networks that change the learning rate as the solution approaches and that automatically try different activation functions. Here we are trying to keep the Neuron class maximally flexible for other neural network applications.

The only other method, other than init(), is output(). output() takes the input signals (inputs) coming to the neuron and applies the formula discussed earlier in the chapter (see figure 7.2). The input signals are combined with the weights via a dot product, and this is cached in outputCache. Recall from the section on backpropagation that this value, obtained before the activation function is applied, is used to calculate delta. Finally, before the signal is sent on to the next layer (by being returned from output()), the activation function is applied to it.

That is it! An individual neuron in this network is fairly simple. It cannot do much beyond take an input signal, transform it, and send it off to be processed further. It maintains several elements of state that are used by the other classes.

NOTE Have you seen an @escaping modifier in Swift before? It indicates that the closures passed to init() for activationFunction and derivative-ActivationFunction will be used outside of the init() method itself. In earlier versions of Swift, you had to mark the opposite: closures that would not "escape." Since Swift 3, one must mark "escaping" closures. The @escaping modifier helps the Swift compiler optimize and is required. If you forget it, you will get a helpful hint before compilation is successful.

7.5.2 *Implementing layers*

A layer in our network will need to maintain three pieces of state: its neurons, the layer that preceded it, and an output cache. The output cache is similar to that of a neuron, but up one level. It caches the outputs (after activation functions are applied) of every neuron in the layer.

```
class Layer {
    let previousLayer: Layer?
    var neurons: [Neuron]
    var outputCache: [Double]
```

At creation time, a layer's main responsibility is to initialize its neurons. Our Layer class's init() method therefore needs to know how many neurons it should be initializing, what their activation functions should be, and what their learning rates should be. In this simple network, every neuron in a layer has the same activation function and learning rate.

```
init(previousLayer: Layer? = nil, numNeurons: Int, activationFunction:
➡ @escaping (Double) -> Double, derivativeActivationFunction: @escaping
➡ (Double) -> Double, learningRate: Double) {
    self.previousLayer = previousLayer
    self.neurons = Array<Neuron>()
    for _ in 0..<numNeurons {
        self.neurons.append(Neuron(weights: randomWeights(number:
        ➡ previousLayer?.neurons.count ?? 0), activationFunction:
        ➡ activationFunction, derivativeActivationFunction:
        ➡ derivativeActivationFunction, learningRate: learningRate))
    }
    self.outputCache = Array<Double>(repeating: 0.0,
    ➡ count: neurons.count)
}
```

As signals are fed forward through the network, the Layer must process them through every neuron (remember that every neuron in a layer receives the signals from every neuron in the previous layer). outputs() does just that. outputs() also returns the result of processing them (to be passed by the network to the next layer) and caches the output. If there is no previous layer, that indicates the layer is an input layer, and it just passes the signals forward to the next layer.

```
func outputs(inputs: [Double]) -> [Double] {
    if previousLayer == nil { // input layer (first layer)
        outputCache = inputs
    } else { // hidden layer or output layer
        outputCache = neurons.map { $0.output(inputs: inputs) }
    }
    return outputCache
}
```

There are two distinct types of deltas to calculate in backpropagation: deltas for neurons in the output layer, and deltas for neurons in hidden layers. The formulas are described in figures 7.4 and 7.5, and the following two methods are rote translations of those formulas. These methods will later be called by the network during backpropagation.

```
// should only be called on an output layer
func calculateDeltasForOutputLayer(expected: [Double]) {
    for n in 0..<neurons.count {
        neurons[n].delta =
        ⇒ neurons[n].derivativeActivationFunction(neurons[n]
        ⇒ .outputCache) * (expected[n] - outputCache[n])
    }
}


// should not be called on output layer
func calculateDeltasForHiddenLayer(nextLayer: Layer) {
    for (index, neuron) in neurons.enumerated() {
        let nextWeights = nextLayer.neurons.map { $0.weights[index] }
        let nextDeltas = nextLayer.neurons.map { $0.delta }
        let sumOfWeightsXDeltas = dotProduct(nextWeights, nextDeltas)
        neuron.delta = neuron.derivativeActivationFunction(neuron
        ⇒ .outputCache) * sumOfWeightsXDeltas
    }
}
}
```

7.5.3   *Implementing the network*

The network itself has only one piece of state—the layers that it manages. The Network class is responsible for initializing its constituent layers.

The init() method takes an Int array describing the structure of the network. For example, the array [2, 4, 3] describes a network with 2 neurons in its input layer, 4 neurons in its hidden layer, and 3 neurons in its output layer. In this simple network, we will assume that all layers in the network will make use of the same activation function for their neurons and the same learning rate.

```
/// Represents an entire neural network. From largest to smallest we go
/// Network -> Layers -> Neurons
class Network {
    var layers: [Layer]

    init(layerStructure:[Int], activationFunction: @escaping (Double) ->
    ⇒ Double = sigmoid, derivativeActivationFunction: @escaping (Double) ->
```

```
➡ Double = derivativeSigmoid, learningRate: Double) {
    if (layerStructure.count < 3) {
        print("Error: Should be at least 3 layers (1 input, 1 hidden,
        ➡ 1 output)")
    }
    layers = [Layer]()
    // input layer
    layers.append(Layer(numNeurons: layerStructure[0],
    ➡ activationFunction: activationFunction,
    ➡ derivativeActivationFunction: derivativeActivationFunction,
    ➡ learningRate: learningRate))

    // hidden layers and output layer
    for x in layerStructure.enumerated() where x.offset != 0 {
        layers.append(Layer(previousLayer: layers[x.offset - 1],
        ➡ numNeurons: x.element, activationFunction:
        ➡ activationFunction, derivativeActivationFunction:
        ➡ derivativeActivationFunction, learningRate: learningRate))
    }
}
```

The outputs of the neural network are the result of signals running through all of its layers. Note how compactly reduce() is used in outputs() to pass signals from one layer to the next repeatedly through the whole network.

```
/// pushes input data to the first layer
/// then output from the first as input to the second
/// second to the third, etc.
func outputs(input: [Double]) -> [Double] {
    return layers.reduce(input) { $1.outputs(inputs: $0) }
}
```

The backpropagate() method is responsible for computing deltas for every neuron in the network. It uses the Layer methods calculateDeltasForOutputLayer() and calculateDeltasForHiddenLayer() in sequence (recall that in backpropagation, deltas are calculated backwards). It passes the expected values of output for a given set of inputs to calculateDeltasForOutputLayer(). That method uses the expected values to find the error used for delta calculation.

```
/// Figure out each neuron's changes based on the errors
/// of the output versus the expected outcome
func backpropagate(expected: [Double]) {
    //calculate delta for output layer neurons
    layers.last?.calculateDeltasForOutputLayer(expected: expected)
    //calculate delta for prior layers
    for l in 1..<layers.count - 1 {
        layers[l].calculateDeltasForHiddenLayer(nextLayer: layers[l + 1])
    }
}
```

backpropagate() is responsible for calculating all deltas, but it does not actually modify any of the network's weights. updateWeights() must be called after backpropagate(), because weight modification depends on deltas. This method follows directly from the formula in figure 7.6.

```
/// backpropagate() doesn't actually change any weights
/// this function uses the deltas calculated in backpropagate()
/// to actually make changes to the weights
func updateWeights() {
    for layer in layers.dropFirst() { // skip input layer
        for neuron in layer.neurons {
            for w in 0..<neuron.weights.count {
                neuron.weights[w] = neuron.weights[w] +
                ➡ (neuron.learningRate * (layer.previousLayer?
                ➡ .outputCache[w])! * neuron.delta)
            }
        }
    }
}
```

Neuron weights are actually modified at the end of each round of training. Training sets (inputs coupled with expected outputs) must be provided to the network. The train() method takes an array of arrays of inputs and an array of arrays of expected outputs. It runs each input through the network and then updates its weights by calling backpropagate() with the expected output (and updateWeights() after that). train() can also optionally print out the error rate as it goes through a training set. Try turning this on to see how the network gradually decreases its error rate as it rolls down the hill in gradient descent.

```
/// train() uses the results of outputs() run over
/// many *inputs* and compared against *expecteds* to feed
/// backpropagate() and updateWeights()
func train(inputs: [[Double]], expecteds: [[Double]], printError: Bool =
➡ false, threshold: Double? = nil) {
    for (location, xs) in inputs.enumerated() {
        let ys = expecteds[location]
        let outs = outputs(input: xs)
        if (printError) {
            let diff = sub(outs, ys)
            let error = sqrt(sum(mul(diff, diff)))
            print("\(error) error in run \(location)")
        }
        backpropagate(expected: ys)
        updateWeights()
    }
}
```

Finally, after a network is trained, we need to test it. validate() takes inputs and expected outputs (not too much unlike train()), but uses them to calculate an accuracy percentage rather than perform training. It is assumed the network is already trained. `validate()` also takes a function, `interpretOutput()`, that is used for interpreting the output of the neural network to compare it to the expected output (perhaps the expected output is a string like "Amphibian" instead of a set of floating-point numbers). `interpretOutput()` must take the floating-point numbers it gets as output from the network and convert them into something comparable to the expected outputs. It is a custom function specific to a data set. `validate()` returns the number of correct classifications, the total number of samples tested, and the percentage of correct classifications.

```
/// for generalized results that require classification
/// this function will return the correct number of trials
/// and the percentage correct out of the total
func validate<T: Equatable>(inputs:[[Double]], expecteds:[T],
➡ interpretOutput: ([Double]) -> T)
➡ -> (correct: Int, total: Int, percentage: Double) {
    var correct = 0
    for (input, expected) in zip(inputs, expecteds) {
        let result = interpretOutput(outputs(input: input))
        if result == expected {
            correct += 1
        }
    }
    let percentage = Double(correct) / Double(inputs.count)
    return (correct, inputs.count, percentage)
}
}
```

The neural network is done! It is ready to be tested with some actual problems. Although the architecture we built is general purpose enough to be used for a variety of problems, we will concentrate on a popular kind of problem—classification.

7.6 *Classification problems*

In chapter 6 we categorized a data set with k-means clustering using no preconceived notions about where each individual piece of data belonged. In clustering, we know we want to find categories of data, but we do not know ahead of time what those categories are. In a classification problem, we are also trying to categorize a data set, but there are preset categories. For example, if we were trying to classify a set of pictures of animals, we might ahead of time decide on categories like mammal, reptile, amphibian, fish, and bird.

There are many machine-learning techniques that can be used for classification problems. Perhaps you have heard of support vector machines, decision trees, or naive Bayes classifiers (there are others too). Recently, neural networks have become widely deployed in the classification space. They are more computationally intensive than some of the other classification algorithms, but their ability to classify seemingly arbitrary kinds of data makes them a powerful technique. Neural network classifiers are behind much of the interesting image classification that powers modern photo software.

Why is there a renewed interest in using neural networks for classification problems? Hardware has become fast enough that the extra computation involved, compared to other algorithms, makes the benefits worthwhile.

7.6.1 Normalizing data

The data sets that we want to work with generally require some "cleaning" before they are input into our algorithms. Cleaning may involve removing extraneous characters, deleting duplicates, fixing errors, and other menial tasks. The aspect of cleaning we will need to perform for the two data sets we are working with is normalization. In chapter 6 we did this via the zscoreNormalize() method in the KMeans class. Normalization is about taking attributes recorded on different scales, and converting them to a common scale.

Every neuron in our network outputs values between 0 and 1 due to the sigmoid activation function. It sounds logical that a scale between 0 and 1 would make sense for the attributes in our input data set as well. Converting a scale from some range to a range between 0 and 1 is not challenging. For any value, V, in a particular attribute range with maximum, max, and minimum, min, the formula is just newV = (oldV - min) / (max - min). This operation is known as *feature scaling*. Here is a Swift implementation.

```
/// assumes all rows are of equal length
/// and feature scale each column to be in the range 0-1
func normalizeByFeatureScaling(dataset: inout [[Double]]) {
    for colNum in 0..<dataset[0].count {
        let column = dataset.map { $0[colNum] }
        let maximum = column.max()!
        let minimum = column.min()!
        for rowNum in 0..<dataset.count {
            dataset[rowNum][colNum] = (dataset[rowNum][colNum]
            ⇨ - minimum) / (maximum - minimum)
        }
    }
}
```

Look at the dataset parameter. It is marked as inout, indicating that the values in the original two-dimensional array can be changed directly in the function. In other words, normalizeByFeatureScaling() does not receive a copy of the data set. It receives a reference to the original data set. This is good for performance and also for situations where we want to make changes to a value rather than receive back a transformation.

Note also that our program assumes that data sets are two-dimensional arrays of Doubles.

7.6.2 The classic iris data set

Just as there are classic computer science problems, there are classic data sets in machine learning. These data sets are used to validate new techniques and compare them to existing ones. They also serve as good starting points for people learning machine learning for the first time. Perhaps the most famous is the iris data set.

Originally collected in the 1930s, the data set consists of 150 samples of iris plants (pretty flowers), split amongst three different species (50 of each). Each plant is measured on four different attributes: sepal length, sepal width, petal length, and petal width.

It is worth noting that a neural network does not care what the various attributes represent. Its model for training makes no distinction between sepal length and petal length in terms of importance. If such a distinction should be made, it is up to the user of the neural network to make appropriate adjustments.

The Playground that accompanies this book contains a comma-separated values (*CSV*) file that features the iris data set.[3] The iris data set is from the University of California's UCI Machine Learning Repository: M. Lichman, UCI Machine Learning Repository (Irvine, CA: University of California, School of Information and Computer Science, 2013), http://archive.ics.uci.edu/ml. A CSV file is just a text file with values separated by commas. It is a common interchange format for tabular data, including spreadsheets.

Here are a few lines from `iris.csv`:

```
5.1,3.5,1.4,0.2,Iris-setosa
4.9,3.0,1.4,0.2,Iris-setosa
4.7,3.2,1.3,0.2,Iris-setosa
4.6,3.1,1.5,0.2,Iris-setosa
5.0,3.6,1.4,0.2,Iris-setosa
```

Each line represents one data point. The four numbers represent the four attributes (sepal length, sepal width, petal length, petal width), which, again, are arbitrary to us in terms of what they actually represent. The name at the end of each line represents the particular iris species. All five lines are for the same species because this sample was taken from the top of the file, and the three species are clumped together, with fifty lines each.

To read the CSV file from disk, we will use a few methods from Foundation. The `Bundle` class will help us access data within a Playground. Foundation adds a method to `String` that can read a text file from disk. Beyond those two lines, the rest of the following function just uses the Swift standard library and functions previously defined in this chapter.

```swift
func parseIrisCSV() -> (parameters: [[Double]], classifications: [[Double]],
    species: [String]) {
    let urlpath = Bundle.main.path(forResource: "iris", ofType: "csv")
    let url = URL(fileURLWithPath: urlpath!)
    let csv = try! String.init(contentsOf: url)
    let lines = csv.components(separatedBy: "\n")
    var irisParameters: [[Double]] = [[Double]]()
    var irisClassifications: [[Double]] = [[Double]]()
    var irisSpecies: [String] = [String]()
```

---

[3] The Playground is available from GitHub at https://github.com/davecom/ClassicComputerScienceProblemsInSwift

```
        let shuffledLines = lines.shuffled()
        for line in shuffledLines {
            if line == "" { continue } // skip blank lines
            let items = line.components(separatedBy: ",")
            let parameters = items[0...3].map{ Double($0)! }
            irisParameters.append(parameters)
            let species = items[4]
            if species == "Iris-setosa" {
                irisClassifications.append([1.0, 0.0, 0.0])
            } else if species == "Iris-versicolor" {
                irisClassifications.append([0.0, 1.0, 0.0])
            } else {
                irisClassifications.append([0.0, 0.0, 1.0])
            }
            irisSpecies.append(species)
        }
    normalizeByFeatureScaling(dataset: &irisParameters)
    return (irisParameters, irisClassifications, irisSpecies)
}
```

irisParameters represents the collection of four attributes per sample that we are using to classify each iris. irisClassifications is the actual classification of each sample. Our neural network will have three output neurons, with each representing one possible species. For instance, a final set of outputs of [0.9, 0.3, 0.1] will represent a classification of iris-setosa, because the first neuron represents that species and it is the largest number. For training, we already know the right answers, so each iris has a premarked answer. For a flower that should be iris-setosa, the entry in irisClassifications will be [1.0, 0.0, 0.0]. These values will be used to calculate the error after each training step. irisSpecies corresponds directly to what each flower should be classified as in English. An iris-setosa will be marked as "Iris-setosa" in the data set.

> **WARNING** The lack of error-checking code and the use of force-unwrapped
> optionals makes parseIrisCSV() a dangerous function. It is not suitable as-is
> for production, but it is fine for testing in a Playground.

Ultimately, parseIrisCSV() returns the parameters, classifications, and species arrays to its caller. We will use the same nomenclature for the variables that will ultimately be fed into the neural network.

```
let (irisParameters, irisClassifications, irisSpecies) = parseIrisCSV()
```

Let's define the neural network itself.

```
let irisNetwork: Network = Network(layerStructure: [4, 6, 3],
    learningRate: 0.3)
```

The layerStructure argument specifies a network with three layers (one input layer, one hidden layer, and one output layer) with [4, 6, 3]. The input layer has 4 neurons, the hidden layer has 6 neurons, and the output layer has 3 neurons. The 4 neurons in the input layer map directly to the 4 parameters that are used to classify each specimen. The 3 neurons in the output layer map directly to the 3 different species that we are trying to classify each input within. The hidden layer's 6 neurons are more the result of trial and error than some formula. The same is true of `learningRate`. These two values (the number of neurons in the hidden layer and the learning rate) can be experimented with if the accuracy of the network is suboptimal.

```
func irisInterpretOutput(output: [Double]) -> String {
    if output.max()! == output[0] {
        return "Iris-setosa"
    } else if output.max()! == output[1] {
        return "Iris-versicolor"
    } else {
        return "Iris-virginica"
    }
}
```

`irisInterpretOutput()` is a utility function that will be passed to the network's `validate()` method to help identify correct classifications.

The network is finally ready to be trained.

```
// train over first 140 irises in data set 20 times
let irisTrainers = Array(irisParameters[0..<140])
let irisTrainersCorrects = Array(irisClassifications[0..<140])
for _ in 0..<20 {
    irisNetwork.train(inputs: irisTrainers, expecteds: irisTrainersCorrects,
    ➥ printError: false)
}
```

We train on the first 140 irises out of the 150 in the data set. Recall that in `parse-IrisCSV()`, the lines read from the CSV file were shuffled. This ensures that every time we run the program, we will be training on a different subset of the data set. Note that we train over the 140 irises 20 times. Modifying this value will have a large effect on how long it takes your neural network to train. Generally, the more training, the more accurately the neural network will perform. The final test will be to verify the correct classification of the final 10 irises from the data set.

```
// test over the last 10 of the irises in the data set
let irisTesters = Array(irisParameters[140..<150])
let irisTestersCorrects = Array(irisSpecies[140..<150])
let irisResults = irisNetwork.validate(inputs: irisTesters, expecteds:
➥ irisTestersCorrects, interpretOutput: irisInterpretOutput)
print("\(irisResults.correct) correct of \(irisResults.total) =
➥ \(irisResults.percentage * 100)%")
```

All of the work leads up to this final question: Out of 10 randomly chosen irises from the data set, how many can our neural network correctly classify? Because there is randomness in the starting weights of each neuron, different runs may give you different results. You can try tweaking the learning rate, the number of hidden neurons, and the number of training iterations to make your network more accurate.

Ultimately you should see a result like this:

```
9 correct of 10 = 90.0%
```

TIP It will take a long time to train your neural network in both this problem and the next. So much so that Xcode can become unresponsive. For that reason, in the Playground that you download to accompany the book, you will find one of the two problems commented out. You should do the same. When you work on the wine problem, comment out the iris problem.

7.6.3 *Classifying wine*

We are going to test our neural network with another data set—one based on the chemical analysis of wine cultivars from Italy.[4] There are 178 samples in the data set. The machinery of working with it will be much the same as with the iris data set, but the layout of the CSV file is slightly different. Here is a sample:

```
1,14.23,1.71,2.43,15.6,127,2.8,3.06,.28,2.29,5.64,1.04,3.92,1065
1,13.2,1.78,2.14,11.2,100,2.65,2.76,.26,1.28,4.38,1.05,3.4,1050
1,13.16,2.36,2.67,18.6,101,2.8,3.24,.3,2.81,5.68,1.03,3.17,1185
1,14.37,1.95,2.5,16.8,113,3.85,3.49,.24,2.18,7.8,.86,3.45,1480
1,13.24,2.59,2.87,21,118,2.8,2.69,.39,1.82,4.32,1.04,2.93,735
```

The first value on each line will always be an integer between 1 and 3 representing one of three cultivars that the sample may be a kind of. Notice how many more parameters there are for classification. In the iris data set there were just four. In this wine data set, there are 13.

Our neural network model will scale just fine. We simply need to increase the number of input neurons. `parseWineCSV()` is analogous to `parseIrisCSV()`, but there are some minor changes to account for the different layouts of the respective files.

```
func parseWineCSV() -> (parameters: [[Double]], classifications:
➡ [[Double]], species: [Int]) {
    let urlpath = Bundle.main.path(forResource: "wine", ofType: "csv")
    let url = URL(fileURLWithPath: urlpath!)
    let csv = try! String.init(contentsOf: url)
    let lines = csv.components(separatedBy: "\n")
    var wineParameters: [[Double]] = [[Double]]()
    var wineClassifications: [[Double]] = [[Double]]()
    var wineSpecies: [Int] = [Int]()

    let shuffledLines = lines.shuffled()
    for line in shuffledLines {
```

---

[4] M. Lichman, UCI Machine Learning Repository (Irvine, CA: University of California, School of Information and Computer Science, 2013), http://archive.ics.uci.edu/ml.

```
        if line == "" { continue } // skip blank lines
        let items = line.components(separatedBy: ",")
        let parameters = items[1...13].map{ Double($0)! }
        wineParameters.append(parameters)
        let species = Int(items[0])!
        if species == 1 {
            wineClassifications.append([1.0, 0.0, 0.0])
        } else if species == 2 {
            wineClassifications.append([0.0, 1.0, 0.0])
        } else {
            wineClassifications.append([0.0, 0.0, 1.0])
        }
        wineSpecies.append(species)
    }
    normalizeByFeatureScaling(dataset: &wineParameters)
    return (wineParameters, wineClassifications, wineSpecies)
}

let (wineParameters, wineClassifications, wineSpecies) = parseWineCSV()
```

The layer configuration for the wine-classification network needs 13 input neurons, as was already mentioned (one for each parameter). It also needs three output neurons (there are three cultivars of wine, just as there were three species of iris). Interestingly, the network works well with fewer neurons in the hidden layer than in the input layer. One possible intuitive explanation is that some of the input parameters are not actually helpful for classification, and it is useful to cut them out during processing. This is not, in fact, exactly how having fewer neurons in the hidden layer works, but it is an interesting intuitive idea.

```
let wineNetwork: Network = Network(layerStructure:
➡ [13, 7, 3], learningRate: 0.9)
```

Once again, it can be interesting to experiment with a different number of hidden layer neurons or a different learning rate.

```
func wineInterpretOutput(output: [Double]) -> Int {
    if output.max()! == output[0] {
        return 1
    } else if output.max()! == output[1] {
        return 2
    } else {
        return 3
    }
}
```

wineInterpretOutput() is analogous to irisInterpretOutput(). Because we do not have names for the wine cultivars, we are just working with the integer assignment in the original data set.

```
// train over the first 150 samples 5 times
let wineTrainers = Array(wineParameters.dropLast(28))
let wineTrainersCorrects = Array(wineClassifications.dropLast(28))
for _ in 0..<5 {
    wineNetwork.train(inputs: wineTrainers, expecteds: wineTrainersCorrects,
    ➥ printError: false)
}
```

We will train over the first 150 samples in the data set, leaving the last 28 for validation. We train 5 times over the samples, significantly less than the 20 for the iris data set. For whatever reason (perhaps innate qualities of the data set, or tuning of parameters like the learning rate and number of hidden neurons), this data set requires less training to achieve significant accuracy than the iris data set. In the sample code for the iris data set's training, we used the range operator (0..<140) to specify the training set. In this data set, we instead use the Sequence method dropLast(). In the next code snippet we will also use dropFirst(). Choose the option that is more readable to you.

```
let wineTesters = Array(wineParameters.dropFirst(150))
let wineTestersCorrects = Array(wineSpecies.dropFirst(150))
let results = wineNetwork.validate(inputs: wineTesters, expecteds:
➥ wineTestersCorrects, interpretOutput: wineInterpretOutput)
print("\(results.correct) correct of \(results.total) =
➥ \(results.percentage * 100)%")
```

With a little luck, your neural network should be able to classify the 28 samples quite accurately.

```
27 correct of 28 = 96.42857142857714%
```

7.7 *Neural network problems and extensions*

Neural networks are all the rage right now, thanks to advances in deep learning, but they have some significant shortcomings. The biggest problem is that a neural network solution to a problem is something of a black box. Even when neural networks work well, they do not give the user much insight into how they solve the problem. For instance, the iris data set classifier we worked on in this chapter does not clearly show how much each of the four parameters in the input affects the output. Was sepal length more important than sepal width for classifying each sample?

It is possible that careful analysis of the final weights for the trained network could provide some insight, but such analysis is nontrivial and does not provide the kind of insight that, say, linear regression does in terms of the meaning of each variable in the function being modeled. In other words, a neural network may solve a problem, but it does not explain how the problem is solved.

Another problem with neural networks is that to become accurate they often require very large data sets. Imagine an image classifier for outdoor landscapes. It may need to classify thousands of different types of images (forest, valley, mountains, stream, steppes, and so on). It will potentially need millions of training images. Not only are such large data sets hard to come by, but for some applications they may be completely non-existent. It tends to be large corporations and governments that have the data-warehousing and technical facilities for collecting and storing such massive data sets.

Finally, neural networks are computationally expensive. As you probably noticed, just training on the iris data set brings a Swift Playground to its knees. A Playground is not a computationally performant environment, but on any computational platform that neural networks are used, it is the sheer number of calculations that have to be performed in training the network, more than anything else, that takes so much time. Many tricks abound to make neural networks more performant (like using SIMD instructions or GPUs), but ultimately training a neural network requires a lot of floating-point operations.

One nice caveat is that training is much more computationally expensive than actually using the network. Some applications do not require ongoing training. In those instances, a trained network can just be dropped into an application to solve a problem. For example, the first version of Apple's Core ML framework does not even support training. It only supports helping app developers run pretrained neural network models in their apps. An app developer creating a photo app can download a freely licensed image-classification model, drop it into Core ML, and start using performant machine learning in their app instantly.

In this chapter we only worked with a single type of neural network: a feed-forward network with backpropagation. As has been mentioned, many other kinds of neural networks exist. Convolutional neural networks are also feed-forward, but they have multiple different types of hidden layers, different mechanisms for distributing weights, and other interesting properties that make them especially well designed for image classification. In recurrent neural networks, signals do not just travel in one direction. They allow feedback loops and have proven useful for continuous input applications like handwriting recognition and voice recognition.

A simple extension to our neural network that would make it more performant would be the inclusion of bias neurons. A bias neuron is like a dummy neuron in a layer that allows the next layer's output to represent more functions by providing a constant input (still modified by a weight) into it. Even simple neural networks used for real-world problems usually contain bias neurons. If you add bias neurons to our existing network, you will likely find that it requires less training to achieve a similar level of accuracy.

7.8 Real-world applications

Although first imagined in the middle of the twentieth century, artificial neural networks did not became commonplace until the last decade. Their widespread application was held back by a lack of sufficiently performant hardware. Today, artificial neural networks have become the most explosive growth area in machine learning because they work!

Artificial neural networks have enabled some of the most exciting user-facing computing applications in decades. These include practical voice recognition (practical in terms of sufficient accuracy), image recognition, and handwriting recognition. Voice recognition is present in typing aids like Dragon Naturally Speaking and digital assistants like Siri, Alexa, and Cortana. A specific example of image recognition is Facebook's automatic tagging of people in a photo using facial recognition. In recent versions of iOS, you can search works within your notes, even if they are handwritten, by employing handwriting recognition.

An older recognition technology that can be powered by neural networks is OCR (optical character recognition). OCR is used every time you scan a document and it comes back as selectable text instead of an image. OCR enables toll booths to read license plates and envelopes to be quickly sorted by the postal service.

In this chapter you have seen neural networks used successfully for classification problems. Similar applications that neural networks work well in are recommendation systems. Think of Netflix suggesting a movie you might like to watch, or Amazon suggesting a book you might want to read. There are other machine learning techniques that work well for recommendation systems too (Amazon and Netflix do not necessarily use neural networks for these purposes—the details of their systems are likely proprietary), so neural networks should only be selected after all options have been explored.

Neural networks can be used in any situation where an unknown function needs to be approximated. This makes them useful for prediction. Neural networks can be employed to predict the outcome of a sporting event, election, or the stock market (and they are). Of course, their accuracy is a product of how well they are trained, and that has to do with how large a data set relevant to the unknown-outcome event is available, how well the parameters of the neural network are tuned, and how many iterations of training are run. With prediction, like most neural network applications, one of the hardest parts is deciding upon the structure of the network itself, which is often ultimately determined by trial and error.

7.9   *Exercises*

1 Use the neural network framework developed in this chapter to classify items in another data set.

2 Create a generic function, parseCSV(), with flexible enough parameters that it could replace both of the CSV parsing functions in this chapter.

3 Try running the examples with a different activation function (remember to also find its derivative). How does the change in activation function affect the accuracy of the network? Does it require more or less training?

4 Take the problems in this chapter and recreate their solutions using a popular neural network framework like Caffe or Keras (both supported by Apple's Core ML).

5 Use Metal to accelerate the execution of the neural network developed in this chapter by taking advantage of the GPU's computational advantages for matrix/vector math.

Miscellaneous problems

Throughout this book we have covered a myriad of problem-solving techniques relevant to modern software development tasks. To study each technique, we have explored famous computer science problems. But not every famous problem fits the mold of the prior chapters. This chapter is a gathering point for famous problems that did not quite fit into any other chapter. Think of these problems as a bonus—more interesting problems with less scaffolding around them.

8.1 *The knapsack problem*

The knapsack problem is an optimization problem that takes a common computational need—finding the best use of limited resources given a finite set of usage options—and spins it into a fun story. A thief enters a home with the intent to rob it. He has a knapsack, and he is limited in what he can steal by the capacity of the knapsack. How does he figure out what to put into the knapsack? The problem is illustrated in figure 8.1.

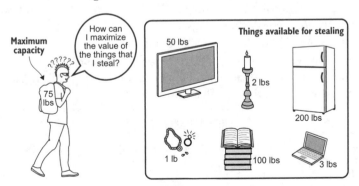

Figure 8.1 The robber must carefully decide what items to steal because the capacity of the knapsack is limited.

If the thief could take any amount of any item, he could simply divide each item's value by its weight to figure out the most valuable items for the available capacity. But to make the scenario more realistic, let's say that the thief cannot take half of an item (such as 2.5 televisions). Instead, we will come up with a way to solve the "0/1 variant" of the problem, so-called because it enforces another rule—the thief may only take one or none of each item.

First, let's define a `struct` to hold our items:

```
struct Item {
    let name: String
    let weight: Int
    let value: Float
}
```

If we tried to solve this problem using a brute force approach, we would look at every combination of items available to be put in the knapsack. For the mathematically inclined, this is known as a *powerset*, and a powerset of a set (in our case, the set of items) has 2^N different possible subsets, where N is the number of items. Therefore, we would need to analyze 2^N combinations ($O(2^N)$). This is okay for a small number of items, but it is untenable for a large number. Any approach that solves a problem using an exponential number of steps is an approach we want to avoid.

Instead, we will use a technique known as *dynamic programming*, which is similar in concept to memoization (chapter 1). Instead of solving a problem outright with a brute-force approach, in dynamic programming one solves subproblems that make up the larger problem, stores those results, and utilizes those stored results to solve the larger problem. As long as the capacity of the knapsack is considered linearly, the problem can be solved with dynamic programming.

For instance, to solve the problem for a knapsack with a 3 lb. capacity and three items, we can first solve the problem for a 1 lb. capacity and one possible item, 2 lb. capacity and one possible item, and 3 lb. capacity and one possible item. We can then use the results of that solution to solve the problem for 1 lb. capacity and two possible items, 2 lb. capacity and two possible items, and 3 lb. capacity and two possible items. And finally we can solve for all three possible items.

All along the way we will fill in a table that tells us the best possible solution for each combination of items and capacity. Our function will first fill in the table, and then it will figure out the solution based on the table.[1]

```
func knapsack(items: [Item], maxCapacity: Int) -> [Item] {
    //build up dynamic programming table
    var table: [[Float]] = [[Float]](repeating: [Float](repeating: 0.0,
    ➥ count: maxCapacity + 1), count: items.count + 1)  //initialize table -
    ➥ overshooting in size
```

---

[1] I studied several resources to write this solution, the most authoritative of which was *Algorithms*, 2nd edition, by Robert Sedgewick (p. 596). I looked at several examples on Rosetta Code of the 0/1 knapsack problem, most notably the Python dynamic programming solution (http://mng.bz/kx8C), which this function is largely a port of.

```
    for (i, item) in items.enumerated() {
        for capacity in 1...maxCapacity {
            let previousItemsValue = table[i][capacity]
            if capacity >= item.weight { // item fits in knapsack
                let valueFreeingWeightForItem = table[i][capacity -
    item.weight]
                table[i + 1][capacity] = max(valueFreeingWeightForItem +
                ➡ item.value, previousItemsValue)  // only take if more
                ➡ valuable than previous combo
            } else { // no room for this item
                table[i + 1][capacity] = previousItemsValue
                ➡ //use prior combo
            }
        }
    }
    // figure out solution from table
    var solution: [Item] = [Item]()
    var capacity = maxCapacity
    for i in stride(from: items.count, to: 0, by: -1) { // work backwards
        if table[i - 1][capacity] != table[i][capacity] {
        ➡ // did we use this item?
            solution.append(items[i - 1])
            capacity -= items[i - 1].weight
            ➡ // if we used an item, remove its weight
        }
    }
    return solution
}
```

The inner loop of the first part of this function will execute N * C times, where N is the number of items and C is the maximum capacity of the knapsack. Therefore, the algorithm performs in O(N * C) time, a significant improvement over the brute-force approach for a large number of items. For instance, for the 11 items that follow, a brute-force algorithm would need to examine 2^11 or 2,048 combinations. The preceding dynamic programmatic function will execute 825 times, because the maximum capacity of the knapsack in question is 75 arbitrary units (11 * 75). This difference would grow exponentially with more items.

```
let items = [Item(name: "television", weight: 50, value: 500),
    Item(name: "candlesticks", weight: 2, value: 300),
    Item(name: "stereo", weight: 35, value: 400),
    Item(name: "laptop", weight: 3, value: 1000),
    Item(name: "food", weight: 15, value: 50),
    Item(name: "clothing", weight: 20, value: 800),
    Item(name: "jewelry", weight: 1, value: 4000),
    Item(name: "books", weight: 100, value: 300),
    Item(name: "printer", weight: 18, value: 30),
    Item(name: "refrigerator", weight: 200, value: 700),
    Item(name: "painting", weight: 10, value: 1000)]
knapsack(items: items, maxCapacity: 75)
```

If you inspect, in the Playground, the results of calling `knapsack(items: items, max-Capacity: 75)`, you will see that the optimal items to take are the painting, jewelry, clothing, laptop, stereo, and candlesticks.

To get a better idea of how this all worked, let's look at some of the particulars of the function.

```
for (i, item) in items.enumerated() {
    for capacity in 1...maxCapacity {
```

For each possible number of items, we loop through all of the capacities in a linear fashion, up to the maximum capacity of the knapsack. Notice that I say "each possible number of items" instead of each item. When i equals 2, it does not just represent item 2. It represents the possible combinations of the first two items for every explored capacity. `item` is the next item that we are considering stealing.

```
let previousItemsValue = table[i][capacity]
if capacity >= item.weight { // item fits in knapsack
```

`previousItemsValue` is the value of the last combination of items at the current `capacity` being explored. For each possible combination of items, we consider if adding in the latest "new" item is even plausible.

If the item weighs more than the knapsack capacity we are considering, we simply copy over the value for the last combination of items that we considered for the capacity in question:

```
else { // no room for this item
    table[i + 1][capacity] = previousItemsValue //use prior combo
}
```

Otherwise, we consider whether adding in the "new" item will result in a higher value than the last combination of items at that capacity that we considered. We do this by adding the value of the item to the value already computed in the table for the previous combination of items at a capacity equal to the item's weight subtracted from the current capacity we are considering. If this value is higher than the last combination of items at the current capacity, we insert it; otherwise we insert the last value:

```
let valueFreeingWeightForItem = table[i][capacity - item.weight]
table[i + 1][capacity] = max(valueFreeingWeightForItem + item.value,
➥ previousItemsValue)  // only take if more valuable than previous combo
```

> **TIP**   `max()` is a Swift standard library function that returns the greater of the `Comparable` arguments supplied to it.

That concludes building up the table. To actually find which items are in the solution, though, we need to work backward from the highest capacity and the final explored combination of items.

```
for i in stride(from: items.count, to: 0, by: -1) { // work backwards
    if table[i - 1][capacity] != table[i][capacity] {
    ➥ // did we use this item?
```

We start from the end and loop through our table from right to left, checking whether there was a change in the value inserted into the table at each stop. If there was, that means we added the new item that was considered in a particular combination because the combination was more valuable than the prior one. Therefore, we add that item to the solution. Also, capacity is decreased by the weight of the item, which can be thought of as moving up the table.

```
solution.append(items[i - 1])
capacity -= items[i - 1].weight  // if we used an item, remove its weight
```

> **NOTE** Throughout both the build-up of the table and the solution search, you may have noticed some manipulation of iterators and table size by 1. This is done for convenience from a programmatic perspective.

Are you still confused? Table 8.1 is the table the `knapsack()` function builds. It would be quite a large table for the preceding problem, so instead let's look at a table for a knapsack of 3 lb. capacity and three items: matches (1 lb.), flashlight (2 lbs.), and book (1 lb.). Assume those items are valued at $5, $10, and $15, respectively.

Table 8.1 An example of a knapsack problem of three items

Weight	0	1	2	3
Matches (1 lb, $5)	0	5	5	5
Flashlight (2 lbs, $10)	0	5	10	15
Book (1 lb, $15)	0	15	20	25

As you look across the table from left to right, the weight is increasing (how much you are trying to fit in the knapsack). As you look down the table from top to bottom, the number of items you are attempting to fit is increasing. On the first row, you are only trying to fit the matches. On the second row, you fit the most valuable combination of the matches and the flashlight that the knapsack can hold. On the third row, you fit the most valuable combination of all three items.

As an exercise to facilitate your understanding, try filling in a blank version of this table yourself, using the algorithm described in the `knapsack()` function with these same three items. Then use the algorithm at the end of the function to read back the right items from the table. This table corresponds to the `table` variable in the function.

8.2   *The traveling salesman problem*

The traveling salesman problem is one of the most classic and talked-about problems in all of computing. A salesman must visit all of the cities on a map exactly once, returning to his start city at the end of the journey. There is a direct connection from every city to every other city, and the salesman may visit the cities in any order. What is the shortest path for the salesman?

The problem can be thought of as a graph problem (chapter 4), with the cities being the vertices, and the connections between them being the edges. Your first instinct might be to find the minimum spanning tree, as described in chapter 4. Unfortunately, the solution to the traveling salesman problem is not so simple. The minimum spanning tree is the shortest way to connect all of the cities, but it does not provide the shortest path for visiting all of them exactly once.

Although the problem, as posed, appears fairly simple, there is no algorithm that can solve it quickly for an arbitrary number of cities. What do I mean by "quickly"? I mean that the problem is what is known as *NP hard*. An NP-hard (non-deterministic polynomial hard) problem is a problem for which no polynomial time algorithm exists (the time it takes is a polynomial function of the size of the input). As the number of cities that the salesman needs to visit increases, the difficulty of solving the problem grows exceptionally quickly. It is much harder to solve the problem for 20 cities than 10. It is impossible (to the best of current knowledge), in a reasonable amount of time, to solve the problem perfectly (optimally) for millions of cities.

8.2.1   *The naive approach*

The naive approach to the problem is simply to try every possible combination of cities. Attempting the naive approach will illustrate the difficulty of the problem and this approach's unsuitability for brute-force attempts at larger scales.

OUR SAMPLE DATA

In our version of the traveling salesman problem, the salesman is interested in visiting five of the major cities of Vermont. We will not specify a starting (and therefore ending) city. Figure 8.2 illustrates the five cities and the driving distances between them. Note that there is a distance listed for the route between every pair of cities.

Perhaps you have seen driving distances in table form before. In a driving-distance table, one can easily look up the distance between any two cities. Table 8.2 lists the driving distances for the five cities in the problem.

Table 8.2   Driving distances between cities in Vermont

	Rutland	Burlington	White River Junction	Bennington	Brattleboro
Rutland	0	67	46	55	75
Burlington	67	0	91	122	153
White River Junction	46	91	0	98	65
Bennington	55	122	98	0	40
Brattleboro	75	153	65	40	0

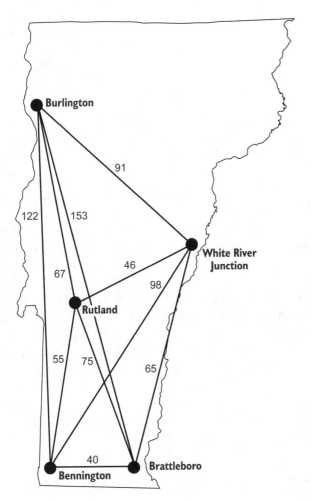

Figure 8.2   Five cities in Vermont and the driving distances between them

We will need to codify both the cities and the distances between them for our problem. To make the distances between cities easy to look up, we will use a dictionary of dictionaries, with the outer set of keys representing the first of a pair, and the inner set of keys representing the second. This will be the type [String: [String: Int]], and it will allow lookups like vtDistances["Rutland"]["Burlington"], which should return 67.

```
let vtCities = ["Rutland", "Burlington", "White River Junction",
➥ "Bennington", "Brattleboro"]

let vtDistances = [
    "Rutland":
        ["Burlington": 67, "White River Junction": 46, "Bennington":
        ➥ 55, "Brattleboro": 75],
```

```
"Burlington":
    ["Rutland": 67, "White River Junction": 91, "Bennington": 122,
    ➥ "Brattleboro": 153],
"White River Junction":
    ["Rutland": 46, "Burlington": 91, "Bennington": 98, "Brattleboro":
    ➥ 65],
"Bennington":
    ["Rutland": 55, "Burlington": 122, "White River Junction": 98,
    ➥ "Brattleboro": 40],
"Brattleboro":
    ["Rutland": 75, "Burlington": 153, "White River Junction": 65,
    ➥ "Bennington": 40]
]
```

FINDING ALL PERMUTATIONS

The naive approach to solving the traveling salesman problem requires generating every possible permutation of the cities. There are many permutation-generation algorithms—they are simple enough to ideate that you could almost certainly come up with one on your own.

One common approach is backtracking. You first saw backtracking in chapter 3 in the context of solving a constraint-satisfaction problem. In constraint-satisfaction problem solving, backtracking is used after a partial solution is found that does not satisfy the problem's constraints. In such a case, you revert to an earlier state and continue the search along a different path than that which led to the incorrect partial solution.

To find all of the permutations of the items in an array (eventually, our cities), we will also use backtracking. After we make a swap between elements and go down a path of further permutations, we will backtrack to the state before the swap was made so we can make a different swap and go down a different path.

```
// backtracking permutations algorithm
func allPermutationsHelper<T>(contents: [T], permutations: inout [[T]], n:
➥ Int) {
    guard n > 0 else { permutations.append(contents); return }
    var tempContents = contents
    for i in 0..<n {
        tempContents.swapAt(i, n - 1) // move the element at i to the end
        // move everything else around, holding the end constant
        allPermutationsHelper(contents: tempContents, permutations:
        ➥ &permutations, n: n - 1)
        tempContents.swapAt(i, n - 1) // backtrack
    }
}
```

This recursive function is labeled a "helper" because it will actually be called by another function that takes fewer arguments. The parameters of `allPermutations-Helper()` are the contents of the original array to be permuted, the current permutations generated so far, and the number of remaining items in the original array to swap around. `permutations` is declared `inout` because the same array will be modified by various calls of `allPermutationsHelper()`.

A common pattern for recursive functions that need to keep multiple items of state across calls is to have a separate outward facing function with fewer parameters that is easier to use. `allPermutations()` is that simpler function.

```
// find all of the permutations of a given array
func allPermutations<T>(_ original: [T]) -> [[T]] {
    var permutations = [[T]]()
    allPermutationsHelper(contents: original, permutations: &permutations, n:
    ➥ original.count)
    return permutations
}
```

`allPermutations()` takes just a single argument: the array for which the permutations should be generated. It calls `allPermutationsHelper()` to find those permutations. This saves the user of `allPermutations()` from having to provide the parameters `permutations` and `n` to `allPermutationsHelper()`.

The backtracking approach to finding all permutations presented here is fairly efficient. Finding each permutation requires just two swaps within the array. However, it is possible to find all the permutations of an array with just one swap per permutation. One efficient algorithm that accomplishes that task is Heap's algorithm (not to be confused with the heap data structure—Heap, in this case, is the name of the inventor of the algorithm).[2] This difference in efficiency may be important for very large data sets (which is not what we are dealing with here).

A quick test of our permutation generator would seem in order.

```
// test allPermutations
let abc = ["a","b","c"]
let testPerms = allPermutations(abc)
print(testPerms)
print(testPerms.count)
```

In the console, you should see all of the possible combinations of "a", "b", and "c." In addition, the total number of generated permutations, 6, should appear.

```
[["b", "c", "a"], ["c", "b", "a"], ["c", "a", "b"], ["a", "c", "b"], ["b",
➥ "a", "c"], ["a", "b", "c"]]
6
```

BRUTE-FORCE SEARCH

We can now generate all of the permutations of the city list, but this is not quite the same as a traveling salesman problem path. Recall that in the traveling salesman problem, the salesman must return (at the end) to the same city that he started in. We can define a simple function that takes an array of arrays and adds the first item in each to the end of each. This can convert our permutations to proper traveling salesman problem paths.

---

[2] Robert Sedgewick, "Permutation Generation Methods" (Princeton University), http://mng.bz/87Te.

```
// make complete paths for tsp
func tspPaths<T>(_ permutations: [[T]]) -> [[T]] {
    return permutations.map {
        if let first = $0.first {
            return ($0 + [first]) // append first to end
        } else {
            return [] // empty is just itself
        }
    }
}
```

Let's quickly test it using our test data from before.

```
print(tspPaths(testPerms))
```

You should see the same letter at the beginning and end of each path.

```
[["b", "c", "a", "b"], ["c", "b", "a", "c"], ["c", "a", "b", "c"], ["a",
➡ "c", "b", "a"], ["b", "a", "c", "b"], ["a", "b", "c", "a"]]
```

We are now ready to try testing the paths we have permuted. solveTSP() painstakingly looks at every path in an array of paths and uses a two-dimensional distance array (the distance between two cities lookup table) to calculate each path's total distance. It returns both the shortest path and that path's total distance.

```
func solveTSP<T>(cities: [T], distances: [T: [T: Int]]) -> (solution: [T],
➡ distance: Int) {
    let possiblePaths = tspPaths(allPermutations(cities))
    ➡ // all potential paths
    var bestPath: [T] = [] // shortest path by distance
    var minDistance: Int = Int.max // distance of the shortest path
    for path in possiblePaths {
        if path.count < 2 { continue }
        ➡ // must be at least one city pair to calculate
        var distance = 0
        var last = path.first! // we know there is one because of above line
        for next in path[1..<path.count] { // add up all pair distances
            distance += distances[last]![next]!
            last = next
        }
        if distance < minDistance { // found a new best path
            minDistance = distance
            bestPath = path
        }
    }
    return (solution: bestPath, distance: minDistance)
}
```

We finally can brute-force the cities of Vermont, finding the shortest path to reach all five.

```
let vtTSP = solveTSP(cities: vtCities, distances: vtDistances)
print("The shortest path is \(vtTSP.solution) in \(vtTSP.distance) miles.")
```

The output should look something like the following, and the best path is illustrated in figure 8.3.

```
The shortest path is ["Bennington", "Brattleboro", "White River Junction",
➡ "Burlington", "Rutland", "Bennington"] in 318 miles.
```

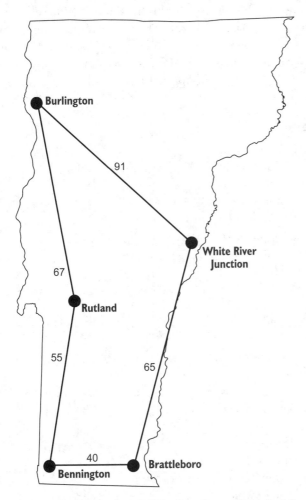

Figure 8.3 **The shortest path for the salesman to visit all five cities in Vermont is illustrated.**

8.2.2 *Taking it to the next level*

There is no easy answer to the traveling salesman problem. Our naive approach quickly becomes infeasible. The number of permutations generated is *n* factorial (n!), where *n* is the number of cities in the problem. If we were to include just one more city (6 instead of 5), the number of evaluated paths would grow by a factor of 6. Then it would be 7 times harder to solve the problem for just one more city after that. This is not a scalable approach!

In the real world, the naive approach to the traveling salesman problem is seldom used. Most algorithms for instances of the problem with a large number of cities are approximations. They try to solve the problem for a near-optimal solution. The near-optimal solution may be within a small known band of the perfect solution (for example, perhaps they will be no more than 5% less efficient).

Two techniques that have already appeared in this book have been used to attempt the traveling salesman problem on large data sets. Dynamic programming, which we used in the knapsack problem earlier in this chapter, is one approach. Another is genetic algorithms, as described in chapter 5. Many journal articles have been published attributing genetic algorithms to near-optimal solutions for the traveling salesman with large numbers of cities.

8.3   *Phone number mnemonics*

Before there were smartphones with built-in address books, telephones included letters on each of the keys on their number pads. The reason for these letters was to provide easy mnemonics by which to remember phone numbers. In the United States, typically the 1 key would have no letters, 2 would have ABC, 3 DEF, 4 GHI, 5 JKL, 6 MNO, 7 PQRS, 8 TUV, 9 WXYZ, and 0 no letters. For example, 1-800-MY-APPLE corresponds to the phone number 1-800-69-27753. Once in a while you will still find these mnemonics in place in advertisements, so the numbers on the keypad have made their way into modern smartphone apps, as evidenced by figure 8.4.

How does one come up with a new mnemonic for a phone number? In the 1990s there was popular shareware to help with the effort. These pieces of software would generate every permutation of a phone number's letters and then look through a dictionary to find words that were contained in the permutations. They would then show the permutations with the most complete words to the user. We will do the first half of the problem. The dictionary lookup will be left as an exercise.

Figure 8.4   The Phone app in iOS retains the letters on keys that its telephone forebears contained.

In the last problem, we looked at permutation generation. We used backtracking to generate the potential paths for the traveling salesman problem. However, as was mentioned, there are many different ways to generate permutations. For this problem in particular, instead of swapping two positions in an existing permutation to generate a new one, we will generate each permutation from the ground up. We will do this by looking at the potential letters that match each numeral in the phone number, and continually add more options to the end as we go to each successive numeral.

First, we will define a mapping of numerals to potential letters. We will work with our phone number split up into Characters, so the mapping will be between Characters.

```
let phoneMapping: [Character: [Character]] = ["1": ["1"], "2": ["a", "b",
➡ "c"], "3": ["d", "e", "f"], "4": ["g", "h", "i"], "5": ["j", "k", "l"],
➡ "6": ["m", "n", "o"], "7": ["p", "q", "r", "s"], "8": ["t", "u", "v"],
➡ "9": ["w", "x", "y", "z"], "0": ["0"]]
```

For readability, we will break up the permutation generator into two functions. The first prepares an initial list of possible letters for each place in the original string containing the phone number. It then passes that initial list of lists to the second function that does the real permutation generation.

Here's the first function.

```
// return all of the possible characters combos, given a mapping, for a
➡ given number
func stringToPossibilities(_ s: String, mapping: [Character: [Character]])
➡ -> [[Character]]{
    let possibilities = s.flatMap{ mapping[$0] }
    return combineAllPossibilities(possibilities)
}
```

It does not do much. The temporary variable possibilities would look like [["g", "h", "i"], ["t", "u", "v"]] if it were provided the string "48" as a starting point.

The next function combines all of those possibilities for each numeral into a list of possible mnemonics.

```
// takes a set of possible characters for each position and finds all
➡ possible permutations
func combineAllPossibilities(_ possibilities: [[Character]])
➡ -> [[Character]] {
    guard let possibility = possibilities.first else { return [[]] }
    var permutations: [[Character]] = possibility.map { [$0] }
    ➡ // turn each into an array
    for possibility in possibilities[1..<possibilities.count] where
    ➡ possibility != [] {
        let toRemove = permutations.count // temp
        for permutation in permutations {
            for c in possibility { // try adding every letter
                var newPermutation: [Character] = permutation
                ➡ // need a mutable copy
                newPermutation.append(c) // add character on the end
```

```
                permutations.append(newPermutation) // new combo ready
            }
        }
        permutations.removeFirst(toRemove) // remove combos missing new
        ⇒ last letter
    }
    return permutations
}
```

Rather than making swaps, like the earlier permutation generator, this permutation generator keeps adding a new letter onto the end until it runs out of letters. It is a less efficient method, but in some ways it is easier to understand. Every iteration of the main loop looks at the existing permutations and extends them by one letter. If there are three potential next letters, there will be three times as many permutations when that iteration finishes. It needs to do some cleanup, though. It needs to take all of the permutations that existed from the last iteration out, because they are now too short (they are missing the last letter). This is the purpose of the toRemove variable. It keeps track of how many permutations there were just before the latest letter was added to create all of the new permutations. It is used to remove that number of old permutations at the end of each iteration.

Now we can find all of the possible mnemonics for a phone number.

```
let permutations = stringToPossibilities("1440787", mapping: phoneMapping)
```

It turns out that the phone number "1440787" can also be written as "1GH0STS". That is easier to remember.

8.4   *Tic-tac-toe*

Tic-tac-toe is a simple game, but it can be used to illustrate the same minimax algorithm that can be applied in advanced strategy games like Connect Four, checkers, and chess. We will build a tic-tac-toe AI that plays perfectly using minimax.

NOTE   This section assumes that you are familiar with the game tic-tac-toe and its standard rules. If not, a quick search on the web should get you up to speed.

8.4.1   *Managing state*

Let's develop some structures to keep track of the state of the game as it progresses.

First, we need a way of representing each square on the tic-tac-toe board. We will use an enum called Piece. A piece can either be X, O, or empty (represented by E in the enum).

```
enum Piece: String {
    case X = "X"
    case O = "O"
    case E = " "
    var opposite: Piece {
        switch self {
```

```
        case .X:
            return .O
        case .O:
            return .X
        case .E:
            return .E
        }
    }
}
```

The enum `Piece` has a computed property, `opposite`, that returns another `Piece`. This will be useful for flipping from one player's turn to the other player's turn after a tic-tac-toe move. To represent moves, we will just use an integer that corresponds to a square on the board where a piece is placed.

```
// a move is an integer, 0-8, indicating a place to put a piece
typealias Move = Int
```

A tic-tac-toe board has 9 positions organized in 3 rows and 3 columns. For simplicity, these 9 positions can be represented using a one-dimensional array. Which squares receive which numeric designation (a.k.a., "index" in the array) is arbitrary, but we will follow the scheme outlined in figure 8.5.

0	1	2
3	4	5
6	7	8

Figure 8.5 The one-dimensional array indices that correspond to each square in the tic-tac-toe board

The main holder of state will be a struct, `Board`. `Board` keeps track of three different pieces of state: the position (represented by the aforementioned one-dimensional array), the player whose turn it is, and the last move made. The last move made will come in handy later when we implement minimax.

```
struct Board {
    let position: [Piece]
    let turn: Piece
    let lastMove: Move
```

A default board is one where no moves have yet been made (an empty board). The constructor for `Board` has default parameters that initialize such a position, with X to move (the usual first player in tic-tac-toe), and `lastMove` being set to the sentinel value -1.

```
    // by default the board is empty and X goes first
    // lastMove being -1 is a marker of a start position
    init(position: [Piece] = [.E, .E, .E, .E, .E, .E, .E, .E, .E], turn:
    ➡ Piece = .X, lastMove: Int = -1) {
        self.position = position
        self.turn = turn
        self.lastMove = lastMove
    }
```

As you probably noticed, all of the instance variables of `Board` are defined with `let`. `Board` is an immutable data structure—Boards will not be modified. Instead, every time a move needs to be played, a new `Board` with the position changed to accommodate the move will be generated.

```
// location can be 0-8, indicating where to move
// return a new board with the move played
func move(_ location: Move) -> Board {
    var tempPosition = position
    tempPosition[location] = turn
    return Board(position: tempPosition, turn: turn.opposite, lastMove:
    ➥ location)
}
```

A legal move in tic-tac-toe is any empty square. The following computed property, `legalMoves`, uses `filter()` to efficiently generate potential moves for a given position.

```
// the legal moves in a position are all of the empty squares
var legalMoves: [Move] {
    return position.indices.filter { position[$0] == .E }
}
```

The `indices` that `filter()` acts on are `Int` indexes into the position array. Conveniently (and purposely), a `Move` is also defined as an `Int`, allowing this definition of `legalMoves` to be so succinct.

There are many ways to scan the rows, columns, and diagonals of a tic-tac-toe board to check for wins. The following implementation of the computed property `isWin` does so with a hard-coded seemingly endless amalgamation of `&&`, `||`, and `==`. It is not the prettiest code, but it does the job in a straightforward manner.

```
var isWin: Bool {
    return
        position[0] == position[1] && position[0] == position[2]
        ➥ && position[0] != .E || // row 0
        position[3] == position[4] && position[3] == position[5]
        ➥ && position[3] != .E || // row 1
        position[6] == position[7] && position[6] == position[8]
        ➥ && position[6] != .E || // row 2
        position[0] == position[3] && position[0] == position[6]
        ➥ && position[0] != .E || // col 0
        position[1] == position[4] && position[1] == position[7]
        ➥ && position[1] != .E || // col 1
        position[2] == position[5] && position[2] == position[8]
        ➥ && position[2] != .E || // col 2
        position[0] == position[4] && position[0] == position[8]
        ➥ && position[0] != .E || // diag 0
        position[2] == position[4] && position[2] == position[6]
        ➥ && position[2] != .E // diag 1
}
```

If all of a row's, column's, or diagonal's squares are not empty, and they contain the same piece, the game has been won.

A game is drawn if it is not won and there are no more legal moves left. The computed property `isDraw` closes out the implementation of `Board`.

```
var isDraw: Bool {
    return !isWin && legalMoves.count == 0
}
}
```

8.4.2 *Minimax*

Minimax is a classic algorithm for finding the best move in a two-player, zero-sum game with perfect information, like tic-tac-toe, checkers, or chess. It has been extended and modified for other types of games as well. Minimax is typically implemented using a recursive function in which each player is designated either the maximizing player or the minimizing player.

The maximizing player aims to find the move that will lead to maximal gains. However, the maximizing player must account for moves by the minimizing player. After each attempt to maximize the gains of the maximizing player, minimax is called recursively to find the opponent's reply that minimizes the maximizing player's gains. This continues back and forth (maximizing, minimizing, maximizing, and so on) until a base case in the recursive function is reached. The base case is a terminal position (a win or a draw).

Minimax will return an evaluation of the starting position for the maximizing player. If the best possible play by both sides will result in a win for the maximizing player, a score of 1 will be returned (in our version, the exact number is arbitrary). If best play will result in a loss, -1 is returned. A 0 is returned if best play is a draw.

These numbers are returned when a base case is reached. They then "bubble-up" through all of the recursive calls that led to the base case. For each recursive call to maximize, the best evaluations one level further down bubble up. For each recursive call to minimize, the worst evaluations one level further down bubble up. In this way, a decision tree is built. Figure 8.6 illustrates this tree that facilitates bubbling-up for a game with two moves left.

> **TIP** For games that have too deep a search space to reach a terminal position (checkers, chess), minimax is stopped after a certain depth (the number of moves deep to search, sometimes called *ply*). Then an evaluation function kicks in, using heuristics to score the state of the game. The better the game is for the originating player, the higher the score that is awarded.

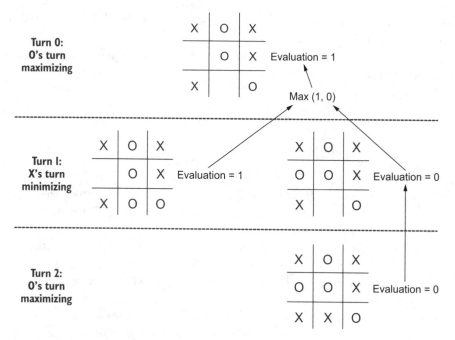

Figure 8.6   A minimax decision tree for a tic-tac-toe game with two moves left. To maximize the likelihood of winning, the initial player, O, will choose to play O in the bottom center.

Here is minimax() in its entirety.

```
// Find the best possible outcome for originalPlayer
func minimax(_ board: Board, maximizing: Bool, originalPlayer: Piece)
➥ -> Int {
    // Base case -- evaluate the position if it is a win or a draw
    if board.isWin && originalPlayer == board.turn.opposite { return 1 }
    ➥ // win
    else if board.isWin && originalPlayer != board.turn.opposite
    ➥ { return -1 } // loss
    else if board.isDraw { return 0 } // draw

    // Recursive case -- maximize your gains or minimize the opponent's gains
    if maximizing {
        var bestEval = Int.min
        for move in board.legalMoves { // find the move with the highest
        ➥ evaluation
            let result = minimax(board.move(move), maximizing: false,
            ➥ originalPlayer: originalPlayer)
            bestEval = max(result, bestEval)
        }
        return bestEval
    } else { // minimizing
        var worstEval = Int.max
        for move in board.legalMoves {
            let result = minimax(board.move(move), maximizing: true,
            ➥ originalPlayer: originalPlayer)
```

```
                worstEval = min(result, worstEval)
            }
        return worstEval
    }
}
```

In each recursive call, we need to keep track of the board position, whether we are maximizing or minimizing, and who we are trying to evaluate the position for (`original-Player`). The first few lines of `minimax()` deal with the base case—a terminal node (a win, loss, or draw). This could alternatively go inside a separate "evaluation" function. The rest of the function is the recursive cases.

One recursive case is maximization. In this situation, we are looking for a move that yields the highest possible evaluation. The other recursive case is minimization, where we are looking for the move that results in the lowest possible evaluation. Either way, the two cases alternate until we reach a terminal state (base case).

Unfortunately, we cannot use our implementation of `minimax()` as-is to find the best move for a given position. It returns an evaluation (an `Int` value). It does not tell us what best first move led to that evaluation.

Instead, we will create a helper function, `findBestMove()`, that loops through calls to `minimax()` for each legal move in a position to find the move that evaluates to the highest value. You can think of `findBestMove()` as the first maximizing call to `minimax()`, but with us keeping track of those initial moves.

```
// Run minimax on every possible move to find the best one
func findBestMove(_ board: Board) -> Move {
    var bestEval = Int.min
    var bestMove = -1
    for move in board.legalMoves {
        let result = minimax(board.move(move), maximizing: false,
        ➡ originalPlayer: board.turn)
        if result > bestEval {
            bestEval = result
            bestMove = move
        }
    }
    return bestMove
}
```

We now have everything ready to find the best possible move for any tic-tac-toe position. Let's try a few examples, starting with an easy win-in-one position.

```
// win in 1 move
let toWinEasyPosition: [Piece] = [.X, .O, .X,
                                  .X, .E, .O,
                                  .E, .E, .O]
let testBoard1: Board = Board(position: toWinEasyPosition, turn: .X,
➡ lastMove: 8)
let answer1 = findBestMove(testBoard1)
print(answer1)
```

You should see 6 printed to the console, indicating X should play in location 6 to win, which is correct.

Now let's try a position that requires the next move to be a block to stop the opponent from winning.

```
// must block O's win
let toBlockPosition: [Piece] = [.X, .E, .E,
                                .E, .E, .O,
                                .E, .X, .O]
let testBoard2: Board = Board(position: toBlockPosition, turn: .X,
➥ lastMove: 8)
let answer2 = findBestMove(testBoard2)
print(answer2)
```

Again, the right answer, location 2, should be printed to the console.

Finally, here is a harder position that requires planning ahead.

```
// find the best move to win in 2 moves
let toWinHardPosition: [Piece] = [.X, .E, .E,
                                  .E, .E, .O,
                                  .O, .X, .E]
let testBoard3: Board = Board(position: toWinHardPosition, turn: .X,
➥ lastMove: 6)
let answer3 = findBestMove(testBoard3)
print(answer3)
```

You should see location 1 being selected for the win.

It does not take much code to implement minimax, and it will work for many more games than just tic-tac-toe. If you plan to implement minimax for another game, it is important to set yourself up for success by creating data structures that work well for the way minimax is designed, like the Board struct. A common mistake for students learning minimax is to use a modifiable data structure that gets changed by a recursive call to minimax and then cannot be rewound to its original state for additional calls.

8.5 *Real-world applications*

Dynamic programming, as used with the knapsack problem, is a widely applicable technique that can make seemingly intractable problems solvable by breaking them into constituent smaller problems and building up a solution from those parts. The knapsack problem, itself, is related to other optimization problems where a finite amount of resources (the capacity of the knapsack) must be allocated amongst a finite but exhaustive set of options (the items to steal). Imagine a college that needs to allocate its athletic budget. It does not have enough money to fund every team, and it has some expectation of how much alumni donations each team will bring in. It can run a knapsack-like problem to optimize the budget's allocation. Problems like this are common in the real world.

The traveling salesman problem is an everyday occurrence for shipping and distribution companies like UPS and FedEx. Package delivery companies want their drivers to travel the shortest routes possible. Not only does this make the drivers' jobs more pleasant, it also saves fuel and maintenance costs. We all travel for work or for pleasure, and finding optimal routes when visiting many destinations can save resources. But the traveling salesman problem is not just for routing travel; it comes up in almost any routing scenario that requires singular visits to nodes. Although a minimum spanning tree (chapter 4) may minimize the amount of wire needed to connect a neighborhood, it does not tell us the optimal amount of wire if every house must be forward-connected to just one other house as part of a giant circuit that returns to its origination. The traveling salesman problem does.

Permutation-generation techniques like the ones used in the naive approach to the traveling salesman problem and the phone number mnemonics problem are useful for testing all sorts of brute-force algorithms. For instance, if you were trying to crack a short password, you could just generate every possible permutation of the characters that could potentially be in the password. Practitioners of such large-scale permutation-generation tasks would be wise to use an especially efficient permutation-generation algorithm, like Heap's algorithm.[3]

Minimax, combined with further extensions like alpha-beta pruning, is the basis of most modern chess engines. It has been applied to a wide variety of strategy games with great success. The deeper the search space for a game, the less effective minimax will be. This is why recent advances in computer play of the board game Go have required exploration of other domains, like machine learning. The search space for Go is simply overwhelming for minimax-based algorithms that attempt to generate trees containing future positions. But Go is the exception rather than the rule. Most traditional board games (checkers, chess, Connect Four, Scrabble, and the like) have search spaces small enough that minimax-based techniques can work well.

8.6   Exercises

1 Reprogram the naive approach to the traveling salesman problem using the graph framework from chapter 4.

2 Implement a genetic algorithm, as described in chapter 5, to solve the traveling salesman problem. Start with the simple data set of Vermont cities described in this chapter. Can you get the genetic algorithm to arrive at the optimal solution in a short amount of time? Then attempt the problem with an increasingly large number of cities. How well does the genetic algorithm hold up? You can find a large number of data sets specifically made for the traveling salesman problem by searching the web. Develop a testing framework for checking the efficiency of your method.

---

[3] Robert Sedgewick, "Permutation Generation Methods" (Princeton University), http://mng.bz/87Te.

3   Use a dictionary with the phone number mnemonics program and return only permutations that contain valid dictionary words.

4   Add a method to the `Board` class in tic-tac-toe that pretty-prints the position.

5   Add tests to tic-tac-toe to ensure that the properties `legalMoves`, `isWin`, and `isDraw` work correctly.

6   Use minimax to make a simple Connect Four engine.

appendix A
Glossary

This appendix defines a selection of key terms from throughout the book.

activation function—A function that transforms the output of a neuron in an *artificial neural network*, generally to render it capable of handling nonlinear transformations or to ensure its output value is clamped within some range (chapter 7).

acyclic—A graph with no *cycles* (chapter 4).

admissible heuristic—A *heuristic* for the A* search algorithm that never overestimates the cost to reach the goal (chapter 2).

artificial neural network—A simulation of a biological *neural network* using computational tools to solve problems not easily reduced into forms amenable to traditional algorithmic approaches. Note that the operation of an artificial neural network generally strays significantly from its biological counterpart (chapter 7).

auto-memoization—A version of *memoization* implemented at the language level, in which the results of function calls without side effects are stored for lookup upon further identical calls (chapter 1).

backpropagation—A technique used for training neural network weights according to a set of inputs with known correct outputs. Partial derivatives are used to calculate each weight's "responsibility" for the error between actual results and expected results. These "deltas" are used to update the weights for future runs (chapter 7).

backtracking—Returning to an earlier decision point (to go a different direction than was last pursued) after hitting a wall in a search problem (chapter 3).

bit string—A data structure that stores a sequence of 1's and 0's represented using a single bit of memory for each. This is sometimes referred to as a "bit vector" or "bit array" (chapter 1).

centroid—The center point in a cluster. Typically, each dimension of this point is the mean of the rest of the points in that dimension (chapter 6).

chromosome—In a genetic algorithm, each individual in the *population* is referred to as a chromosome (chapter 5).

cluster—See *clustering* (chapter 6).

clustering—An *unsupervised learning* technique that divides a data set into groups of related points, known as *clusters* (chapter 6).

codon—A combination of three nucleotides that together form an amino acid (chapter 2).

compression—Encoding data (changing its form) to require less space (chapter 1).

connected—A graph property that indicates there is a path from any vertex to any other vertex (chapter 4).

constraint—A requirement that must be fulfilled in order for a constraint-satisfaction problem to be solved (chapter 3).

crossover—In a genetic algorithm, combining individuals from the population to create offspring that are a mixture of the parents, and that will be a part of the next generation (chapter 5).

CSV—A text interchange format in which rows of data sets have their values separated by commas, and the rows themselves are generally separated by newline characters. CSV stands for "comma-separated values." CSV is a common export format from spreadsheets and databases (chapter 7).

cycle—A path in a graph that visits the same vertex twice without backtracking (chapter 4).

decompression—Reversing the process of *compression*, returning the data to its original form (chapter 1).

deep learning—Something of a buzzword, deep learning can refer to any of several techniques that use advanced machine-learning algorithms to analyze "big data." Most commonly, deep learning refers to using multilayer artificial neural networks to solve problems using large data sets (chapter 7).

delta—A value that is representative of a gap between the expected value of a weight in a neural network and its actual value. The expected value is determined through the use of *training* data and *backpropagation* (chapter 7).

digraph—See *directed graph* (chapter 4).

directed graph—Also known as a *digraph*, a directed graph is a graph in which edges may only be traversed in one direction (chapter 4).

domain—The possible values of a variable in a constraint-satisfaction problem (chapter 3).

dynamic programming—Instead of solving a large problem outright using a brute-force approach, in dynamic programming the problem is broken up into smaller subproblems that are each more manageable (chapter 8).

edge—A connection between two *vertices* (nodes) in a graph (chapter 4).

exclusive or—See *XOR* (chapter 1).

feed-forward—A type of neural network in which signals propagate in one direction (chapter 7).

fitness function—A function that evaluates the effectiveness of a potential solution to a problem (chapter 5).

generation—One round in the evaluation of a genetic algorithm. Also used to refer to the population of individuals active in a round (chapter 5).

genetic programming—Programs that modify themselves using the *selection, crossover,* and *mutation* operators to find solutions to programming problems that are non-obvious (chapter 5).

gradient descent—The method of modifying an *artificial neural network's* weights using the *deltas* calculated during *backpropagation* and the *learning rate* (chapter 7).

graph—An abstract mathematical construct that is used for modeling a real-world problem by dividing the problem into a set of connected nodes. The nodes are known as *vertices*, and the connections are known as *edges* (chapter 4).

greedy algorithm—An algorithm that always selects the best immediate choice at any decision point, hopeful that it will lead to the globally optimal solution (chapter 4).

heuristic—An intuition about the way to solve a problem that points in the right direction (chapter 2).

hidden layer—Any layers between the input layer and the output layer in a *feed-forward artificial neural network* (chapter 7).

infinite loop—A loop that does not terminate (chapter 1).

infinite recursion—A set of recursive calls that does not terminate, but instead continues to make additional recursive calls. Analogous to an *infinite loop*. Usually caused by the lack of a base case (chapter 1).

input layer—The first layer of a *feed-forward artificial neural network* that receives its input from some kind of external entity (chapter 7).

learning rate—A value, usually a constant, used to adjust the rate at which weights are modified in an *artificial neural network*, based on calculated *deltas* (chapter 7).

memoization—A technique in which the results of computational tasks are stored for later retrieval from memory, saving additional computation time to recreate the same results (chapter 1).

minimum spanning tree—A *spanning tree* that connects all vertices using the minimum total weight of edges (chapter 4).

mutate—In a genetic algorithm, randomly changing some property of an individual before it is included in the next generation (chapter 5).

natural selection—The evolutionary process by which well adapted organisms succeed and poorly adapted organisms fail. Given a limited set of resources in the environment, the organisms best suited to leverage those resources will survive and propagate. Over several generations, this leads to helpful traits being propagated amongst a population, hence being naturally selected by the constraints of the environment (chapter 5).

neural network—A network of multiple neurons that act in concert to process information. The neurons are often thought about as being organized in layers (chapter 7).

neuron—An individual nerve cell, such as those in the human brain (chapter 7).

normalization—The process of making different types of data comparable (chapter 6).

NP-hard—A problem that belongs to a class of problems for which there is no known polynomial time algorithm to solve (chapter 8).

nucleotide—One instance of one of the four bases of DNA: adenine (A), cytosine (C), guanine (G), and thymine (T) (chapter 2).

output layer—The last layer in a *feed-forward artificial neural network* that is used for determining the result of the network for a given input and problem (chapter 7).

path—A set of edges that connects two vertices in a graph (chapter 4).

ply—A turn (often thought of as a move) in a two-player game (chapter 8).

population—In a genetic algorithm, the population is the collection of individuals (each representing a potential solution to the problem) competing to solve the problem (chapter 5).

priority queue—A data structure that pops items based on a "priority" ordering. For instance, a priority queue may be used with a collection of emergency calls in order to respond to the highest priority calls first (chapter 2).

queue—An abstract data structure that enforces the ordering FIFO (First-In-First-Out). A queue implementation provides at least the operations "push" and "pop" for adding and removing elements, respectively (chapter 2).

recursive function—A function that calls itself (chapter 1).

selection—The process of selecting individuals in a generation of a genetic algorithm for reproduction, to create individuals for the next generation (chapter 5).

sigmoid function—One of a set of popular *activation functions* used in *artificial neural networks*. The eponymous sigmoid function always returns a value between 0 and 1. It is also useful for ensuring results beyond just linear transformations can be represented by the network (chapter 7).

SIMD instructions—Microprocessor instructions optimized for doing calculations using vectors, also sometimes known as "vector instructions." SIMD stands for "single instruction, multiple data" (chapter 7).

spanning tree—A tree that connects every vertex in a graph (chapter 4).

stack—An abstract data structure that enforces the Last-In-First-Out (LIFO) ordering. A stack implementation provides at least the operations "push" and "pop" for adding and removing elements, respectively (chapter 2).

synapses—Gaps between *neurons* in which neurotransmitters are released to allow for the conduction of electrical current. In layman's terms, these are the connections between *neurons* (chapter 7).

supervised learning—Any machine-learning technique in which the algorithm is somehow guided toward correct results using outside resources (chapter 7).

training—A phase in which an *artificial neural network* has its weights adjusted by using *backpropagation* with known correct outputs for some given inputs (chapter 7).

tree—A graph that has only one path between any two vertices. A tree is *acyclic* (chapter 4).

unsupervised learning—Any machine-learning technique that does not use foreknowledge to reach its conclusions. In other words, a technique that is not guided, but instead runs "on its own" (chapter 6).

variable—In the context of a constraint-satisfaction problem, a variable is some parameter that must be solved for as part of the problem's solution. The possible values of the variable are its *domain*. The requirements for a solution are one or more *constraints* (chapter 3).

vertex—A single node in a *graph* (chapter 4).

XOR—A logical bitwise operation that returns `true` when either of its operands is true, but not when both are true or neither is true. The abbreviation stands for *exclusive or*. In Swift, the ^ operator is used for XOR (chapter 1).

z-score—The number of standard deviations a data point is away from the mean of a data set (chapter 6).

appendix B
More resources

Where should you go next? This book covered a wide swath of topics, and this appendix will connect you with great resources that will help you explore them further.

Swift

As was stated in the introduction, *Classic Computer Science Problems in Swift* assumes you have a foundational knowledge of the syntax and semantics of the Swift language. Hence, we call it "a great second book on Swift." If you feel like your Swift fundamentals are still a bit shaky, you should check out these books.

- Apple, *The Swift Programming Language* (Apple, 2018), http://mng.bz/8A3K.
  - Free
  - Available both on the web and as an eBook
  - Comprehensive, up-to-date coverage of the entire language, suitable for both beginners and experienced programmers
- Tjeerd in 't Veen, *Swift in Depth* (Manning, 2018), www.manning.com/books/swift-in-depth.
  - A new offering from Manning that covers design patterns and advanced Swift features

iOS development

Although Swift can be used for more than just iOS development, iOS development remains its bread and butter. Here are some resources that offer a tutorial-style approach to teaching iOS development.

- Craig Grummitt, *iOS Development with Swift* (Manning, 2017), www.manning.com/books/ios-development-with-swift.
  - An up-to-date tutorial from Manning

- Christian Keur and Aaron Hillegass, *iOS Programming: The Big Nerd Ranch Guide*, 6th edition (Pearson, 2017), www.bignerdranch.com/books/ios-programming/.
  - A classic iOS text co-written by one of the Apple world's most famous developers
- Paul Hudson, *Hacking with Swift*, www.hackingwithswift.com/read.
  - Free version available (with ads)
  - A wide swath of different application types approached
  - Consistently updated for the latest versions of Swift
- RayWenderlich.com
  - A huge number of high-quality tutorials on every aspect of iOS development
  - Video tutorials also available on many topics

Mac development

It might not be quite as popular as the iPhone, but the Mac is still an exciting environment for Swift development. UIKit, the UI framework on iOS, was originally an evolution of AppKit, the Mac's UI framework. As a rule of thumb, writing a Mac app is slightly more complicated than writing an iOS app, simply because the UI paradigm encompasses more modes of interaction.

- Aaron Hillegass, Adam Preble, and Nate Chandler, *Cocoa Programming for OS X: The Big Nerd Ranch Guide*, 5th edition (Pearson, 2015).
  - The definitive guide to Mac programming co-written by a legend in the industry
  - Unfortunately it has somewhat outdated examples (built around Swift 1); hopefully a new edition of the book will come out

Algorithms and data structures

To quote this book's introduction, "This is not a data structures and algorithms textbook." There is little use of big-O notation in this book, and no mathematical proofs. This is more of a hands-on tutorial to important programming techniques, and there is value in having a real textbook too. Not only will it provide you with a more formal explanation of why certain techniques work, it will also serve as a useful reference. Online resources are great, but sometimes it is good to have information that has been meticulously vetted by academics and publishers.

- Thomas Cormen, Charles Leiserson, Ronald Rivest, and Clifford Stein, *Introduction to Algorithms*, third edition (MIT Press, 2009), https://mitpress.mit.edu/ books/introduction-algorithms.
  - This is one of the most-cited texts in computer science, so definitive that it is often just referred to by the initials of its authors: CLRS
  - Comprehensive and rigorous in its coverage
  - Its teaching style is sometimes seen as less approachable than other texts, but it is still an excellent reference
  - Pseudocode is provided for most algorithms

- Robert Sedgewick and Kevin Wayne, *Algorithms*, fourth edition (Addison-Wesley Professional, 2011), http://algs4.cs.princeton.edu/home/.
  - A very approachable yet comprehensive introduction to algorithms and data structures
  - Well organized with full examples of all algorithms in Java
  - Popular in college algorithms classes
- Steven Skiena, *The Algorithm Design Manual*, second edition (Springer, 2011), www.algorist.com.
  - Very different in its approach than other textbooks in this discipline
  - Offers less code but more descriptive discussion of appropriate uses of each algorithm
  - Offers a "choose your own adventure"-like guide to a wide range of algorithms
- Aditya Bhargava, *Grokking Algorithms* (Manning, 2016), www.manning.com/books/grokking-algorithms.
  - A very graphical approach to teaching basic algorithms, with cute cartoons to boot
  - Not a reference textbook, but instead a guide to learning some basic selected topics for the first time
- Erik Azar and Mario Eguiluz Alebicto, *Swift Data Structures and Algorithms* (Packt, 2016), https://www.packtpub.com/application-development/swift-data-structure-and-algorithms.
  - One of the only algorithms and data structures texts entirely in Swift
- Swift Algorithm Club, https://github.com/raywenderlich/swift-algorithm-club.
  - Very wide in its breadth, so a great starting point for most topics
  - Updated for new Swift versions
  - Explanations and code vary in quality and are provided by many different authors, so there is no unified voice or ability to presume reader knowledge

Artificial intelligence

Artificial intelligence is changing our world. In this book you not only were introduced to some traditional artificial intelligence search techniques like A* and Minimax, but also to techniques from its exciting subdiscipline, machine learning, like k-means and neural networks. Learning more about artificial intelligence is not only interesting, it also will ensure you are prepared for the next wave of computing.

- Stuart Russell and Peter Norvig, *Artificial Intelligence: A Modern Approach*, third edition (Pearson, 2009), http://aima.cs.berkeley.edu.
  - The definitive textbook on AI, often used in college courses
  - Wide in its breadth
  - Excellent source code repositories (implemented versions of the pseudo-code in the book) available online

- Stephen Lucci and Danny Kopec, *Artificial Intelligence in the 21st Century*, second edition (Mercury Learning and Information, 2015), http://mng.bz/1N46.
  - An approachable text for those looking for a more down-to-earth and colorful guide than Russell and Norvig
  - Interesting vignettes on practitioners and many references to real-world applications
- Andrew Ng, "Machine Learning" course (Stanford University), www.coursera.org/learn/machine-learning/.
  - A free online course that covers many of the fundamental algorithms in machine learning
  - Taught by a world-renowned expert
  - Often referenced as a great starting point in the field by practitioners

Functional programming

Swift can be programmed in a functional style, and indeed this style is popular amongst many Swift enthusiasts. Delving into the reaches of functional programming is possible in Swift itself, but it can also be helpful to work in a purely functional language and then take some of the ideas one learns from that experience back to Swift.

- Harold Abelson and Gerald Jay Sussman with Julie Sussman, *Structure and Interpretation of Computer Programs* (MIT Press, 1996), https://mitpress.mit.edu/sicp/.
  - A classic introduction to functional programming often used in introductory computer science college classes
  - Teaches in Scheme, an easy-to-pick-up, purely functional language
  - Available online for free
- Aslam Khan, *Grokking Functional Programming* (Manning, 2018), www.manning.com/books/grokking-functional-programming.
  - A very graphical and friendly introduction to functional programming
- Chris Eidhof, Florian Kugler, and Wouter Swierstra, *Functional Swift* (objc.io, 2016), www.objc.io/books/functional-swift/.
  - A deep dive into functional programming in Swift

Open source projects mentioned in this book

I maintain several open source projects that chapters in this book were built from. The projects offer more features and utility than could be made use of in the book.

- SwiftPriorityQueue by David Kopec, https://github.com/davecom/SwiftPriorityQueue.
  - A generic priority queue useful with A* and Dijkstra's algorithm
  - Used in chapters 2 and 4
- SwiftCSP by David Kopec, https://github.com/davecom/SwiftCSP.
  - Chapter 3's constraint-satisfaction problem framework is based on SwiftCSP

- SwiftGraph by David Kopec, https://github.com/davecom/SwiftGraph.
  - A complete library for graph data structures and algorithms
  - The graph framework in chapter 4 is a mini-version of SwiftGraph
- SwiftSimpleNeuralNetwork by David Kopec, https://github.com/davecom/SwiftSimpleNeuralNetwork.
  - Chapter 7's simple neural network is based on SwiftSimpleNeuralNetwork

appendix C
A brief history of Swift

Where did Swift come from, and where is it going? This appendix aims to answer both of these questions. To fully appreciate Swift's purpose requires understanding the ecosystem that it emerged from. Swift is a young language, but it incorporates many old ideas.

> **WARNING** This appendix is not meant to provide reference-quality material. It contains speculation, suppositions, and opinion.

A brief history of programming language paradigms incorporated in Swift

Swift contains all of the features that have become standard in class-based, object-oriented programming languages. These are features like objects, inheritance, polymorphism, and many more that are exposed when you build using the class reference semantics in Swift. Object-oriented programming languages can trace their history to at least as far back as Simula 67 from 1967, and they were influenced by ideas from even earlier languages, like Lisp (1958). Simula 67 was not a particularly widely used language, but its ideas emerged in popular programming languages of the 1970s, 1980s, and 1990s.

Object-oriented programming found perhaps its most pure expression in Smalltalk (1972). Smalltalk, in turn, was highly influential on Objective-C (1984), which Swift is a replacement for. Objective-C did not find large-scale adoption outside of NeXT and later Apple (after its purchase of NeXT). Objective-C is a thin superset of C (1972), providing Smalltalk-like message-passing, but C++ (1983), another object-oriented evolution of C with a much larger feature set, found far wider industry adoption. Android's main programming language, Java (1995), was heavily influenced by C++.

Although C++, Java, and other similar languages have made object-oriented programming the dominant paradigm in software development since the 1990s, another thread of language development has also sought to succeed procedural code. Functional programming emphasizes the primacy of functions acting on immutable data structures, without global state changes. In other words, in pure functional languages, a function's return value only depends on the arguments supplied to its parameters (with no global state affecting the outcome). Functional programming languages ironically also sometimes trace their lineage to Lisp.

Functional programming languages have long been popular in the academic world, where languages like Scheme (1970), a dialect of Lisp, and ML (1973) continue to be seen in the computer science classroom and in research. Their close proximity to the mathematical models that underlie code is sometimes cited as the attraction. More recently, ideas from the world of functional programming have started to find their way into mainstream emerging languages. Although it is unlikely that pure functional programming languages like Haskell (1990) and Clojure (2007) will ever be completely mainstream, ideas from the functional world can be seen in popular modern languages like JavaScript (1995) and Swift.

In particular, the value semantics when working with `enum` and `struct` types in Swift have functional programming roots. Functions are first-class citizens in Swift. The standard library has built-in support for popular functional programming methods like map, reduce, and filter. In other words, Swift has all of the tools you need to program in a fully functional style. This strong support has attracted functional programming devotees from other functional language communities into the Swift world. Sometimes they have clashed with the old guard of object-oriented developers coming from Objective-C backgrounds.

But the truth is that Swift is a multi-paradigm language. Like other modern emerging languages, such as Rust (2010) and Dart (2011), it draws inspiration from a myriad of prior languages. The great thing about developing a programming language today is that there are decades of hindsight. Modern language designers can pick and choose from what has worked well for other languages, and can remix their features into a cohesive whole. And there is still room for experimentation. Swift even introduces a paradigm of its own—"protocol-oriented programming," as was described in chapter 4.

Some Swift practitioners are adamant about programming in a functional style, protocol-oriented style, or object-oriented style. Perhaps the best way to approach programming in Swift is like the language designers did with the language itself, picking and choosing the best features of the language for the particular app in question. Swift enables flexibility, and there is no reason to use a flexible language in a rigid style.

Programming languages at Apple before Swift

In Apple's four-decade history, many programming languages have come and gone from their day of sunshine and Apple's stamp of approval. The Apple II (1977), like most personal computers of its day, included a built-in BASIC (1964) interpreter. A lot of serious development was done in 6502 (the name of the microprocessor in the Apple II) assembly, and there was some high-level development in popular languages of the day, like Pascal. The Macintosh (1984) was a Pascal (1970) stronghold in the 1980s through the early 1990s, by which time C and C++ began to become industry standards, and they eventually displaced Pascal, even on the Mac.

The acquisition of NeXT in 1997 brought Objective-C and the advanced object-oriented frameworks that underlay NeXTStep/OpenStep to the Mac, with the release of Mac OS X in 2001. Apple supplied a path for older C/C++ apps to be updated for Mac OS X with the release of Carbon, but future development using the updated frameworks from NeXT (Objective-C using the Cocoa APIs) was promoted. From 2001 through the public release of Swift in 2014, Objective-C was the first-class language for both macOS and iOS development.

Apple made two major updates to Objective-C's programming model during this time. The introduction of Objective-C 2.0 alongside Mac OS X 10.5 (2007) brought some modern syntax sugar to make life in Objective-C a little more succinct (it is notoriously verbose). Traditional memory management in Objective-C was done using manual reference counting (programmers littering their code with retain and release calls). Apple experimented with a garbage collector for Objective-C, but eventually replaced it with Automatic Reference Counting (ARC), which involves the compiler inserting retain and release calls at compile time in the appropriate places. ARC lives on as the memory management model in Swift.

Apple has also had many interesting programming language detours in its lifetime. Hypercard (1987), Apple's famous multimedia, card-based development environment for regular people, included the English-like HyperTalk (1987) language. Apple also brought an English-like dialect to scripting the Macintosh with AppleScript (1993), which lives on in the modern macOS. During the development of the Newton (1993), Apple developed both the Dylan (1992) and NewtonScript (1993) programming languages, neither of which ever achieved widespread use. At the time of Mac OS X's introduction, Java was the hot industry programming language. For several years, Apple supplied a bridge between Java and Objective-C, enabling developers to program Cocoa apps in Java (similar to how we now interact with Cocoa from Swift, in a sense). The Java route was never especially popular, and Apple eventually deprecated the bridge.

Swift history

Swift was started as a project by Chris Lattner in 2010.[1] For some time, Mac (and later iOS) developers had been clamoring for a modern replacement for Objective-C, given some of its perceived limitations. Due to its nature as a superset of C, Objective-C lacks language-level memory and type safety. Its syntax is sometimes seen as too verbose and

---

[1] *Chris Lattner's Homepage* is at http://nondot.org/sabre/.

different from other mainstream programming languages, especially for those new to it. Message-passing is at the core of Objective-C and enables its incredible dynamism, but is also responsible for some performance limitations.

Lattner had achieved notoriety for the development of LLVM, a compiler infrastructure project that serves as the backend for not only Swift but many other programming language compilers as well. Lattner was also the lead developer of LLVM's most famous front end, Clang, which compiles C, C++, and Objective-C code. By the time Swift was in heavy development, Lattner had risen to be a senior manager in Apple's developer tools group. In 2013, Swift became a major focus of the group, leading to its eventual release the following year.

Milestones

In its short public history, Swift has already achieved several major milestones, including four production (by version number, not necessarily by readiness!) releases.

SWIFT'S UNVEILING

Swift was unveiled to the world in a surprise announcement at Apple's World Wide Developer Conference (WWDC) in June 2014. Initial reactions were mostly positive, including surprise and excitement. Swift Playgrounds were a major feature promoted by Apple at WWDC, allowing a kind of interactive programming environment not previously seen in many mainstream platforms. At its announcement, Apple's Vice President of Software Engineering, Craig Federighi, called Swift "fast, modern, and designed for safety." He contrasted this with Objective-C by calling Swift "Objective-C without the C."[2] Swift was made available to developers in beta form during the conference.

It was clear during the announcement of Swift that Objective-C was not going anywhere. Apple's frameworks on both macOS and iOS were built over decades using Objective-C. Apple and third-party developers had millions of lines of Objective-C code that needed to be supported going forward. It is not as if Apple announced Swift and had rewritten their operating systems in it. Therefore, another major feature of Swift promoted during WWDC and responsible for several design decisions in the language is Objective-C interoperability. It is common for languages to offer interoperability with other languages. For instance, many programming languages offer C interoperability (including Swift) because C is so ubiquitous. Languages that run in the JVM usually have full Java interoperability. What was interesting at the unveiling of Swift was the depth of Objective-C interoperability. Apple clearly designed Swift to be as seamless as possible for use with its existing Objective-C frameworks.

Part of working with Apple's Objective-C frameworks meant bridging between the Foundation types in Objective-C (NSString, NSArray, NSDictionary, and so on) and their equivalents in Swift's standard library. This "toll-free" bridging happens seamlessly when working with Objective-C frameworks and was a large part of enabling

---

[2] Harrison Weber, "Apple announces 'Swift,' a new programming language for OS X & iOS," *VentureBeat* (June 2, 2014), http://mng.bz/98s0.

Swift's easy adoption by iOS and Mac app developers. It is an underappreciated technology, but imagine having to constantly convert between types every time a Cocoa API is accessed.

SWIFT 1

Swift 1 came out of beta and shipped in "final" form alongside Xcode 6 in September 2014. This first "production" release of the Swift language and compiler was criticized for slow compile times, crashing support tools, and a lack of perceived dynamism.[3] The language itself was not so much the issue (except with regards to dynamism) as much as the tooling built around the language. Apple warned developers that future versions of Swift might break syntax compatibility with this first release, and this was to happen several times in Swift's future.

The discussion surrounding the support of dynamism in the language (or lack thereof) would be a theme of critique from old-guard Objective-C developers for years to come. In fact, since its first release, Swift has supported many of the dynamic features of Objective-C for Objective-C interoperability when code is explicitly marked as usable from the Objective-C runtime. In modern releases of Swift, one turns on these features by marking it with `@objc`. However, running code inside of the Objective-C runtime is not the long-term goal of the language (and is not even supported on Linux).

SWIFT 2

Swift 2, released in final form in September 2015, made major syntactic and semantic changes to the language.[4] Swift 2 added support for error handling with `do`, `try`, and `catch`. It added the `guard` and `defer` statements. It included significant renames to major portions of the standard library. However, perhaps most significantly, it added support for protocol extensions to the language (protocols can have actual method definitions), enabling protocol-oriented programming.

Swift 2 was a major step in maturing the language, giving it syntactic and semantic features that set it apart from some of its predecessor languages. However, Swift continued to suffer from troubled tooling. Developers continued to complain about slow build times and notorious crashes of `SourceKitService` during development. At this point in Swift's development, it became common for third-party developers to do all new development in Swift, whereas during the Swift 1 era, many Objective-C developers held off.

Xcode included a migration tool for taking Swift 1 code and updating it for Swift 2. This important tool was the only help developers had for dealing with the numerous syntax changes between Swift 1 and 2, and later Swift 2 and 3. The repeated changes to syntax were one reason developers cited for holding off on Swift adoption. In the Swift 4 release cycle, Apple included explicit support for compiling with the last revision of the language (Swift 3).

---

[3] Maxim Zaks, "Is Swift dynamic enough?" *Medium* (August 19, 2014), http://mng.bz/Q1l7.

[4] Greg Heo, "What's New in Swift 2?" raywenderlich.com (June 12, 2015), http://mng.bz/P2Ue.

SWIFT GOES OPEN SOURCE

In December 2015, Apple released Swift and its supporting infrastructure as an open source project hosted at Swift.org, with source code repositories available on GitHub. Apple maintained control of Swift, but developed a community proposal process for non-Apple employees to get changes included in the language. Swift was released under a permissive open source license (Apache 2.0). Swift was promised to be released in an open source form since its early days, and Apple's follow-through was applauded. Since its open source release, Swift has accumulated many contributors outside of Apple, and it has been ported to numerous other platforms.

SWIFT 3

Swift 3, released alongside Xcode 8 in September 2016, did not include as many breaking changes and new pieces of syntax as Swift 2 did, but nonetheless Swift 3 was a major upgrade to the language that included significant cleanup.[5] Part of that cleanup eliminated legacy syntax, like C-style for loops as well as the ++ and -- operators. This caused some consternation, but it ultimately enabled Swift to develop its own unique style. Swift 3 made many changes to the way that standard library functions and properties are named and how calls to Objective-C system libraries are named.

Swift 3 also marked the first official release of the Swift Package Manager, an important tool for working with the language on larger multimodule, interdependent, and even multiplatform projects. The previous package management situation in the Cocoa world involved the use of the third-party tools CocoaPods and Carthage. But neither tool had official, sanctioned, Apple support, and each would sometimes break with new releases of Xcode. Swift Package Manager aims to unify package management in the Swift world, but it has yet to fully displace the use of CocoaPods and Carthage.

Swift 3 included numerous other changes, but it will probably be best remembered by developers as the point at which Swift began to mature. By the release of Swift 3, Swift had overtaken Objective-C in both programmer rankings of language popularity, and certainly in mindshare. Swift 3 included more extensive support for Swift on Linux and began to see actual adoption of Swift on the server side. Many of the early tooling issues with Swift had been resolved, or at least improved, by the Swift 3 release.

Not every change made in a Swift release cycle has been for the better. Some changes to access control in Swift 3 (`fileprivate` vs. `private`, for instance) were derided and modified in the Swift 4 cycle. There have been other reversals in Swift's short history, including various changes to the String APIs between Swift 1 and Swift 4.

SWIFT 4

Compared to the Swift 2 and Swift 3 releases, Swift 4, released in September 2017, was a more muted affair. Perhaps a sign of increasing maturity, few syntax changes were present in Swift 4. But although the language itself did not include many changes,

---

[5] Ted Kremenek, "Swift 3.0 Released," Swift blog (September 13, 2016), https://swift.org/blog/swift-3-0-released/.

many improvements were made to the standard library and the Swift Package Manager.[6] One of the most notable improvements was the inclusion of a fairly easy-to-use, standard interface for serialization and archiving, a much debated topic in earlier versions of Swift (numerous JSON parsers, for instance, were developed by third parties). Other notable improvements were related to the String and Collection APIs in the standard library.

Swift 4 was the first release of the compiler to include backward compatibility. A special version of Swift 3, Swift 3.2, can be compiled with the Swift 4 compiler. This enables developers to stick with Swift 3 while still upgrading to the latest version of the tools. Ironically, developers likely needed to do less of this with Swift 4, because most Swift 3 code compiles with little change in Swift 4, unlike prior version upgrades of the language.

Swift on other platforms

As Swift has advanced, it has been ported to multiple other platforms. Apple itself ported Swift to Linux and released the port at the same time that Swift went open source. Unfortunately, the port is only officially supported on a few releases of the Ubuntu Linux distribution. Third-party developers have gotten Swift building on Raspberry Pi, where there is something of a community, and a Windows port is in development. There is a group working on Swift support for Android, and there was even speculation at one point that major companies like Facebook and Google were encouraging the effort.[7] Google later adopted Kotlin, a language with syntax similar to Swift, although significantly divergent in semantics, as a first-class alternative to Java on Android.

Swift on Linux led to an interest in server-side Swift. There is an official work group cooperating to create standards for server-side APIs. In the meantime, three fairly popular high-level frameworks have sprung up for building back ends (especially of web apps) in Swift—Perfect, Vapor, and Kitura. Kitura is backed by IBM and is part of a larger initiative by the company to build products using Swift technologies. Apple has a high-level alliance with IBM as well.

Swift's future directions

It seems Swift has begun to mature. Developers can likely expect the fewer breaking changes in the Swift 4 release cycle to be more of the norm going forward. Publicly stated goals for Swift in the future include ABI stability, concurrency primitives, and more fine-grained control of memory. These will likely all be additive features that will not break existing code. ABI stability will bring the ability to distribute precompiled frameworks that work across Swift versions. Grand Central Dispatch, the current concurrency

---

[6] Ted Kremenek, "Swift 4.0 Released," Swift blog (September 19, 2017), https://swift.org/blog/swift-4-0-released/.

[7] Nate Swanner, "Google is said to be considering Swift as a 'first class' language for Android," *The Next Web* (April 27, 2016), http://mng.bz/38MR.

solution on Apple platforms, is a C library that does not take advantage of any specific language features. Adding language primitives will hopefully enable even more transparent use of concurrency—think of what Go Routines are to the Go programming language, or Async/Await is to C#/Python/JavaScript. There is discussion of bringing Async/Await to Swift and/or an Actor-based model, similar to Erlang. Fine-grained memory control enables performance optimizations for high-demand programs. Rust has such control built into the language, and there is talk of bringing similar constructs for "ownership" to Swift.

Swift is at an exciting point in its evolution. It has surpassed Objective-C in popularity and is beginning to gain steam as it branches out beyond the Apple ecosystem and entrenches on Linux with server-side Swift. As additional features continue to add to the capabilities of the language, its tooling continues to mature, performance continues to improve, and it gets ported to further platforms, Swift is on a trajectory for tremendous growth. As of early 2018, it has already cracked the top 10 list, according to several indicators of the most popular programming languages in the world. Where it will end up long term is anyone's guess, but keep in mind that the language is still only a few years old!

index

iOS Development with Swift
by Craig Grummitt

ISBN: 9781617294075
568 pages
$49.99
November 2017

Grokking Algorithms
An illustrated guide for programmers
and other curious people
by Aditya Y. Bhargava

ISBN: 9781617292231
256 pages
$44.99
May 2016

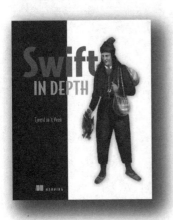

Swift in Depth
by Tjeerd in 't Veen

ISBN: 9781617295188
475 pages
$49.99
June 2018

For ordering information go to www.manning.com

MORE TITLES FROM MANNING

Functional Programming in Scala
by Paul Chiusano and Runar Bjarnason

> ISBN: 9781617290657
> 320 pages
> $44.99
> September 2014

The Quick Python Book, Third Edition
by Naomi Ceder

> ISBN: 9781617294037
> 400 pages
> $39.99
> April 2018

Deep Learning with Python
by François Chollet

> ISBN: 9781617294433
> 384 pages
> $49.99
> November 2017

For ordering information go to www.manning.com